THE AMERICAN HOME ADVISOR

The American Home Advisor

by

James Sanders

Illustrations by
Olga Tuimil

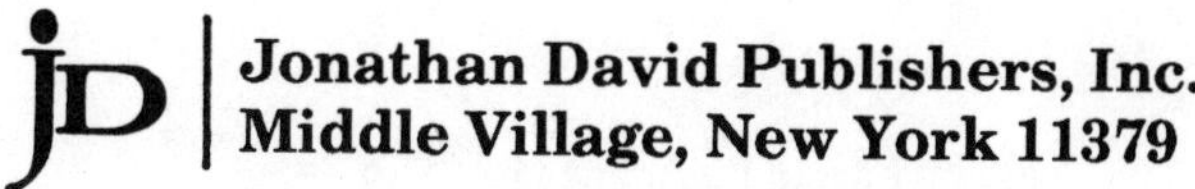

Jonathan David Publishers, Inc.
Middle Village, New York 11379

THE AMERICAN HOME ADVISOR

Copyright © 1991
by
Jonathan David Publishers, Inc.

No part of this book may be reproduced in any form without the prior written consent of the publisher. Address all inquiries to:

Jonathan David Publishers, Inc.
68-22 Eliot Avenue
Middle Village, New York 11379

1992 1994 1995 1993 1991
2 4 6 8 10 9 7 5 3 1

Library of Congress Cataloging-in-Publication Data

Sanders, James, 1925-
The American home advisor/by James Sanders.
p. cm.
Includes index.
ISBN 0-8246-0349-4
1. Home economics. I. Title.
TX158.S26 1991
640—dc20
91-18405
CIP

Layout by Arlene Goldberg

Printed in the United States of America

In Appreciation

Putting together a book of this magnitude is more than I could have accomplished without the help of family, friends, and neighbors. My thanks to all those who shared so generously of their time and knowledge.

Special thanks are due to my wife, Charlotte, who carefully reviewed the manuscript and offered many insightful comments.

To the various companies who provided information on the uses of their products, my sincere appreciation.

To the staff at Jonathan David Publishers, Inc., particularly Fiorella Torre, who worked closely with me for almost a year, wading through what seemed an endless amount of paperwork, a very special thank you.

And to Florence Weissman and Rose Marie Wasiak, I extend my thanks for typing and retyping the many drafts of the manuscript.

Contents

Introduction

Although it is true that "You can't know everything," that doesn't salve the wound of having to pay a plumber the minimum service charge of $29 or $35 to change a leaky bathroom washer whose ping-ping and pong-pong prevents you from counting sheep and falling asleep—or of paying a lawyer $200 for directing you to a standard contract form in a stationery store.

Which brings us to a parallel truism. In this minimum-charge-for-everything society, "You have to know a little bit about everything," unless of course you are independently wealthy. And that is what this book dedicates itself to: providing bits of random information that others have found useful and that might be directly applicable to the situation in which you find yourself.

To assemble this book, I've combed reams of material searching for solutions to household problems, whether in the area of basic plumbing and electricity, home beautification in its many aspects, financial management, growing and preserving fruits and vegetables, and on and on. Most of all, though, I've spent thousands of hours speaking with countless people—professionals and commoners alike—and what I've found is that there is nothing comparable to learning directly from the experiences of others.

Last winter, I was going over my lawn tractor at the end of the year as I always do, and I noticed a big crack in the wall of the fan belt. "This," I said, "is next season's trouble. Better take care of it now." And I proceeded to start to remove the belt. But, there were snags. The screw that holds the belt tight had frozen and had to be drilled out. And then a new hole had to be drilled to accommodate a new screw. But I couldn't drill the new hole deep enough because that required a special tool that isn't easy to find.

When the mechanic finally stopped by for seasonal maintenance two months later, he took a quick look before setting to work and asked, "Whatcha changin' the belt fer?" And I pointed to the crack in the V-belt that penetrated almost to the ply material surrounding the outer circumference. "Doesn't matta," he responded. "Doesn't matter?" I said. "Doesn't matta," he said. And he went on to explain that almost all of the strength of a fan belt lies in the ply material and almost none in the V-shaped sidewall, which only serves as a guide. In most cases the only time to change a belt, he said, is when it snaps. That valuable bit of information is not easy to come by, and I'm grateful to my mechanic for passing it on to me.

So I urge you to keep your eyes open, talk to people, and build on your and their experiences. What you'll learn is "Where there is a problem, there is a solution. And, where there's a solution, there might be a better solution." I hope that *The American Home Advisor* helps you in your search.

Good luck!

JIM SANDERS

1
In the Kitchen

Introduction

The kitchen used to be the exclusive domain of the woman of the house. But that was before women's lib. Today, with microwaves, blenders, dishwashers, salad shooters, and food processors at our disposal, anyone can turn out a creditable meal—and the kitchen has become the domain of the entire family.

Not everyone has the ability to become a great cook, but everyone should become familiar with kitchen basics. Today, that means first learning to explore to the fullest the capabilities of the various kitchen appliances. Nothing is more helpful than to read the instruction manuals that come with the appliances and then to reread them several months later, when the basic operations have been mastered and the finer points can be focused on.

The second kitchen essential is cleanliness. Dirt is not a natural consequence of protracted use. Every item in the kitchen—appliances, flatware, copperware, serving dishes—can be made to sparkle. All that is needed is the technique and the will.

And the third kitchen essential is order. To function well it is necessary that the kitchen be well organized. Pots and pans should be easy to reach. Flatware drawers should be neatly arranged. Take the time to organize the kitchen well at the outset, and you will reap ample rewards later.

GENERAL KITCHEN TIPS

Shopping List at Arm's Reach

Make use of small magnets to hang your shopping list on the refrigerator door. This can also be achieved by attaching a sheet of paper to the refrigerator door with a plastic adhesive called Holdit, sold in houseware stores. It is easy to remove and replace the sheet of paper as necessary.

Transferring Liquids

It is not necessary to spill a liquid when transferring it to a narrow-mouthed bottle. Hold a long thin knife (or long pointed object of any kind) alongside the mouth of the container you are pouring from and inside the mouth of the container you are pouring to. The liquid will flow down the sides of the knife in a fine stream and will enter the narrow-mouthed bottle without a drop being spilled.

A Foil Funnel

If you need a funnel in a hurry and one is not handy, make one

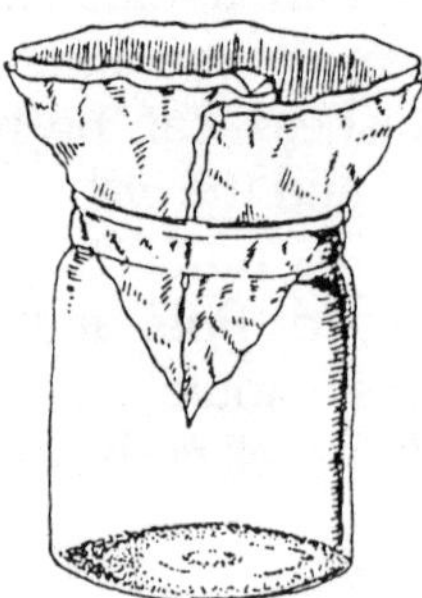

out of aluminum foil. Double the foil for added strength, then roll it into a cone, reducing the small end to the required size. You will find this improved funnel useful for pouring products like salt and sugar from one container into another.

Delayed Dishwashing

If you do not have the time to do the dishes as soon as the meal is over, rinse them off and let them soak for a half-hour in hot water to which detergent has been added. The work you will have to do later will be greatly reduced. Use very hot soaking water for greasy or sugary pans. Use cold water for pans that have held milk, eggs, or flour.

Protecting Kitchen Cabinets

The moisture that usually saturates the atmosphere of a kitchen will take its toll on wooden cabinets whose surfaces are not protected by paint, varnish, shellac, or wax. Often most neglected is the inside of the kitchen cabinets, which will deteriorate in time if attacked by dry rot and fungus growths. It is worth taking the time to apply shellac to these surfaces.

Shelving Paper

For dishes stored in kitchen cabinets to stay clean, it is important to line the shelves with paper. If the shelf-paper tends to curl up, secure it with cellophane tape rather than thumbtacks.

When dishes are shifted around, the paper will not tear as easily.

A Quieter Kitchen

If noise is a problem in your kitchen, consider lining the counters and shelves with linoleum or vinyl tile. The sound will be muffled and the surfaces will wipe clean with ease.

Lining Shelves

If light objects (like empty jars) tend to slide around on your kitchen shelves, you might want to try lining the shelves with sheets of fine sandpaper. The very lightest grade of sandpaper or emery paper will do the trick.

Hanging Cups on Hooks

To save space and to avoid chipping, store mugs and cups on hooks screwed into the underside of kitchen closet shelves.

Free-flowing Salt

A popular method of keeping salt moisture-free and free-flowing is to pour a small mount of uncooked rice into the salt shaker. If you have no rice handy, use aluminum foil to keep moisture out of the salt. Mold a small piece of foil tightly over the top of the shaker and leave it there when the shaker is not in use.

See-through Containers

Try to use glass or see-through containers for dry ingredients. They are both more attractive and more practical. You will be able to see at a glance when your supply is running low.

Emery Board as a Sharpener

An emery board can be used effectively to sharpen knives or scissors. Always be sure to follow the existing bevel.

Stubborn Cans

If after you have removed the lid of a can with a can opener you find it difficult to get the food product out (as when opening cans of cranberry jelly or dog food), turn the can upside down and pierce the bottom of the can. The food will now slide out easily.

Hot Water on Lids

Hard-to-open jar lids are often easily loosened after hot water has been allowed to run on the side of the cap for a minute or two. The hardened sugar or other matter that binds the lid to the jar often breaks down under the heat and loosens the seal.

Nutcrackers for Bottle Caps

Nutcrackers have more than one use—if they're the squeeze

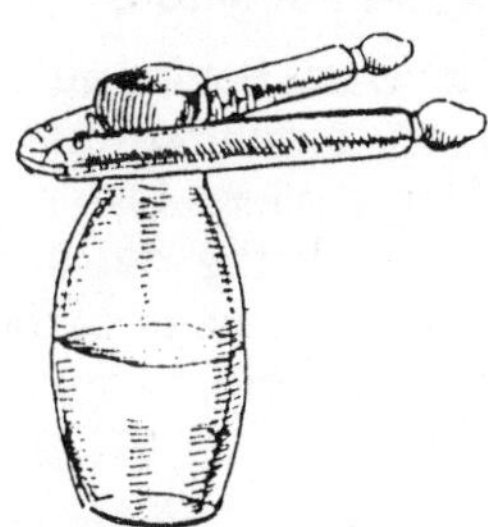

type. Use them for turning tight-fitting caps on small-mouthed bottles.

Unlikely Jar Opener

Although designed to remove oil filters, "The Grabber"—which comes in two sizes with specially designed handles—will make it easy to open tight-capped jars. Arthritics will especially appreciate this tool. If not available in your auto parts store, write to The Pine Co. See the Appendix for the address.

Kitchen Pliers

Locking pliers make a handy (though expensive) kitchen tool, particularly for loosening the lids of hard-to-open jars. Adjust the

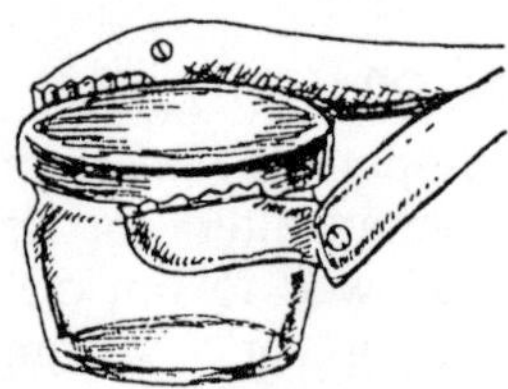

pliers to the size desired, grasp the lid, and turn. Ordinary pliers will do if the jar lid is not too large.

A word of CAUTION: Be very careful when using pliers on glass jars.

Nutcracker Substitute

If you do not have a nutcracker handy, try cracking nuts with a pair of large pliers. Use the open jaws to crush the nut shells, or you can use the inside of the pliers (the part you hold) to crush larger nuts.

Sandpaper for Stubborn Jar Lids

When you are having difficulty getting a good grip on a jar lid, a piece of sandpaper may help. Hold the sandpaper in the palm of your hand and press against the sides of the stubborn lid. It should turn without slipping.

Examine All Cans

Cans of food that bulge at the ends or are discolored at the seams should not be used. There is a very good chance that the contents are contaminated.

Enlarging Corks

Corks dry out and shrink with the passage of time. To return a cork to its original shape, boil it in a covered pan. This will sterilize it at the same time.

Foil-wrapped Corks

If a cork is too small for a bottle, make it bigger by wrapping as much aluminum foil around the cork as is needed to give it a snug fit.

Sticking Corks

Corks in bottles that contain sugary liquids often stick. To avoid this problem, wrap wax paper around the cork before inserting it into the bottle.

Cutting Boards

Use separate wood surfaces for slicing meats and vegetables. Using the same surface for both can lead to bacterial contamination. Cutting boards can be renewed periodically with sandpaper.

Stuck Tumblers

To loosen glasses that have become stuck together, pour

cold water into the inner glass and follow this by dipping the bottom of the outer one into hot water. The tumblers will come apart without being forced.

Airtight Containers

In warm weather, a food product kept in its original cardboard container tends to encourage the growth of bacteria. The same food stored in an airtight glass jar will not invite bacteria. For this reason it is a good idea to save screw-top glass jars for storing cereals, flour, and flour mixes during the warmer months. In locations where there is prolonged heat, and where items are not used too often, it is best to refrigerate.

Wooden Knife Handles

Knife blades that are attached to wooden handles with an adhesive should not be soaked in water for prolonged periods. Water may weaken the adhesive. Painted knife handles are also likely to be damaged by protracted soaking.

Operating Blenders

If your blender is too full, it will probably not work at all, or at least not efficiently. For best results do not fill the blender more than two-thirds of capacity.

Kitchen Space-savers

Bulky wooden spoons and spatulas that usually congest kitchen drawers can be hung from a rack. A piece of wood cut to the desired width and length will provide a good base for the pegs. Using an electric drill fitted with a quarter-inch bit, make holes in the board every three inches, starting three inches from the end. Hold the drill at a slight downward angle. Then cut off

three-inch lengths of quarter-inch doweling and force them into the holes, tapping with a hammer if necessary. Sand off the edges of the doweling if the fit is too tight. Stain or paint the piece, then attach it to your kitchen wall.

Nonslip Bases

Rest your whipping bowl on a

damp, folded cloth to keep it from slipping around while you work. You might also want to tack or staple a large piece of sandpaper to a block of wood of the same size—or do the same with a piece of rubber matting—and keep it handy for kitchen activity.

Shifty Grinders

A food grinder that will not stay firmly in place is very irritating. You can prevent the grinder from moving around by placing a piece of folded sandpaper, rough side out, between the clamp and the table.

Use Drip Pans

Save elbow grease by lining stove-top drip pans with aluminum foil. When foods boil over, it is the foil rather than the pan that will be soiled.

Stuck Food

To remove food stuck to the bottom and sides of a pot, fill the pot with warm water and let it stand until the food has softened. For even quicker results, bring the water to a boil and turn off the heat. After a few minutes, rinse out the pot; most of the stuck food should come free easily.

Nonstick Skillets

Use nonstick skillets for frying and thereby reduce your fat intake. Avoid frying in cast iron because foods so cooked tend to dry out quickly, making it necessary to add fats to the pan to prevent the food from burning.

Frying Pan Odors

Charcoal briquets heated in a frying pan will eliminate the odors the pan has absorbed.

Freshening Up Cutting Boards

Odors from fish, onions, or garlic that penetrate cutting boards can be reduced greatly, and even eliminated, by rubbing a half-peeled lemon briskly over the board surfaces. You may also want to try a tablespoon of baking soda to which enough water has been added to make a paste. Rub well for one or two minutes, then rinse.

Cutting-board Stains

To remove stains from cutting boards, first bleach the stains with a mixture of lemon juice and salt. Rub vigorously into the board and rinse with clean water. If another application is needed, wait until the board has dried.

Temporary Care for Stickiness

After removing a label, stickiness often persists. Dusting the sticky area with talcum powder is a temporary solution to the annoying condition.

Removing Bottle Labels

Place the jar with the label to be removed in a container of hot water. Allow to sit completely immersed for one-half hour. The label will usually peel off without difficulty. If a residue remains, remove it with acetone or a cleaning solution such as Goo Gone, which is specifically designed for this purpose.

Laminated Kitchen Tops

Do not use abrasive cleansers such as Ajax to clean laminated countertops. They scratch and dull the surface. Instead, use a mild dishwashing detergent. To remove stubborn stains, sprinkle fresh lemon juice on the countertop and let it stand for about one hour.

Formica Cleaning

Formica, the most popular covering for kitchen surfaces, is a plastic laminate that can be best cleaned with mild detergent. Persistent stains can be removed with a product such as Bon Ami. Hot pots and pans should not be placed on formica; the heat can cause scorching or buckling of the surface.

Cleaning a Can Opener

Electric can openers get sticky and clogged after repeated use. If you want to avoid the trouble of removing yours from the wall when it needs a cleaning, dip a hard-bristled toothbrush in hot water containing a detergent, and scrub the can opener until clean. However, now and then it is best to remove the opener from the wall and soak it in hot water containing detergent. (Make sure not to immerse the motor.) Allow it to sit for about ten minutes, then give it a good scrubbing.

Cleaning Beaters and Choppers

Immerse egg beaters, potato mashers, grinders, food choppers, and the like in water as soon as you are through using them. Clean difficult-to-get-at spots with a toothbrush.

Liquid Cleansers on Appliances

All liquid cleansers, even those advertised as containing mild abrasives, must be used sparingly. When applying these cleaning agents to appliances, use a soft cloth and rub gently to avoid scratching and dulling.

Safe Microwave Cleaner

Add four tablespoons of baking soda to a quart of warm water to produce a nonabrasive solution capable of cleaning your microwave.

General Oven Cleaning

Let the range cool before you clean it. Wash with warm water and detergent, rinse, then dry with a soft cloth.

When wiping off spills from a warm oven, use a dry cloth or paper towel. Remove stubborn spots by rubbing with dry baking soda and a damp cloth.

Cleaning Ovens

Ovens require a thorough cleaning from time to time to remove accumulated grease and burned-on food. Place one-half cup of household ammonia in a bowl and set the bowl in a cold oven. Allow to stand at least four hours, or overnight. Remove the bowl and add one quart of warm water to the contents. Use this solution to clean the inside walls of the oven. Scouring powder or steel wool may be used to remove stubborn stains.

Cleaning Oven Spills

If oven spills are covered with salt immediately, when the oven cools the burnt food and stain can be wiped clean with a damp sponge or rag.

Oven Spray Cleaners

Aerosol oven cleaners are available in hardware stores and supermarkets. After spraying the oven interior, close the door and allow the cleaner to eat away the grease and grime. After several hours, wearing rubber gloves, wash out the interior and wipe clean with paper towels.

Glass Oven Doors

The glass on oven doors can be cleaned with liquid detergent and warm water. Doors with chrome trim can be cleaned with a nonabrasive cleanser like Bon Ami. A paste made of baking soda is another way of cleaning chrome. After cleaning, rinse with water and dry with a clean cloth.

Gas Burner Cleaning

If the flame on your gas range is yellow, the burner may be clogged. The burner on a gas stove can be lifted out by pulling the tubular end out of the gas

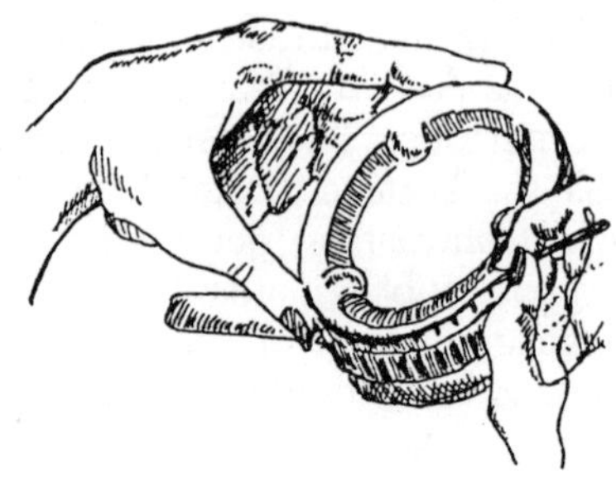

port. It should then be soaked in a detergent solution. With a needle or pin, clean out clogged holes in the burner ring. Do not use a toothpick, which might break off and clog the hole. After drying, return the burner to its original position.

Hard-to-Clean Burners

If a burner is hard to get clean, allow it to soak for 30 minutes in a mixture of one cup of vinegar and one gallon of boiling hot water. Then, place it in the oven for 15 minutes with the temperature set at 300 degrees F. This will dry out the unit, and it will then be ready for use.

Electric Stove Cleaning

The burner coils on an electric stove do not have to be cleaned, because the heat burns off spilled food. However, the drip pans under the coils do need regular cleaning.

To remove the coil of an electric stove, first be sure the stove is turned off and the coil is cool. Note where the two electrodes are plugged in, then pull. The coil will come out and drip pans can be removed for soaking in a detergent solution to soften the congealed drippings. (Never immerse the coil itself in water.) Scrub the pans with a nonabrasive cleanser and, after drying, replace by pushing the electrodes in firmly.

Cleaning the Refrigerator

Bleach kills odor-causing bacteria and, if used on the interior surfaces of the refrigerator, will leave it fresh and clean. Pour some bleach on a cloth or sponge and, after a thorough wiping, rinse with water. Leave the door open for a few minutes to air-dry before replacing the food.

Baking Soda in the Fridge

Aside from its use as a cooking agent, baking soda can serve as an odor absorber in the refrigerator. Place an open box on one of the refrigerator shelves. After one month, replace with a new box and pour the contents of the old one down the sink drain to sweeten and clean it.

Vanilla Instead of Baking Soda

Aside from the baking soda method of keeping odors out of the refrigerator, another method is to soak a ball of cotton in vanilla extract and then place it in a small saucer on a shelf. It will keep the interior smelling sweet.

Keeping Refrigerators Fresh

Keep an open container of charcoal briquets on a shelf, towards the back. Charcoal is particularly effective in absorbing onion and fish odors.

Vinegar and Mildew

To help keep your refrigerator mildew-free, wipe the walls and shelves periodically with a sponge dipped in vinegar.

Glycerin as a Refrigerator Cleansing Agent

Pour glycerin (available in drug stores) on a sponge and rub onto the interior walls and shelves of the refrigerator. This will enable you to clean up spills with ease.

Refrigerators Can Mar Floors

Protect kitchen floors against scratches (or cracked tiles) by placing a covering on the floor when pulling out the refrigerator. An old shower curtain is very useful for this purpose because of its durability.

Dishwasher Sweetener

From time to time add four or five tablespoons of baking soda and place it in the dishwasher when it is running through the rinse cycle. This will deodorize the inside of the unit.

Cleaning Your Dishwasher

If the walls or bottom of the dishwasher is soiled or discolored, place one cup of liquid bleach in the bottom rack of the machine and run it through the wash cycle.

Dishwasher Detergents

Detergents designed for use in dishwashers are highly alkaline and are entirely different from those used in automatic washers and when doing hand laundry. Dishwasher detergents will not keep for a long time once opened.

COOKWARE, SILVERWARE, AND GLASSWARE

Cooking With Woks

The Chinese wok, because of its shape, is particularly good for stir-frying. Consumers Union (May 1990) found the traditional-looking nonstick Maxim EW-70 wok and the Farberware 343A stainless steel wok to be among the best on the market. Both have a list price of under $100.00.

Preparing Enamelware

Enamelware should be treated before being used for the first time. Immerse the product in warm water and bring the water to a slow boil. Preparing enamelware in this manner will add years to its life.

Seasoning Skillets

If you want new skillets and frying pans (especially those made of cast iron) to do an effective job, grease them well and place them in the oven for 30 minutes at 450 degrees Fahrenheit. Let them cool, then wash with warm soapy water. Skillets with nonstick surfaces such as Teflon should be treated following manufacturer's directions.

Cleaning Enameled Pots

Enameled pots should be washed with a soft sponge or a nylon mesh dish pad and scraped with a rubber scraper. Metal sponges, steel wool, and scouring powder are harmful to enamel finishes.

Aluminum Cookware

Aluminum, a soft metal, will show scratch marks if scrubbed hard with steel wool or another abrasive material. To minimize scratching, use a straight back-and-forth motion rather than a circular one.

Lightening Aluminum Pots

The inside of aluminum pots darkens when alkaline foods such as spinach and potatoes are cooked in them. Brighten pot interiors by cooking acidic foods, such as apples, in them.

Waxing Cast Iron

To prevent rusting of cast-iron pots and pans, after washing them in hot water and drying, and while they are still warm, rub a piece of wax paper over the surfaces.

Hot Metal Pans

Metal pans in which hot water has been boiled or food has been heated will warp if immediately immersed in cold water.

Teflon Coatings

Cookware that has been coated with teflon should never be scoured with abrasive cleansers, steel wool, or metal scouring pads. Use hot, sudsy water and clean with a rubber scrubber or a sponge to remove food and grease.

Charred Pots

Make a paste by adding a small amount of water to baking soda and apply the paste to portions of the pot that have been burned. Allow to stand overnight, then rub off the burned matter.

This paste is also effective in removing food that stubbornly clings to pots and pans. But first fill the casserole with boiling water and let sit for five minutes.

Stained Pots

Pot stains can usually be removed by a solution of one cup of water, two tablespoons of baking soda, and one-half cup of chlorine bleach. Use enough of the solution to cover the stains, then boil for up to 10 minutes, until the stains have disappeared. Rinse with clean water several times, then dry before storing away.

Shiny Copper Cookware

A mixture of salt and vinegar, salt and lemon juice, or ammonia and water will shine copper cookware without leaving scratches. Use one tablespoon of salt to two tablespoons of vinegar or lemon juice. Use equal parts of ammonia and water. Dip a soft cloth or paper towel into the mixture and rub the soiled spots. Alternatively, dip a half-lemon into salt and rub it over the copper. Complete the job and restore the shine by rubbing the entire utensil with a wet steel-wool soap pad. Use fine steel wool only.

Cleaning Silverware

Fill an aluminum pan with warm water and laundry detergent. The pan should be large enough to hold all the silverware you wish to clean. To clean very large objects, fill a plastic pail with warm water and drop in a piece of aluminum foil. After 15 minutes, remove the silver pieces from the solution and give them a good rinsing. The silver will shine.

Speedy Silverware Cleaning

Fill a pot with a quart of water to which one teaspoon of baking soda and one teaspoon of salt has been added. Bring to a boil, then place the silverware in the pot and allow to boil for two to three minutes, until the tarnish disappears. Dry thoroughly and buff with a soft cloth.

Glassware and Earthenware

Glassware and earthenware that have been used for cooking should never be immersed in cold water until they have been allowed to cool off.

Fine China Test

When buying chinaware, if the article being sold is advertised as genuine, you can test it by holding it up to the light. You will see light through it if it is genuine, because genuine china is translucent. In the case of earthenware or imitation china, on the other hand, light will not shine through.

Improving China

Do not be afraid to "spoil" your good china by using it often. Genuine china is strong and does not suffer from regular normal use. Many, in fact, believe that china improves in strength and appearance with usage.

China Cracks

Hairline cracks in china can often be concealed by boiling the dish in sweet milk. The boiling should last for about an hour at low heat.

Preserving China

China that has been stored in a cool cupboard should be allowed to come to room temperature before hot liquids are poured onto it. This will reduce the chance of cracking.

Washing Fine China

Fine china should be washed by hand, not in a dishwasher. Use mild detergents, for harsh ones wear away the overglaze and damage the metallic decorations found on some china.

Stains on China

Use salt and baking soda to remove stains from china. This is less abrasive than the usual kitchen cleansers.

Gold-trimmed Dishes and Glassware

Dishes and glassware decorated with gold trim should not be washed in dishwashers. This will prevent the decorations from being damaged or scratched.

Strengthening Glassware

Glassware can be strengthened so that it will be less fragile and will last longer. Put the glassware in lightly salted water and bring the water to a slow boil. The slower you boil the water, the stronger the glassware will become.

Glassware Luster

You can add sparkle and life to glassware by rinsing it in water to which a splash of vinegar has been added. Another procedure for restoring luster to glass is to put a few pinches of borax in the wash water.

Lemon juice applied to glass surfaces also makes them sparkle. After drying the glass, buff with paper towels.

Protecting Glassware

When pouring hot liquids into glassware, cushion the shock caused by the sudden change in temperature by inserting a spoon (preferably a silver one) into the

glass. Pour the hot liquid directly onto the spoon and allow it to flow into the glass receptacle.

Protecting Glassware

Glassware can survive the hottest water if you remember to slip it into the water sideways—and slowly. This is particularly true of stemware, which should be held by the stem and slipped slowly into the hot water.

Washing Glassware

When washing glassware, be sure not to do it together with your greasy dishes. If you do, the grease from the dishes will be transferred to the glassware.

Cleaning Glassware

To remove brown stains from glassware, rub with dry baking soda. Then, if necessary, follow through with a mild scouring powder, and complete the procedure with a thorough rinse. Do not use abrasive pot scrubbers because they will scratch the surface of the glass. Fine steel wool, used carefully, can help greatly.

Nicked Glassware

You can round off the sharp edges of nicked glassware with "OO" sandpaper. Wrap the paper around the handle of a pencil and rub the paper across the nicked area until the sharp edges have disappeared. An emery board will also be useful for this purpose.

Toothpaste on Glassware

To remove scratches from glassware, polish the surface with toothpaste.

Wine-stained Glass

Drinking glasses or decanters stained by red wine can be cleaned easily by rinsing with bleach. Of course, this should be followed by a thorough washing with water.

Stained Decanters

Stains that have developed in glass vases and decanters can be removed by soaking them in hot water containing a bit of vinegar. Areas smudged by grease can be cleaned with ginger ale or a cola drink.

Glass Stains

For cleaning stains or cloudiness in glass tumblers, fill the tumblers with water, add one or two teaspoonfuls of ammonia, and allow to stand overnight. An ammonia/water mixture is also a good windowpane cleaner.

Beer Glasses

Beer glasses can be thoroughly cleaned by washing them in a mixture of water and vinegar: one tablespoon of vinegar to one quart of water.

Cleaning Bottles With Tacks

Carpet tacks can sometimes be used to remove the sediment that has gathered on the bottom

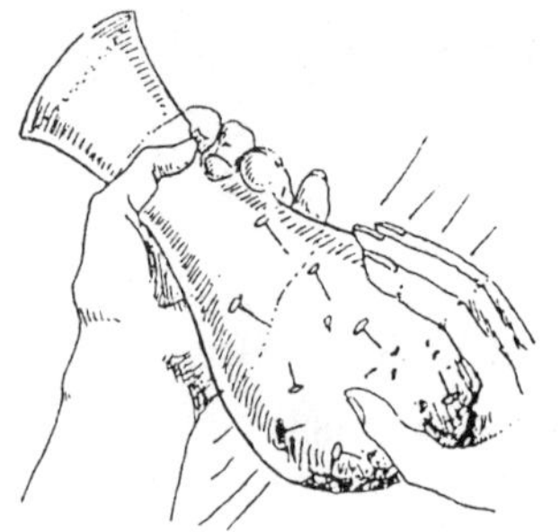

of a glass bottle or vase. Shake vigorously and the tacks will loosen the sediment.

Tough Stains on Porcelain

Porcelain dishes, such as Corningware, can be freed from discoloration by pouring full strength chlorine bleach on them.

Cleaning Porcelain Dishes

Porcelain dishes (which includes chinaware) are best cleaned with a mild detergent in hot water. Scrub, then dry immediately. Commercial cleansers effective in removing stains from porcelain are Dip-It, M-E Cleaner, and Maid Easy. These are generally available in housewares stores.

Teakettle Stains

To remove tea stains from teakettles, fill the pot halfway with water and drop in several pieces of lemon. Boil the water, pour it off, let it cool, then rinse. Rub lemon rind directly on any mineral stains that remain.

Lime Scale in Kettles

The white lime scale that accumulates on the inside of kettles can be eliminated by filling the kettle with water and vinegar, an equal amount of each, and boiling for about fifteen minutes. The acid vinegar will neutralize the lime.

Coffee and Tea Stains on Mugs and Cups

If coffee or tea is allowed to sit in a mug or cup for too long, the liquid is likely to stain the receptacle. The easiest way to remove such stains is to fill the stained cup with liquid bleach and allow it to sit for one or two minutes. The stain will disappear, and the bleach can be reused. Wash out the cup with a sudsy detergent.

Another suggestion for removing coffee and tea stains from porcelain (china) dishware is to rub the stained area with a soft damp cloth that has been dipped into baking soda.

MONEY-SAVING TIPS

A Time for Shopping

If you have little shopping patience, the best time to visit a supermarket is early in the morning or late in the evening, after eight if possible.

Lid Coasters

The plastic lids which come on containers of coffee, peanuts, and shortening cans make good coasters for glasses and cups.

Saving on Bread

Many stores have a separate section for day-old bread. Although it is sold at reduced prices, it has the same nutritive value as fresh bread and will keep for as long as a week.

Buy the store's own brand of bread. It is cheaper and usually not inferior to the bread supplied by well-known baking companies.

Finally, buy bread by weight, not by size.

Save Aluminum Foil

Aluminum foil can be washed off and used repeatedly. When the foil is no longer suitable for baking, for covering leftovers, or for wrapping food for the freezer, crumple it and use it as a pot scrubber.

Cheapest Dishwashing Detergent

If you add two or three tablespoons of vinegar to the dishwater, you can use the cheapest dishwashing detergent and get excellent results.

Steel Wool

When buying steel wool scouring pads, make sure they are labeled "stainless." Otherwise, the pads will rust after one use.

Nylon Netting

If you buy onions and potatoes that are packaged in nylon net bags, save the bags for use as dish scrubbers. Stuff them with a piece of old towel or sponge and use.

Pouring Liquids

Transfer liquids that come in wide-mouthed bottles to bottles with smaller openings. There is generally less spillage when pouring from narrow-mouthed bottles.

KITCHEN SAFETY

Kitchen Accidents

Avoid kitchen accidents by refraining from standing on a chair to reach articles on high shelves. Keep a stool or small stepladder handy at all times.

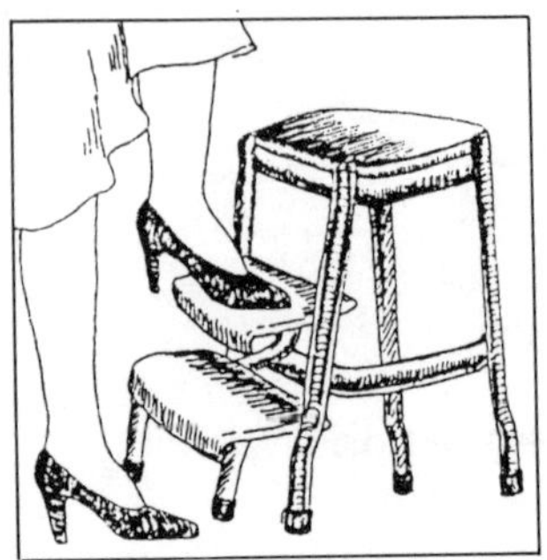

Protect Your Children

Do not store items kids are fond of in cabinets above the range or on the backsplash. Children will be tempted to climb on the range to reach those items and could be seriously injured.

Toaster Caution

While a toaster is plugged into an outlet, never use a metal knife to remove a piece of toast from it. Toasters carry considerable current and are to be handled with caution.

Kids and Kitchen Appliances

If you have young children at home, immediately after using an electric toaster, waffle iron, food processor, and similar items, it is wise to unplug them. To minimize the chance of accidents, try to keep all appliances out of the reach of very young children.

Safe Knife Handling

Keep all kitchen knives sharp, and never cut food as it is being held in the palm of your hand.

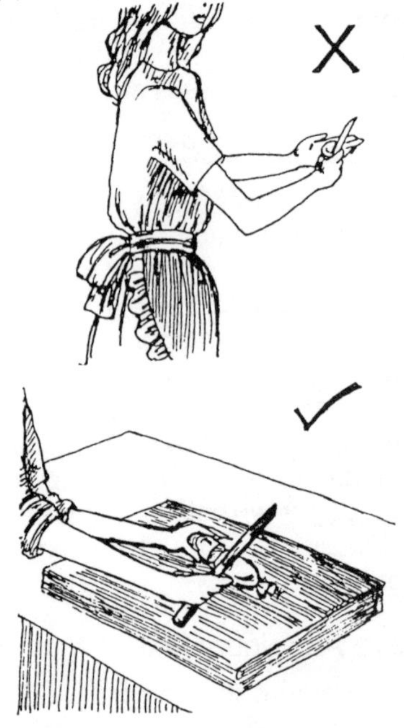

Place the food on a firm surface, and cut away from your body, not towards it.

Cooks Beware

Do not wear loose-fitting clothing, especially loose hanging sleeves, when operating a range. Flammable materials can be easily ignited.

Do not leave pots with their handles sticking out so that one can accidentally bump into them.

Keep Your Eyes on the Burner

Never leave the kitchen while something is cooking on one of the burners; you could become side-tracked. Complete all boiling and frying before taking on another task. If the phone rings, turn off the range before answering it; and ask if you can return the call.

Aluminum Foil Fires

Meats broiled on a sheet of aluminum foil may produce enough melted fat to start a small fire. So, be cautious. First of all, trim all excess fat from the meat before you begin broiling. Secondly, make sure the foil placed beneath the meat has slits cut into it through which the melted fat can drain into the broiler pan.

Heating Food in Cans

Do not heat unopened canned foods in the oven. The buildup of pressure could cause the containers to burst, resulting in severe injury.

Extinguishing Oven Fires

Always have on hand in the kitchen an open box of baking soda ready to throw on flames caused by burning grease or electrical failure. In case of a small fire douse the flames with the baking soda; do not use water.

Flaming Pans

Smother a flaming pan on your range surface by covering it completely with a well-fitting lid, cookie sheet, or flat tray. Do not pour water on grease fires. Flaming grease outside a pan can be put out by dousing it with baking soda.

2
General Cooking Hints

Introduction

The days when preparing a tasty, nutritious meal required an entire afternoon's time have long since passed. With precooked foods and take-out items for sale virtually everywhere, and with microwave ovens available to prepare them in, the job of the meal preparer has become greatly simplified. Nevertheless, almost any dish—even those ready-to-eat—can be improved by judicious seasoning. Experiment with herbs and flavored vinegars to turn the ordinary into the piquant. Herbs are particularly useful to those who wish to reduce their dependence on salt without sacrificing flavor.

In these times of escalating food prices, the wise, innovative cook will find ways of turning leftovers into tasty dishes. With imagination, it is easy to consign the "Tuesday is salmon croquettes, Thursday is chicken" syndrome to history. Bread past its prime can be turned into delicious garlic toast; spaghetti can be combined with leftover vegetables, meat, and fish to create a Chinese delight (add soy sauce or sesame oil for that touch of authenticity); pouting leftover burgers can be brought back to life with a quick sizzle in the oven. Cooking is one area where momma doesn't necessarily know best. Don't be afraid to experiment. Your critics are waiting.

Selecting Pot Sizes

Generally speaking, it is most efficient to cook in flat-bottomed pots that correspond to the size of the burners. Small pots used on large burners waste heat, and

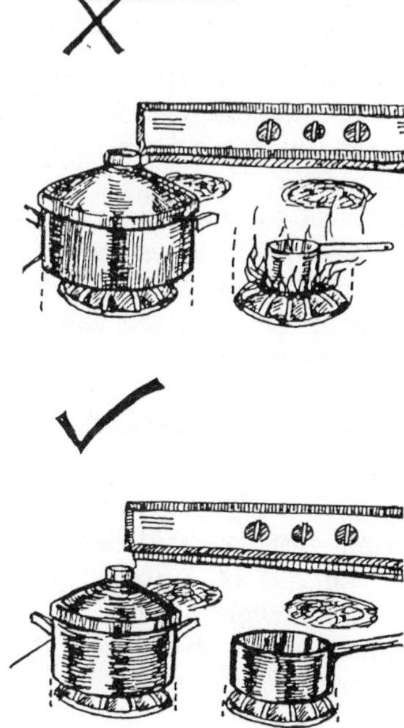

large pots on small burners do not cook evenly. Match the pot to the burner as closely as possible.

Microwaving Casseroles

Microwaves cook more evenly if the food is placed in a shallow casserole with vertical, rather than slanting, sides.

Microwaving to Cut Calories

Since microwaving seals in moisture, it is unnecessary to add oil or butter. Consequently, less fat is consumed, thus cutting down on calorie intake.

Makeshift Double Boiler

If you need a double boiler and don't have one handy, create one by placing a stainless steel mixing

bowl inside a pot with a half-inch to one inch of water. Make sure that the bottom of the bowl does not touch the water.

Frying Without Sticking

Prevent food being fried from sticking to the pan by heating the pan before adding the fat.

Spattering Grease

To keep grease from spattering when fish or meat is being fried, cover the skillet with a colander. The openings in the colander will allow the steam to escape and thus permit the food to brown.

Turning Omelettes

Flipping omelettes and keeping them in one piece is an elusive undertaking. An almost foolproof method is to slide the egg onto a plate and cover it with another plate of like size. Turn the plates upside down and slide the omelette back into the fryer.

Spattering Butter or Oil

To prevent butter or oil from spattering, sprinkle some salt in the frying pan.

Lining a Pan With Foil

If a recipe instructs that the inside of a pan be lined with foil, the foil can be made to fit close to exactly, as follows: First, invert the pan and lay the foil over the bottom of the pan. Then, remove the foil, turn the pan right side up, and insert the shaped foil into the pan.

Reduce Cooking Time

To save money and time when broiling, food to be cooked should be removed from the refrigerator an hour or two before broiling time. Food at room temperature cooks more quickly than cold food.

Preventing Sticking

Precooked french fries and other frozen foods are commonly heated in the oven on a sheet of aluminum foil. To prevent sticking, try crinkling the foil and respreading it before placing the food on the foil. With less foil surface contacting the food, the food will be less prone to stick.

Eliminating Cooking Odors

To rid the kitchen of unpleasant cooking odors, boil three teaspoons of ground cloves for 15 minutes in two cups of water. This will sweeten the air. If you do not have cloves handy, try heating vinegar in a pot for five minutes, allowing the vapors to permeate the room.

Eliminating Smoke Odor

A dish of vinegar left standing in a room will dispel the odor of smoke from cooking food. To get smoke out of a room quickly, soak a towel in water, wring it out, then swish it around the room.

Odors on Hands

To remove the odors of onions and fish from your hands, try rinsing with vinegar. If that doesn't work, try rubbing the palms with damp salt.

Broiling Over Charcoal

When broiling outdoors, it is important to start with a heaping pile of charcoal in order to end up with a large bed of burning coals. After the flames have died down, allow sufficient time for most of the charcoal to turn white before placing meat on the grill.

Trim away excess fat and keep the grill far enough from the coals so that the flames that shoot up periodically from the dripping fat do not burn the meat. It is wise, at the outset, to turn meat over about 30 seconds after first placing it on the grill so that both sides are seared. This will seal in most of the juices.

Barbecue Fires

Never pour lighter fluid or other flammable liquids onto smoldering charcoal. Flames are liable to leap up at you unexpectedly. When lighting charcoal it is also wise to position yourself so that the prevailing wind is at your back.

Charcoal and Cardboard

Instead of using gasoline or charcoal starter to get the barbecue going, place small pieces of cardboard under and in between the charcoals. Burning cardboard (from ordinary cartons) gives off significant heat and in most cases will start the coal burning.

Laying a pine cone or two in the middle of the coals will serve the same purpose as cardboard.

Reusing Charcoal

Charcoal broiling can be rather expensive, but one way to cut the cost is to put the fire out as soon as cooking is finished. Douse the coals with a pot of water, allow to dry, and use the charcoal again. Alternately, the charcoal can be placed in a metal pan with a tight-fitting lid. Position the lid when you wish to extinguish the fire.

Cooking Oils

Corn oil, like safflower oil, is mostly polyunsaturated. Both are good for deep-frying and stir-frying.

Peanut and olive oils are especially recommended for frying. The oils don't pick up odors and tastes as readily as do other oils and will burn only at high temperatures (500 degrees F. or more). They can be strained and used again.

Coconut oil is mostly saturated and therefore tough to digest.

Fruit-flavored Vinegars

Add seasonal berries (or herbs) of your choice to bottles of ordinary white vinegar (blueberries and raspberries are good choices). After two or more weeks, strain and store in attractive bottles.

Reducing Saltiness

Soups and stews that are too salty can be saved by cutting in a few raw potatoes. As the potatoes cook, they will absorb some of the salt. Or, you might try reducing the saltiness by adding a teaspoon of vinegar and/or a pinch of sugar.

Salt Substitute

If you are curtailing your salt intake, try using liberal amounts of fresh lemon and fresh or dried herbs in its place.

Doubling Recipes

Even when a recipe states that the yield of the recipe can be doubled by doubling the ingredients, be careful about doubling the amount of salt called for. A little salt goes a long way, and you will not need twice the amount of salt. Spices should likewise be added sparingly.

Sweetness Antidote

To offset the sweetness of a dish, add a few pinches of salt or a teaspoon of vinegar.

Use Your Pepper Mill

Freshly ground pepper is infinitely more flavorful than the preground kind. So, grind your pepper as needed for a recipe or at the table.

Licorice Flavor

If you are looking to add a hint of licorice taste to a dish, add a dash of crushed anise or fennel seeds.

Cutting Down on Gravy Grease

If your gravy is too greasy, add approximately one-half teaspoon of baking soda and stir well.

Thickening Gravies and Sauces

To thicken one cupful of gravy or sauce, mix one tablespoon of cornstarch with three tablespoons of water. Whisk into the gravy or sauce.

Salad Dressings Without Fat

Instead of using heavy, fatty, oil-based salad dressings, try substituting vinegar or lemon juice flavored with herbs or spices of choice.

Manual Grinder

To crush nuts, place them in a plastic bag and hit lightly with

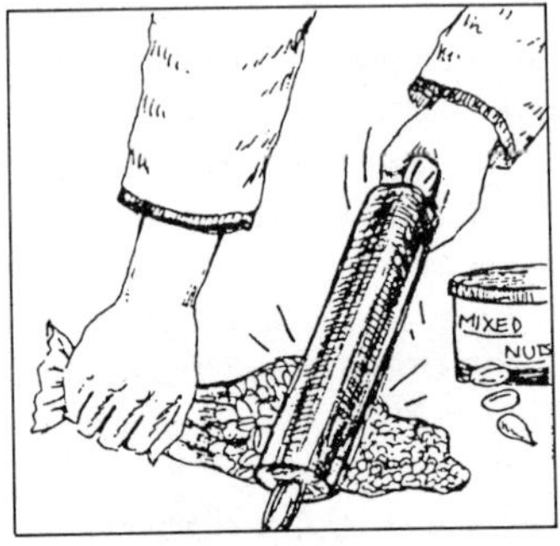

a rolling pin, hammer or similar blunt implement.

Cooling Food Naturally

Because oxygen destroys some of the nutrients in food, try not to stir cooked or hot food in order to cool it off. If food is too hot to eat, allow it to cool off naturally before serving.

Boiling More Efficiently

When boiling water in order to cook spaghetti or potatoes, keep the lid on the pot until the water comes to a boil. Then reduce the heat and keep the top of the pot partially covered. This will enable you to boil at lower heat while providing an avenue for steam to escape.

Pilot Lights

The supply of heat produced by a pilot light can be put to good use. Here are two suggestions:

- Keep a kettle of water on it, and you will enjoy a continual supply of warm water.
- Prunes and similar foods, placed in a pot with a small amount of water, will cook slowly for you.

Hard-cooking Eggs With Residual Heat

When cooking eggs in a shell, bring water to a boil, gently boil the eggs for three minutes, then turn off the heat. Cover the pan with a lid and allow the residual heat to continue the cooking. After ten minutes the eggs will be hard-cooked.

Slicing Apples

Use stainless steel knives to slice apples. Other metals may cause the apples to turn brown.

Cutting Sticky Foods

Sticky foods, such as candied fruits, will cut apart more easily if the knife is dipped in hot water and wiped clean before each cut is made.

Wet Noodles

Wet noodles dropped on a counter or on the floor can be picked up more easily if they are first sprinkled with cornstarch. The cornstarch makes the noodles less slippery and easier to hold on to.

Kitchen Shears

Instead of using a knife to slice, dice, or chop, you may find some kitchen chores easier to execute with shears. Try shears when

- cutting raisins, candied fruits, and marshmallows.
- trimming crusts from bread.
- cutting thin slices of cooked meats.
- cutting away the pulp and seeds from peppers.
- cutting parsley, chives, and other herbs.

If the substance to be cut is sticky, dip the shears in flour first.

Revive Potato Chips and Crackers

Potato chips and crackers that have lost their crispness can be revived by heating them through in an oven or toaster and then letting them cool uncovered.

Brewing Coffee With Distilled Water

Coffee brewed with distilled water is said to be tastier than that brewed with tap water—and the coffeemaker will not have to be cleaned as vigorously.

Old Bread

Don't throw away bread that is too dry to eat. Allow it to stand in the open until it has become hard, then put it in the oven after you have finished a baking project, while the oven is still cooling off. Later, convert the bread to crumbs in a blender or a meat grinder or by placing it in a paper bag and crushing it with a rolling pin. Use the crumbs for meat loaves, croquettes, meatballs, casseroles, and to dip fish before frying or baking.

Softening Hardened Brown Sugar

To soften hardened brown sugar, place a moist but not wet paper towel in a glass jar or plastic bag together with the sugar. The moisture from the towel will transfer to the sugar and soften it within a day or two.

Vinegar and Gelatin

To keep a gelatin mold firm for an extended period of time, add a teaspoon of white vinegar to the gelatin mixture before placing it in the refrigerator to set.

Toasting Coconut

Toast packaged or freshly grated coconut by spreading it in thin layers on a cookie sheet and placing it in an oven at 350 degrees Fahrenheit. Leave the coconut in the oven until golden brown, stirring often for even toasting.

Blanching Almonds

Blanch almonds yourself by pouring boiling water over the shelled nuts. Let them stand in the water for 30 seconds, then remove. When cool, rub the skins off between the thumb and forefinger.

Toasting Blanched Almonds

To toast blanched almonds, place either whole, sliced, or slivered nuts in a large shallow pan. Bake at 350 degrees Fahrenheit for 10 minutes or until toasted golden.

Peanut Butter Spreadability

Avoid wasted energy and save money by adding a teaspoon of hot water to a jar of very thick peanut butter. The peanut butter will spread more easily and will go much farther.

Oven Circulation

For best baking results, the hot air in the oven must circulate freely. To be sure it does, stagger

pans on the oven shelves when baking several items at the same time.

Baking Biscuits

Biscuits bake best on a flat baking surface without sides. For maximum heat circulation, make sure that there is an inch or two of space between the edges of the baking sheet and the sides of the oven.

Opening Oven Door

When baking, avoid opening the oven door frequently. When it is absolutely necessary to open the oven, do so as briefly as possible.

Self-rising Flour

Flour labeled as "self-rising" contains baking powder as a leavening agent. Do not use self-rising flour in a recipe unless it is specifically called for.

Nonstick Sprays

Using a nonstick spray instead of vegetable shortening will save on calorie and fat intake. A nonstick spray will give good results when a recipe calls for a greased and floured baking pan.

Eggs for Baking

If a cake requires two whole eggs and the frosting calls for egg whites, it is possible, by doing a bit of juggling, to save eggs. Use one whole egg in the cake plus two egg yolks. The cake will be moist and you will have two egg whites left for the frosting, instead of two extra egg yolks sitting in the refrigerator. Of course, the finished cake will be altered slightly.

The Sheen on a Pie Crust

If you want an attractive sheen on top of your pie crust, add a teaspoon of water to egg white, beat well, and brush on. Return the pie to the oven for a few minutes. For a darker crust, brush with egg yolk that has been mixed with a teaspoon of water.

Easier Frosting

Frosting can be spread on easily if the cake layers are frozen. The frosting itself should be at room temperature.

Puff Pastry Weather

Don't make puff pastry on a hot summer's day. The butter will warm up very quickly and start to melt, leaving you with a disastrous result. Wait for a nice cool day to undertake puff pastry.

OVEN TEMPERATURES

Degrees Fahrenheit		Degrees Celsius
200	extremely low	100
225	very low	110
250	very low	120
275	low	135
300	low	150
325	moderately low	165
350	moderate	175
375	moderately hot	190
400	hot	205
425	hot	220
450	very hot	230
475	very hot	245
500	extremely hot	260
525	extremely hot	275

Boiling Point: 212 degrees Fahrenheit
100 degrees Celsius

TEMPERATURE CONVERSION

Fahrenheit	subtract 32 and multiply by 5/9 to find Celsius temperature
Celsius	multiply by 9/5, then add 32 to find Fahrenheit temperature

TABLE OF EQUIVALENT AMOUNTS

dash	⅛ teaspoon	2 to 3 drops
1 teaspoon	⅓ tablespoon	⅙ ounce
3 teaspoons	1 tablespoon	½ ounce
1 tablespoon	3 teaspoons	½ ounce
2 tablespoons	⅛ cup	1 ounce
4 tablespoons	¼ cup	2 ounces
5⅓ tablespoons	⅓ cup	2⅔ ounces
6 tablespoons	⅜ cup	3 ounces
8 tablespoons	½ cup	4 ounces
10 tablespoons	⅝ cup	5 ounces
10⅔ tablespoons	⅔ cup	5⅓ ounces
12 tablespoons	¾ cup	6 ounces
14 tablespoons	⅞ cup	7 ounces
16 tablespoons	1 cup	8 ounces
⅛ cup	2 tablespoons	1 ounce
¼ cup	4 tablespoons	2 ounces
⅜ cup	¼ cup plus 2 tablespoons	3 ounces
⅝ cup	½ cup plus 2 tablespoons	5 ounces
⅞ cup	¾ cup plus 2 tablespoons	7 ounces
1 cup	16 tablespoons	8 ounces
1 cup	½ pint	8 ounces
2 cups	1 pint	16 ounces
4 cups	1 quart	32 ounces
16 cups	1 gallon	128 ounces

CAKE PAN CONVERSIONS

If cake calls for:	It will also bake in:
1 8-inch layer	1 11 × 4½ × 2¾-inch rectangle
	9 to 12 2½-inch cupcake pans
2 8-inch layers	2 thin 8 × 8 × 2-inch squares
	18 to 24 2½-inch cupcake pans
	1 13 × 9 × 2-inch rectangle
3 8-inch layers	2 9 × 9 × 2-inch squares
1 9-inch layer	1 8-inch square
	15 2½-inch cupcake pans
2 9-inch layers	2 8 × 8 × 2-inch squares
	3 thin 8-inch layers
	1 15 × 10 × 1-inch rectangle
	30 2½-inch cupcake pans
1 8-inch square	1 9-inch layer
2 8-inch squares	2 9-inch layers
	1 13 × 9 × 2-inch rectangle (with leftover batter)
1 9-inch square	2 thin 8-inch layers
2 9-inch squares	3 8-inch layers (with leftover batter)
	1 15 × 10½ × 1-inch rectangle
1 12 × 8 × 2-inch rectangle	2 8-inch layers
1 13 × 9 × 2-inch rectangle	2 thin 9-inch layers
	2 8 × 8 × 2-inch squares
	2 8-inch rounds
1 8 × 4 × 3-inch loaf	1 8 × 8 × 2-inch square
1 9 × 5 × 3-inch loaf	1 8-inch round
	1 9 × 9 × 2-inch square
	1 11 × 4½ × 2¾-inch rectangle
	24 to 30 2½-inch cupcake pans
1 9 × 3½-inch tube pan	2 9-inch layers
	24 to 30 2½-inch cupcake pans
1 10 × 4-inch tube pan	2 9 × 5 × 3-inch loaves
	1 13 × 9 × 2-inch rectangle
	2 15 × 10 × 1-inch rectangles

WHAT MAKES WHAT

When your recipe calls for:	You will need:
Crumbs	
1 cup soft breadcrumbs	2 slices bread
1 cup dry breadcrumbs	3 slices dry bread
1 cup crushed cereal flakes (corn or wheat)	3 cups cereal
1 cup potato chip crumbs	2 cups firmly packed potato chips
1 cup pretzel crumbs	24 thin pretzels
1 cup fine graham cracker crumbs	12 crackers
1 cup fine gingersnap crumbs	18 2-inch crackers
1 cup fine vanilla wafer crumbs	28 to 30 2-inch crackers
Macaroni and rice products	
2 cups cooked cornmeal	½ cup uncooked
2 cups cooked elbow macaroni	1 cup uncooked or half an 8-ounce package
4 cups cooked small shells	2 cups uncooked
3½ cups cooked noodles	5 cups uncooked or one 8-ounce package
4 cups cooked spaghetti	8-ounce package
4 cups cooked rice	1 cup uncooked rice or 2 cups uncooked instant rice
Dairy	
8 tablespoons butter or margarine	¼ pound or 1 stick or ½ cup
2 cups butter or margarine	1 pound
1 cup freshly grated cheese	¼ pound
1 cup cottage cheese	8 ounces or ½ pound
1 cup whipped cream	½ cup cream for whipping
1 cup sour cream	8 ounces or ½ pint
⅔ cup evaporated milk	1 small can

Eggs	
1 cup whole eggs	4 to 6 eggs
1 cup egg whites	8 to 10 whites
1 cup egg yolks	12 to 14 yolks
Meats	
2 cups ground raw meat	1 pound raw meat
2 cups ground cooked meat	1 pound cooked meat
3 cups diced cooked meat	1 pound cooked meat
4 cups diced cooked chicken	a 5-pound cooked chicken
Fruits, juices, and peels	
1 cup candied fruits	8 ounce jar
1 cup cut-up dates	8 ounces or ½ pound
2 cups cooked prunes	½ pound prunes
4 cups sliced apples	4 medium-sized apples
2 cups sliced strawberries	1 pint strawberries
2 cups pitted cherries	4 cups unpitted cherries
4 cups sliced fresh peaches	2 pounds or 8 medium-sized peaches
4 cups cranberries	1 pound cranberries
1 teaspoon grated orange rind	½ orange
1 cup orange juice	3 medium-sized oranges
1½ teaspoons grated lemon rind	1 lemon
3 tablespoons lemon juice	1 lemon
1 cup lemon juice	4 to 6 lemons
1 cup mashed bananas	3 medium-sized bananas
3 cups seedless raisins	1 pound raisins
Nuts	
1 cup blanched whole almonds	5 ounces shelled almonds
1 cup toasted slivered almonds	5 ounces shelled almonds
1 cup chopped walnuts	¼ pound or 4 ounces shelled walnuts
1 cup pecans	3 ounces shelled pecans
1½ cups whole peanuts	7 ounces
1½ cups chopped peanuts	7 ounces

TO CONVERT A RECIPE TO METRIC MEASURE

Approximate conversion for weight

When you know	*Multiply by*	*To find*
ounces	28	grams (gr.)
pounds	.45	kilograms (kg.)

Approximate conversion for volume

teaspoons	5	milliliters (ml.)
tablespoons	15	milliliters
fluid ounces	30	milliliters
cups	.24	liters (l.)
pints	.47	liters
quarts	.95	liters
gallons	3.8	liters

Approximate conversion for length

inches	2.5	centimeters (cm.)

TO CONVERT A RECIPE FROM METRIC MEASURE

Approximate conversion for weight

When you know	*Multiply by*	*To find*
grams	.035	ounces
kilograms	2.2	pounds

Approximate conversion for volume

milliliters	.03	fluid ounces
liters	2.1	pints
liters	1.06	quarts
liters	.26	gallons

Approximate conversion for length

centimeters	0.4	inches

METRIC EQUIVALENTS FOR COOKING

- Gram (gr.) is the basic unit of weight (mass). There are about 28 grams to the ounce.
- A kilogram equals 1,000 grams.
- A kilogram is just under 2¼ pounds.
- ½ kilogram equals 500 grams, slightly more than 1 pound.
- ¼ kilogram equals 250 grams, marginally more than ½ pound.
- ⅛ kilogram equals 125 grams, slightly more than ¼ pound.
- 1 ounce equals 28 grams.
- ½ ounce equals 14 grams.
- A kilogram is frequently referred to as a kilo.

- Milliliters (ml.) and liter (l.) are the basic units used for measuring liquid volume. There are about 28 milliliters in a fluid ounce.
- 5 milliliters equal 1 teaspoon.
- 15 milliliters equal 1 tablespoon.
- A liter is a little more than 1 quart. Used for milk, wines, or cooking oil.

PORTION CONVERTER

When you want to alter the yield of a recipe, here are some helpful hints to help you save time.

Amount	One-half recipe	One-third recipe
¼ teaspoon	⅛ teaspoon	pinch
½ teaspoon	¼ teaspoon	pinch
1 tablespoon	1½ teaspoons	1 teaspoon
2 tablespoons	1 tablespoon	2 teaspoons
3 tablespoons	1 tablespoon plus 1½ teaspoons	1 tablespoon
4 tablespoons	2 tablespoons	1 tablespoon plus 1 teaspoon

5 tablespoons	2 tablespoons plus 1½ teaspoons	1 tablespoon plus 2 teaspoons
6 tablespoons	3 tablespoons	2 tablespoons
7 tablespoons	3 tablespoons plus 1½ teaspoons	2 tablespoons plus 1 teaspoon
8 tablespoons	4 tablespoons or ¼ cup	2 tablespoons plus 2 teaspoons
⅛ cup	1 tablespoon	2 teaspoons
¼ cup	2 tablespoons	1 tablespoon plus 1 teaspoon
⅓ cup	2 tablespoons plus 2 teaspoons	1 tablespoon plus 2⅓ teaspoons
⅜ cup	3 tablespoons	2 tablespoons
½ cup	¼ cup or 4 tablespoons	2 tablespoons plus 2 teaspoons
⅝ cup	¼ cup plus 1 table-spoon or 5 tablespoons	3 tablespoons plus 1 teaspoon
⅔ cup	⅓ cup or 5 table-spoons plus 1 teaspoon	3 tablespoon plus 1⅔ teaspoons
¾ cup	¼ cup plus 2 table-spoons or 6 tablespoons	¼ cup or 4 tablespoons
⅞ cup	¼ cup plus 3 table-spoons or 7 tablespoons	4 tablespoons plus 2 teaspoons
1 cup	½ cup or 8 table-spoons	⅓ cup or 5 table-spoons plus 1 teaspoon

TEMPORARILY OUT?

For best results, use the ingredients called for in the recipe, but, in an emergency, chances are that you might have a suitable substitute on hand. There may be a slight variation in the texture or taste, but the results will still be fine.

Instead of:	You may use:
1 cup whole milk	4 tablespoons nonfat dry milk plus 2 teaspoons fat (butter or margarine) blended in 1 cup water 1 cup fruit juice or 1 cup potato water in baking
1 cup light cream	⅞ cup milk and 3 tablespoons melted butter—for cooking only
1 cup heavy cream	¾ cup milk plus ⅓ cup melted butter—for cooking only, not whipping
1 cup buttermilk for baking	1 cup sweet milk mixed with 1 tablespoon lemon juice. Let stand for 5 minutes.
1 cup butter	1 cup margarine or ⅞ cup oil
1 whole egg for thickening	2 egg yolks
1 cup honey	1¼ cups sugar plus ¼ cup liquid
1 cup tomato juice	½ cup tomato sauce plus ½ cup water
1 cup canned tomatoes	1½ cups chopped fresh tomatoes simmered for 10 minutes, or ½ cup tomato sauce plus ½ cup water

Instead of:	You may use:
1 cup ketchup	1 cup tomato sauce plus ¼ cup sugar and 2 tablespoons vinegar—for cooking only
½ pound mushrooms	4-ounce can of mushrooms
½ cup seedless raisins	½ cup dried prunes
1 small clove garlic	⅛ teaspoon garlic powder
1 medium-sized onion	1 teaspoon onion powder or 1 tablespoon instant minced onion, rehydrated

3
Meat, Poultry & Fish

Introduction

There is no question that American eating habits are changing. People are consuming more poultry, fish, and vegetables and less fatty red meats. Nevertheless, we continue to consume large amounts of meat, what the beef industry calls "real food for real people."

The enjoyment and nutrition we receive from the meat, poultry and chicken we eat depends largely on how we store, season, and cook them. Uncooked foods should not be stored in the refrigerator for very long before being eaten—a few days at most. That which will not be cooked within that period should be properly wrapped and frozen. Frozen, uncooked meat, poultry and fish will keep from several months to a year.

Consumers should be aware of how fresh meat, poultry and fish are priced and where the best buys are to be found. Gourmet cuts of meat, sold in exclusive shops, can carry price tags several times those of more popular cuts. And yet, imaginatively prepared, cheaper cuts can be as tasty and as nutritious. Like other food items, meats and fishes are more economical at certain times of the year. Turkeys, for example, are sometimes heavily discounted before Thanksgiving. Those with large freezers can realize significant savings if they make large purchases when market prices are favorable.

MEAT

Beef Grades

The United States Department of Agriculture grades beef according to the following classifications:

- *U.S. Prime:* Excellent quality, usually tender and juicy, good distribution of fat through the lean meat.
- *U.S. Choice:* Combines a moderate amount of fat with desirable eating quality. Graded beef sold at a butcher shop is most likely to be U.S. Choice.
- *U.S. Good:* Relatively tender beef with a high ratio of lean to fat.
- *U.S. Commercial:* Most beef of this grade is produced from mature animals. It has a fairly thick fat covering and lacks natural tenderness. Such meat is low-priced and usually requires long, slow cooking.

Government vs. Private Markings

All graded meat is inspected, but not all inspected meat is graded. Although the United States Department of Agriculture (USDA) grade name appears in purple on most retail cuts of meat, meat packers, wholesalers, or retailers may use their own brand names, and these should not be confused with USDA grades. Letters such as A and AA are never used as meat grades by the USDA.

Signs of Good Beef

You can be reasonably sure of the high quality of beef if

- the lean part is light red.
- the lean part looks velvety.
- the lean part is veined with fat.
- the fat is flaky.
- the bones are red.

Meat Prices and Quality

Market prices for a particular cut of meat vary with the supply of that cut available in the commercial market. Loin steaks and center-cut chops cost more because there is less of them on each animal. There are only about 40 pounds of porterhouse, T-bone, and club steak on a steer that weighs 1,000 pounds. A 250-pound porker dresses down to only about 10 pounds of center-cut chops, and a 100-pound lamb yields only about three pounds of loin chops.

Variety Meats

Liver, kidney, heart, and sweetbreads spoil more rapidly than other meats. They should be prepared and cooked on the day of purchase and stored promptly in the coldest part of the refrigerator.

Kosher Franks

Kosher brands of hot dogs, salami, and bologna are made from beef rather than pork and contain less fat and additives than their nonkosher counterparts.

For Best Taste

To derive the best taste from meat products, cook as soon as possible after purchase. Smaller cuts should be used first. Steaks and chops should be refrigerated for only two or three days before cooking or broiling, while roasts will keep a bit longer.

Tenderized Meat

Meat sometimes is treated before cooking so as to increase tenderness. Some tenderizing treatments are applied by the butcher before the meat is sold; others are applied in the home. In the home, round steak and flank steak can be made more tender by pounding it with a mallet. Steaks can also be scored by cutting slashes across the surface or by pounding with a mallet.

Tenderizing With Lemon

To tenderize and flavor meats—particularly veal— pour lemon juice over the meat and allow to stand for 30 minutes before cooking.

Tenderizing With Vinegar

Tough meat may be made tender by rubbing in some vinegar before cooking. Marinating the meat in wine vinegar produces an interesting taste.

Seasoning Meat

To enhance the flavor of beef and veal choose from, but don't limit yourself to, these seasonings: celery, onion, garlic, pepper, parsley, basil, bay leaf, marjoram, thyme.

Extracting Meat Flavor

To get the full flavor from broiled meats, season with salt *after* broiling, not before.

Broiling Steaks and Chops

Proper broiling temperature is 550 degrees Fahrenheit. When the meat is on the broiler rack and the rack is in place, there should be about two inches between the surface of the meat and the heat. If the chops or steaks are very thick, increase the distance.

When broiling in a gas range, keep the door closed. When broiling in an electric range, leave the door slightly ajar. When the meat is well browned, season it with salt and pepper, then turn and brown the other side. Turn only once. For maximum succulence, serve the meat as soon as it is done.

Preserving Flavor

Simmered meat is more flavorful and juicy if it is chilled quickly in the stock in which it was cooked than if the stock is drained from the meat before chilling.

Beef Roasting Procedure

Sprinkle the meat with salt and pepper before placing it fat side up in an open roasting pan or on an oven rack. Insert a meat thermometer through the outside fat into the thickest part of the meat, making sure that the thermometer tip does not rest on bone or fat. Roast at 325 degrees Fahrenheit without adding water or covering the pan.

A sirloin tip, standing rib, or rolled rib roast of about six pounds will be rare when the meat thermometer reaches 140 degrees, medium at 160 degrees, and well done at 170.

Veal Roasting Procedure

Regardless of the cut, when roasting veal, follow the above preparation directions for roasting beef. Your oven should be set at 325 degrees Fahrenheit until the meat thermometer reaches 180 degrees.

Roasting Fresh Pork

Follow the above preparation directions for roasting beef. Keep the oven temperature at 325 degrees Fahrenheit throughout the roasting. Pork loin, as well as shoulder or crown roast cuts of about four pounds, will be done when the meat thermometer reaches 185 degrees. If there is even so much as a tinge of pink in the meat, increase roasting time until the pink color disappears.

Storing Venison

An excellent candidate for freezer storage is venison. If wrapped well, it will retain its freshness for a year and make an unusually attractive main dish.

Freezing Small Cuts of Meat

Small cuts of meat that are to be kept for more than three days should be frozen. Meats to be stored in the freezer for only a week or two should be wrapped first in heavy wax paper, then in aluminum foil. Wrap chops and patties individually in wax paper, then overwrap several at a time in foil. Use special freezer paper for long-term storage.

POULTRY

Selecting a Chicken

Before buying a whole chicken, examine the thighs and neck. They should be neither thin or scrawny. Also, check the skin color before making a purchase. You'll find that chickens with a light yellow skin-color have the best meat.

Chicken Sizes

When purchasing ready-to-cook chicken for broiling, allow one-quarter to one-half of a bird per serving. When buying ready-to-cook birds for roasting, stewing, or frying, purchase three-quarters of a pound per serving. Small chickens are best for broiling. Young birds have smooth, tender skin, soft tender meat, and a flexible breastbone.

Selecting Poultry for Freezing

Freeze only fresh, high-quality poultry. Choose well-fleshed birds with few skin blemishes.

Select poultry according to how you plan to use the frozen product. Young chickens or turkeys are suitable for roasting, frying, and broiling. Mature poultry can be used for braising and stewing.

Poultry that is properly frozen and stored only for the recommended time can be as good as fresh poultry.

Freezing Poultry Pieces

To freeze, place meaty pieces, such as the breast, legs, and wings, close together in a freezer bag or freezer wrap. To shorten thawing time, place a double layer of freezer wrap or wax paper between the pieces so they can be easily separated for thawing. Seal, label, and freeze.

Defrosting a Bird

Experts advise that, for safety's sake, it is best to avoid defrosting poultry at room temperature. After removing the chicken, goose, or turkey from the freezer, defrost it in the refrigerator, in a microwave oven, under cold running water, or in a cold water bath, changing the water at least once every 30 minutes. Frozen poultry should be completely thawed before cooking.

Refreezing Poultry

Frozen raw or cooked poultry that has thawed may be safely refrozen if it still contains ice crystals or if it is still below 40 degrees Fahrenheit and has been held no longer than one or two days at refrigerator temperatures after thawing. Thawing and refreezing may lower the eating quality of the food.

Stewing Chicken

Place small pieces of chicken in a pot and add boiling water to cover. Add vegetables and seasonings. Cover and simmer over low heat for about two hours, then remove the vegetables and add a paste of two tablespoons of flour mixed with cold water for every cup of broth, stirring a bit of the broth into the paste first. While cooking continues over low heat, stir until the gravy thickens and comes to a boil. Stir for an additional minute and serve.

Baked Chicken Pieces

First, in a skillet brown pieces to be baked, then put the pieces in an open or covered casserole. Bake in the oven at 325 degrees Fahrenheit for one hour or until done.

Baked Foil-wrapped Chicken

Before baking, brush the chicken halves (or quarters) with melted butter and sprinkle on salt, pepper, and other seasonings, including garlic if desired. Wrap the pieces in foil so that the juices will not be lost. Place in a shallow pan or on a cookie sheet and bake for 50 minutes at 400 degrees Fahrenheit. When the baking is finished, pull back the foil and brown the chicken in the broiler. Periodically baste the bird with its own juices during broiling.

Deep-fried Chicken

Small fryers of two pounds or less are best for frying. Roll the pieces in seasoned flour and fry for ten minutes in deep fat at 350 degrees Fahrenheit. Drain before serving.

Broiling Chicken

Broil halves or parts of small broiler-fryers, skin side down, in a preheated broiler. The heat source should be about five inches from the surface of the chicken. Brush the bird with melted butter or margarine, and broil for about 15 minutes. Season and turn. A whole chicken or individual parts weighing about one pound will require 25 to 30 minutes cooking time.

Chicken in Cream Sauce

To bake chicken in cream sauce, roll the chicken parts in flour with salt and pepper, then brown them in butter. Combine a cup of sour cream with a cup of water, add sliced mushrooms, and bake the chicken in the sauce.

Roasting Fowl

To roast chicken and small turkeys, place in a 325-degree Fahrenheit oven, breast up. Use a shallow, uncovered pan. Protect the breast skin and top of the legs with a loose piece of aluminum foil. During roasting, occasionally baste the chicken with melted fat. On the average, two hours for a three-pound bird is adequate roasting time.

Roasting Ducks and Geese

Place a V-shaped rack in the roasting pan and set the bird breast-up on the rack. Prick the breast skin of a large goose in several places so that the fat can drain off. During roasting, do *not* brush the bird with the melted fat.

During the first half of the roasting period, protect the breast and legs with a loose piece of aluminum foil, then remove it. Prick the skin a second time and finish the roasting at 350 degrees Fahrenheit.

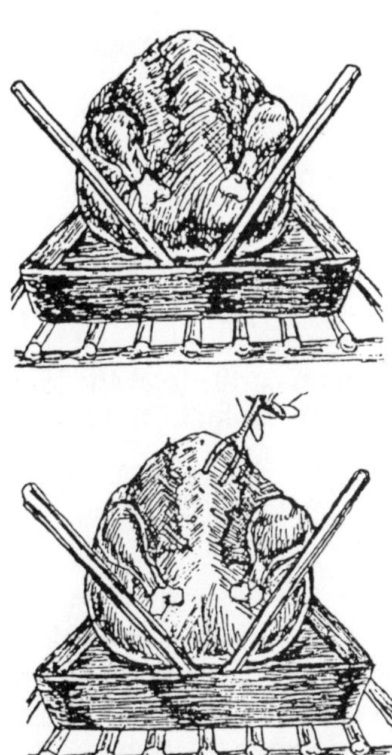

Begin the roasting of ducks at 325 degrees and allow two hours for a three-pound duck and three hours for a bird that weighs over four pounds.

A goose of approximately six pounds requires three hours roasting time, beginning at 325 degrees Fahrenheit.

The Turkey Market

Most turkeys are marketed when young. They are tender-meated and suitable for roasting. Small, young turkeys that can be broiled or fried as well as roasted are available in some stores. These will suit the needs of small families. Generally, turkeys range from four to 24 pounds, ready to cook.

Storing Turkey

Refrigerate leftover turkey as you would any other fowl. However, if the turkey has been stuffed, first remove the stuffing and store separately.

CARVING A TURKEY

1. Remove the drumstick by pulling the leg from the body, loosening it as much as possible. Then cut through the skin and soft part of the joint. Press the knife firmly. If you hit bone rather than cartilage at the joint, move the knife to one side or the other until the knife can cut through without undue difficulty.

2. Make an incision into the white meat in a horizontal line parallel to the wing. Cut deep into the breast until you feel the body frame.

3. Now, starting halfway up the breast, slice down into the white meat. Cut thick or thin slices to suit your taste. End each downward cut at the horizontal cut first made. Don't carve more than is needed for the meal. Store uncut turkey as a whole. This will keep the meat from drying out.

FISH

Fish and Heart Attacks

Scientific studies have shown that eating a fish meal two or three times a week helps prevent heart attacks. Even if a person has suffered one such attack, eating several servings of fish per week is said to help substantially reduce the chances of recurrence.

Shellfish and Cholesterol

While some varieties of shellfish—crayfish, shrimp, and squid, for example—are high in cholesterol, many—including crab, mussels, scallops, and clams—are lower in cholesterol than even chicken.

Kosher Fish

Do not offer anyone who observes the Jewish dietary laws shellfish or fish that does not have fins and scales. These are prohibited foods in Chaper 11 of the Book of Leviticus.

Choose Tuna in Water

Tuna packed in water rather than oil is more healthful.

Looking a Fish in the Eye

You can tell a fresh fish by looking it straight in the eye. The eyes should be clear, unclouded, and shiny.

In addition to checking the eyes, when selecting a fish take note of the following:

- The gills should be reddish-pink and not slimy.
- The scales should be bright and shiny and not loose.
- The flesh should be firm to the touch. It should spring back when pressed in.

Fillet vs. Whole Fish

Although whole fish is cheaper than fillets or steaks, do not forget that there is considerable waste in whole fish. There is no waste in fillets, and only a small amount of waste in steaks. Keep these facts in mind when comparing prices.

Preserving Fish

For maximum flavor, eat fresh fish the same day you buy it. If you must keep it for a few days, freeze the uncooked fish in a container filled with water. Be sure to remove the head. When ready to use, allow the fish to thaw, then cook immediately.

Fish Scales

Fish scales will come off easily if the fish is dipped in hot water very briefly before it is cleaned.

Washing Fish

Fish and seafood need only be

dipped in water and wiped dry before cooking. Holding either fish or seafood under running water for extended periods of time detracts from its succulence.

Slippery Fish

You can prevent fish from slipping through your fingers by dipping your fingers in salt.

Overcooking Fish

Fish, unlike meat, does not become more *tender* with cooking. Fish becomes more flavorful as it is cooked, but only to a point. Overcooking adds nothing to the flavor; it only toughens the fish.

Broiling Fish Fillets

When broiling fish fillets, remember that they generally do not have to be turned, and neither do shrimp or scallops. Broil for three to ten minutes, depending on thickness, until the fish feels firm when touched.

Broiling Whole Fish and Fish Steaks

Depending on the thickness, broil *thick* fish steaks and whole fish for three to eight minutes before turning. Turn only once. After turning, brush with butter and sprinkle with seasonings.

Baking Fish

Bake fish at 350 degrees Fahrenheit for ten to 20 minutes per pound. Bake tiny fish at the same temperature for one or two minutes per ounce. When the fish feels firm to the touch, it is cooked.

Baking a Whole Fish

Remove the head of the fish only *after* baking. If removed beforehand, the fish will be dry and tough at the cut end. By leaving the head on, the flavor and juices of the fish are sealed in and the amount of cooking required is reduced.

Pan-fried Fish

Before pan-frying, dip fillets, fish steaks, shellfish, and split or whole small fish in milk to which has been added a beaten egg and two tablespoons of water. After dipping, roll the fish in bread or cracker crumbs. Fry in hot oil (375 degrees Fahrenheit) until light brown on both sides, making sure the fat doesn't burn.

Smoking Fat

The odor that fried fish sometimes gives off comes not from the fish but from the smoking fat. To keep deep fat from reaching the smoking point, watch the flame. Make sure the heat is not too intense.

Avoiding Fish Odor

To keep your hands from smelling fishy, soak the fish in cold water to chill it before handling.

Fish Odors

To get rid of a fish odor, wash your hands with vinegar and rinse off with water. A solution of one tablespoon of salt in a glass of tap water will also yield good results.

Fish Garnishes

Tomatoes, mushroom caps, and baked potatoes (split and topped with cheese or sour cream) make wonderful garnishes for broiled fish.

4
Dairy Products & Eggs

Introduction

Because they are inexpensive sources of protein, dairy products and eggs are a staple in almost every household. For those interested in a modified vegetarian diet, these foods often take the place, nutritionally, of meat and fish. A traditional objection to consumption of eggs and milk products as a protein source has been that these items contribute to increased blood cholesterol levels. One answer to this is that the body actually requires relatively little protein to sustain itself, and for most people it is thus possible to reduce egg and dairy intake without denying the body what it needs. A recent far-ranging dietary study in China shows that Americans consume, on average, one-third more protein than do Chinese. Yet, the lifespan of the average Chinese, despite vastly inferior living conditions and health care, is almost equal to that of the average American.

For those who rely heavily on dairy products and are concerned about their intake of saturated fats, a solution lies in low-fat products. Virtually all dairy products—cheeses, milk, yogurt, ice cream, sour cream—come in low-fat formulations. Because butterfat contributes much to the taste of these foods, those containing reduced amounts of fat will not be as rich as their full-fat counterparts. It should be remembered, however, that fat intake reduction is not an either/or proposition. In most cases, choosing low-fat dairy alternatives *selectively* will provide significant health benefits without forcing you to sacrifice eating enjoyment.

MILK AND CREAM

Storing Milk

Take milk out of the refrigerator only when you are ready to use it. Left standing at room temperature, milk quickly loses its freshness. Store it in the coldest part of the refrigerator (never in the door) and keep it covered, otherwise it will quickly take on the flavor of other foods.

Low-fat Milk Keeps Longer

Whole milk will keep in the refrigerator under normal circumstances for seven to ten days. Low-fat milk, however, will sometimes keep for up to three weeks. The exact period that milk will store depends on how old the milk was when purchased, how often it is removed from the refrigerator, and how cold the refrigerator is.

Freezing Milk

If you have a large quantity of milk on hand and are about to go on vacation, or if you wish to keep milk on hand for an emergency, do not be afraid to freeze it. Thaw the milk in the refrigerator or at room temperature. Although the texture of the thawed product will not always be the same as the original, it will be suitable for use.

Evaporated Milk

Cover opened cans of evaporated milk before storing them in the refrigerator. Use wax paper, plastic wrap, or aluminum foil and secure it with a rubber band. The covering will stop the milk from drying out around the lip where the can was opened and will prevent flavors of other foods from penetrating the milk.

Dry Milk

Keep dry milk in unopened packages at room temperature, preferably not above 75 degrees Fahrenheit. Once you have opened the package, be careful to reseal it tightly, and keep it in a tightly covered can or jar in the refrigerator.

Scalding Milk

The best way to scald milk is to heat it over simmering water in the top of a double boiler. In this way the milk will not be scorched.

Reducing Fat Intake

To reduce fat intake, substitute skim milk, 1% milk, or 2% milk for whole milk or buttermilk.

Delaying Spoilage

If you must leave milk or cream unrefrigerated for an extended period, retard spoilage by adding an ice cube or two to the container.

Milk and Cream Spoilage

To delay spoilage of milk or cream, transfer it from its cardboard container to a glass jar.

Preventing Cream From Curdling

Often, when poured over fruits and berries, cream tends to curdle. You can prevent this by adding a pinch of baking soda to the cream before pouring.

Whipping Heavy Cream

Heavy cream whips more easily if the cream, the beaters, and the mixing bowl are chilled. Place them in the refrigerator or freezer for about ten minutes before whipping.

Cream as Decoration

If you wish to decorate your cake with whipped cream, it would be wise to use a stabilizer to give the cream extra body.

Combine one teaspoon of unflavored gelatin with one to two tablespoons of water. Let stand for five minutes, until the liquid has been absorbed, then place over simmering water until the gelatin is clear. Let cool to room temperature, then gradually whisk the gelatin into the cream, making sure it is incorporated thoroughly. When the cream has reached the desired degree of stiffness, cover and refrigerate until needed. Use within 12 to 24 hours. Whipped cream so stabilized can be piped through a pastry bag or spread with a spatula.

Lemon for Rapid Whipping

Use four drops of lemon juice per half pint (one cup) of cream. This will make cream whip more rapidly. Count the drops, because too much lemon juice will sour the cream. If you have an eyedropper on hand, use it to count the drops.

Ultra-pasteurized Cream

Heavy cream that has been ultra-pasteurized keeps much longer than regular pasteurized cream, but it is considerably harder to whip and is not as tasty.

EGGS

Storing Whole Eggs

Contrary to conventional wisdom, egg racks on refrigerator doors are not the best place to store whole eggs. Experts now tell us that fresh eggs are best stored in the cartons in which they are sold.

A covered container is best for storing whole shelled eggs because the membrane is porous and will absorb the odors of foods stored near them.

Refrigerating Eggs

Eggs always require refrigeration. This is also true for cooked or uncooked foods containing eggs. Do not buy unrefrigerated eggs, and when using eggs for baking do not leave them at room temperature for more than two hours.

Brown vs. White Eggs

In some parts of the country, brown eggs are considered to be of higher quality than white eggs. The reverse is believed to be true in other parts of the country. Actually, there is no difference in the quality, so buy whichever is cheaper.

Dried Eggs

Keep dried eggs in unopened packages in a cool place (50 to 60 degrees Fahrenheit), but preferably in the refrigerator. Once opened, keep in a tightly covered jar in the refrigerator.

Cracked Eggs in a Carton

If the eggs in a carton have cracked and some have stuck to the carton, simply wet the box and you will easily be able to remove the eggs that were stuck without further cracking them.

How Long to Keep Eggs

Do not allow raw eggs to sit in the refrigerator for more than five weeks. Hard-cooked eggs can be kept safely for one week.

Testing the Age of an Egg

If you're in doubt about the freshness of an egg, put it in a deep container of cold water. A fresh egg will sink to the bottom. An egg that inclines at an angle is several days old. An egg that

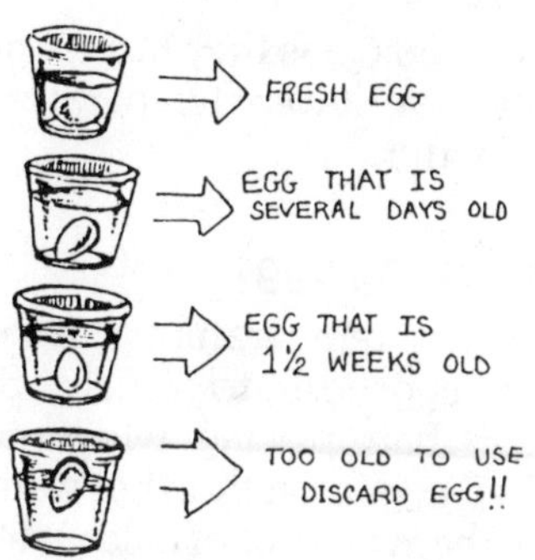

stands upright is about a week-and-a-half old. An egg that floats to the top is too old to use and should be discarded.

Raw or Cooked?

If you're not sure whether an egg is raw or cooked, lay it on its side and give it a whirl. If the egg wobbles while rotating, it's raw.

Simmer, Don't Boil

Because egg whites and yolks tend to coagulate at temperatures below the boiling point, it's better to simmer eggs than cook them in vigorously boiling water. For soft-cooked eggs, simmer for three minutes; for firm but soft yolks, simmer for four minutes; for eggs even more firm but still soft, simmer for five minutes. Hard-cooked eggs should be simmered for ten minutes.

By simmering rather than boiling hard-cooked eggs, you'll avoid that green division that appears between yolk and white—and you'll avoid that hard-boiled egg odor. Also, cooking at a high temperature toughens the protein in eggs, and the tougher eggs are, the less delicious they taste. Eggs cooked at lower temperatures taste better.

Hard-boiling Eggs

Sudden temperature changes cause eggshells to crack. So, rather than placing whole uncooked eggs directly in hot water, place them in a pot of cold waters then place the pot over the heat source.

As an extra precaution, after placing eggs in the pot with cold water, add a few pinches of salt or a teaspoonful of vinegar. Should the eggs crack, the salt and vinegar will usually prevent them from oozing.

Another Way to Hard-boil an Egg

To make perfect hard-boiled eggs, bring a pot of water to a boil. Turn off the heat. Place room-temperature eggs into the water. Cover the pot and let stand for 15 minutes.

Cracked Shells

If the egg you are about to boil is cracked on one side, crack it a little on the other side. If you do this, you will find that the egg will stay inside the shell while it boils.

Shelling Hard-boiled Eggs

The shells of hard-boiled eggs can be removed easily if you rinse them in cold water as soon as they are taken out of the hot water.

Eggs in Cake Recipes

If a cake recipe calls specifically for large eggs, it is best not to substitute extra-large ones. Doing so might cause the cake to fall when cooled.

Separating Whites From Yolks

One way of separating egg white and yolk without breaking the yolk is to puncture a small hole in one end of the shell and let the white drain into a dish while the yolk stays unbroken inside. Afterwards, break open the shell and remove the yolk.

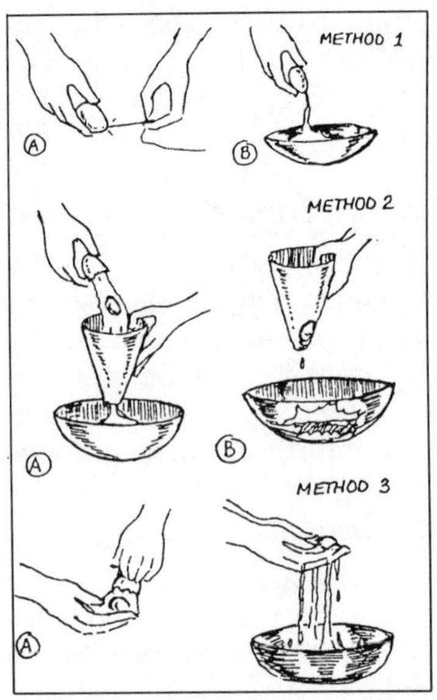

An alternative is to pour both the yolk and the white of the egg into a funnel held above a bowl. The yolk will stay in the funnel while the white runs into the bowl.

Still another way to successfully separate white and yolk is to crack the egg and pour the contents into the palm of the hand. Allow the white to slide through your fingers into a bowl below.

Adding Eggs to Batter

It's not a good idea to drop eggs directly from the shell into the batter. One bad egg will spoil the batter. Crack each egg open in a separate bowl. If the egg is rotten, you will smell it. Also, if a bit of eggshell falls into it, you will be able to remove it with ease.

Fluffy Meringue

Adding white vinegar to egg whites before beating them helps produce fluffy meringue. Use one-half teaspoon of vinegar to six egg whites.

Fluffier Omelets

If you want your omelets to be fluffly, use eggs that have been left out of the refrigerator for at least one-half hour. Adding a pinch of cornstarch or a few tablespoons of milk or water to the eggs before beating also helps turn out fluffy omelets.

Beating Egg Whites

Eggs darken aluminum, so it's a good idea not to beat egg whites in an aluminum bowl. Use bowls made of stainless steel, glass, porcelain, or enamel.

Centering the Yolk

Storing eggs with the wide end up helps to keep the yolk centered.

Storing Egg Yolks

For short-term storage of egg yolks, place the yolks in a container and add water to cover. Then close the container and refrigerate. Drain the water and use the yolks within three to four days. For long storage for future use in baking, mix each yolk with a teaspoon of sugar and freeze.

CHEESE

Buy Cheese in a Busy Store

Buy cheese only in a store that does a brisk business. Chances are that the greater a store's turnover, the fresher the cheese will be.

Moldy Cheese

Being a high-moisture food, cheese is susceptible to mold. Moldy cheese should be discarded. Simply cutting away the mold does *not* solve the problem, because fungi have roots, and these roots may extend deep into the cheese.

Don't Overstock

Buy only as much cheese as will be used within a few days of purchase. Freshness is one assurance of tastiness and quality.

Sampling Cheese

Whenever possible, sample cheeses before buying. Many stores will cut off a sliver for tasting.

ON MEASURING CHEESE

When a recipe calls for a specific measure of cheese—a cup, for example—it is easy to determine how much to purchase by following these rules of thumb:

- 4 ounces or ¼ pound of cheese = 1 cup shredded. This rule applies to all varieties of natural or process cheese. When measuring, be sure to lightly pack the cheese level with the top of the measuring cup.
- When measuring cottage cheese or cream cheese, use the following guide:

1 pound cottage cheese = 2 cups
3 ounces cream cheese = 6 tablespoons
8 ounces cream cheese = 1 cup or 16 tablespoons

Serving Temperatures for Cheese

Since full flavor cannot be released when cheese is cold, the correct serving temperature is vital. All cheeses, except cottage or pot cheese, should be served at room temperature.

Firm and semifirm cheeses, such as Swiss Emmentaler and Gouda, should be removed from the refrigerator at least one hour before serving. Extra-large chunks will require two to three hours to come to room temperature.

Soft and semisoft cheeses, such as Bonbel, Muenster, Camembert, and Brie, need from 20 to 30 minutes to come to room temperature.

Leaving Cheese Out Too Long

Cheese left at room temperature for too long will dry out. Therefore, take only as much cheese out of the refrigerator as you think will be eaten within two hours after guests begin arriving.

Strong and Mild Cheeses

Strong and mild cheeses should be kept apart so that flavors and odors do not mix. A small branch of rosemary or thyme set on the serving platter will help offset the odor of strong cheeses.

Storing Hard Cheese

Wrap cheese in wax paper, aluminum foil, or plastic wrap so that air will not make contact with it. Then, store it in the refrigerator. Packaged cheese can be stored in its original wrapping, but use additional wrapping if the original has been torn or opened.

Treatment of Soft-ripening Cheese

After removing a cut piece of a soft-ripening cheese (Brie, Camembert, Coulommiers, etc.)

from the refrigerator, to prevent it from running, press strips of wood against the cut surfaces of the cheese. Allow the cheese to come to room temperature before serving.

Dried-out Cheese

Cheese that has dried out and is no longer suitable for serving can be grated and stored for use in future cooking.

Grating Cheese

A small grater is a very valuable kitchen tool, for cheeses grated at home usually have more flavor than pregrated packaged counterparts. Use the small coarse openings of a grater to grate cheese. Firm or hard cheeses grate most easily into very fine particles.

Easier Grating

Thoroughly chilled cheese will shred or grate more easily than cheese at room temperature.

When Freezing Cheese

To retain its consistency, cheese should be frozen as quickly as possible. To hasten the freezing process, large pieces of cheese should therefore be cut into half-pound chunks that are no thicker than one inch.

Be sure to wrap the cheese tightly in a moistureproof material such as foil or plastic wrap. Or place it in a plastic bag and draw out as much air as possible. This will prevent the cheese from losing moisture and will thereby insure freshness.

Which Cheeses to Freeze

Most firm or semifirm cheeses can be kept frozen for as long as six months, provided that they are properly wrapped. Soft to semisoft cheeses and blue-veined cheeses are generally more fragile and may not take well to freezing. Before freezing a large supply, it is best to experiment with a small quantity of a given cheese and then test it for flavor and consistency.

Warming Up Frozen Cheese Dishes

To heat up frozen cheese dishes, cover them tightly with foil and place in a moderate oven.

Making Cheese Sauce

When making a cheese sauce, add the cheese to the other ingredients at the last minute. Allow the sauce to cook only until the cheese melts. When reheating cheese sauces, *warm* them over hot water in the top part of a double boiler.

Cooking With Cheese

When you cook with cheese, keep the heat at a very low temperature. This will prevent the cheese from curdling or scorching. Don't overcook.

On Melting Cheese

When melting cheese, instead of using direct heat, use a double boiler and keep the heat moderate.

Broiling Cheese Dishes

When broiling a dish topped with cheese, place the pan so that the cheese is several inches below the heat source. Broil just until the cheese melts.

Cheese and Fruit

Some cheeses taste better with particular fruits than others. You might want to try:

- Swiss with orange sections.
- Camembert with apples.
- Roquefort with pears.
- Liederkranz with grapes.

Serve apples, pears, and cheese cut into pieces and speared on toothpicks.

Buying a Fondue Set

Be careful when purchasing a fondue set. The market is saturated with imitations of the original Swiss equipment. In too many cases this colorful equipment not only performs inadequately but is actually dangerous to use. Be aware that most fondue sets on the market are designed for beef fondue; few are suitable for cheese.

Entertaining With Cheese

When serving cheese to guests, plan on purchasing about one-quarter pound of cheese per guest (that is, for eight guests you will need two pounds of cheese in all). Vary the forms and shapes of the cheeses served. For example, serve Swiss slices, Cheddar cubes or fingers, and wedges of blue cheese as part of an arrangement.

CHEESE KNIVES

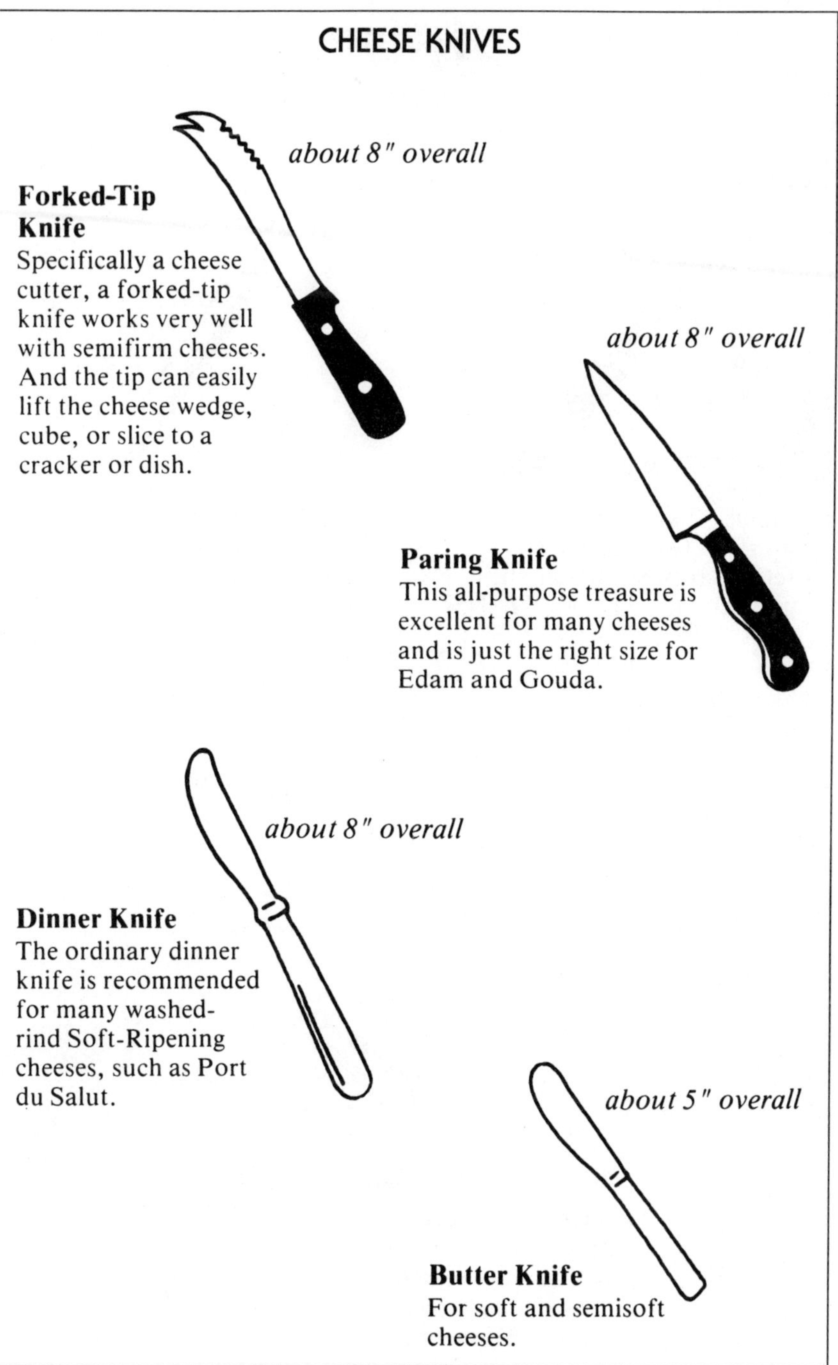

Forked-Tip Knife
Specifically a cheese cutter, a forked-tip knife works very well with semifirm cheeses. And the tip can easily lift the cheese wedge, cube, or slice to a cracker or dish.

Paring Knife
This all-purpose treasure is excellent for many cheeses and is just the right size for Edam and Gouda.

Dinner Knife
The ordinary dinner knife is recommended for many washed-rind Soft-Ripening cheeses, such as Port du Salut.

Butter Knife
For soft and semisoft cheeses.

CHEESE CUTTERS

about 9″ overall

Double-Wire Cheese Cutter
The perfect cutter for cheeses that crumble, this cutter consists of two taut wires stretched between handle and cap at the end of a 5″ steel rod.

about 6″ overall

Cheese Sampler
You will find this professional tool most useful, for with it you can pierce the center of a Soft-Ripening cheese to check for ripeness without disturbing the ripening process. Its blade is sharp and trough-like and works like a simple corkscrew.

about 9″ overall

Scandinavian Cheese Slicer and Server
This is the most common special cheese cutter. The slit in its stainless steel blade is used to shave semifirm cheeses.

CHEESE CUTTERS

about 20" overall

Double-Handled Cheese Cutter
Made specifically to cut great wheels of firm cheese. When used, equal pressure should be exerted on both sides.

about 13" overall

Single-Handled Cheese Cutter
A more practical tool for the beginner than its double-handled counterpart, it is equally well constructed and made to cut firm cheeses from one side.

about 9" x 6" overall

Cheese Chopper
The huge blade and small handle make the cheese chopper less than ideal for cutting large firm cheeses, but it is an especially good device to mince slices or small chunks for cooking.

Cheese Scraper and Gouger
Shaped much like a sculptor's tool, the scraper can be used for gouging chunks or extra-hard cheese for grating or nibbling. It is also ideal for Raclette.

HOW TO CUT CHEESES

CUT SQUARE CHEESES AND WHEELS IN WEDGES...

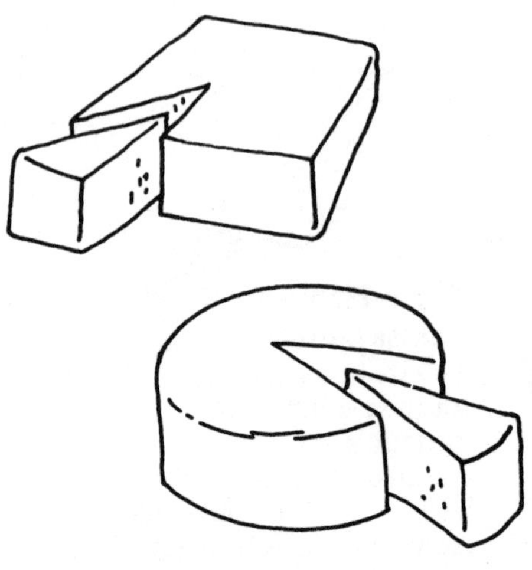

CUT SOFT SURFACE-RIPENED CHEESES IN TAPERED SLICES

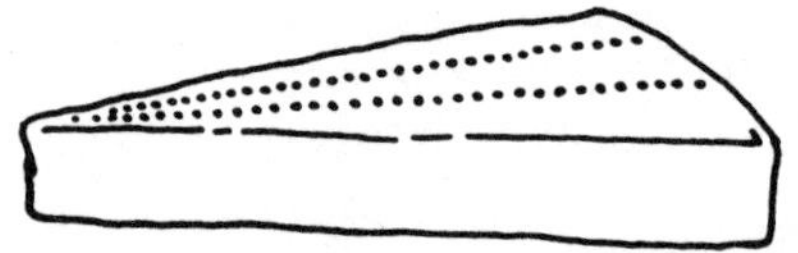

CUT BLUE-VEINED CHEESES ON THE BIAS....

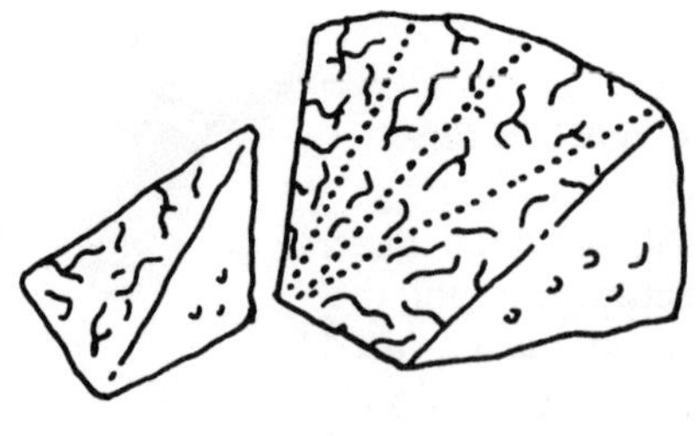

CUT CYLINDRICAL AND RECTANGULAR CHEESES IN SLICES...

CUT SMALL GOAT CHEESES IN HALF...

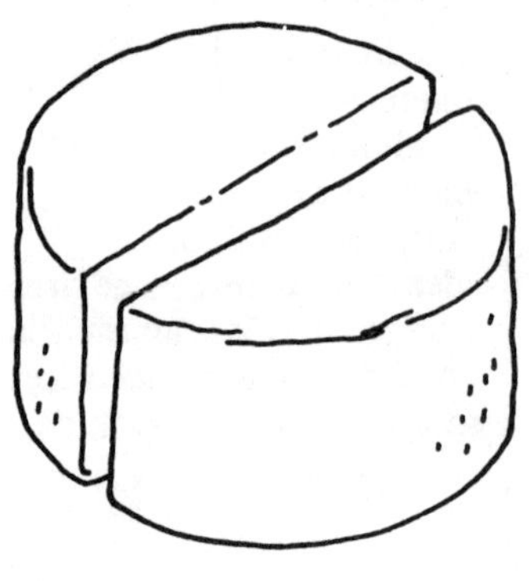

5
Fruits, Vegetables, Grains & Herbs

Introduction

Improved storage and transportation methods have made fruits and vegetables that used to be considered seasonable available the year 'round. Sweet corn from Florida can be found in northern supermarkets in the dead of winter, together with peaches and plums from South America. But this convenience comes with a steep price, and the consumer would do well to buy with the market and the season. He or she should also become acquainted with the best ways of preserving and storing fresh produce. Apples and pears bought at favorable prices in season, for example, can be stored successfully in the refrigerator for up to several months if proper procedures are followed.

Much about the quality of fresh produce can be gleaned from its appearance. Succulent, shiny leaves and skins indicate healthy, fresh fruits and vegetables, while dull, limp, shriveled produce has passed its prime. Purchasers should, however, be aware that many produce outlets sprinkle their fruits and vegetables. While misting can certainly prolong the life of prime produce, it should not be allowed to mask that which is inferior. Nor should consumers be deceived by the plastic coatings on apples and cucumbers, which can heighten the eye appeal and conserve the natural moisture of the product but do nothing to enhance its inherent quality.

That Fresh-squeezed Taste

There is good reason why canned juice doesn't have the tang of fresh-squeezed: there's something missing. That something is the air that was removed during the canning process. Bring canned juice back to life by stirring it well with a spoon, with a rotary beater, or in a blender. You can also aerate the juice by pouring it from one container to another several times.

Serving Fresh Fruit

Fresh fruit should be served cold—but not too cold. Take fruit out of the refrigerator at least 15 minutes before serving so that it can warm up slightly.

Serving Frozen Fruit

Thawed frozen fruit will be most flavorful if served just as soon as it has thawed, when there are still a few ice crystals left.

Dried Fruit

Keep dried fruit in a tightly covered jar at room temperature, preferably not above 70 degrees Fahrenheit. In warm, humid weather store in the refrigerator.

Fruit Stains

Fruit stains can be removed from the hands by rubbing on a mixture of lemon juice and salt then rinsing off with water.

Fruit Discoloration

To prevent peaches, pears, apples, and other peeled fruits from discoloring after peeling, dip them in cool water mixed with citrus juice.

Where the Citrus Flavor Is

Whether it's a lemon, a lime, or an orange, the flavor is in the colored (outer) part of the peel (rind). The white part that is next to the actual fruit has a bitter taste. When grating, be careful to avoid this part of the rind.

Grated Orange Peel

To improve flavor, grated orange peel can be added to pudding mixes or to the batters of cakes and cookies. Grated orange peel not used immediately can be dried out in the oven and stored in tightly closed containers for future use.

Peeling Thin-skinned Fruits

The skin can be peeled from peaches, nectarines, tomatoes, and other fruits with thin skins by first placing the fruit in a pot, covering with hot water, and allowing it to stand for three or four minutes, or by bringing water to a boil for one minute.

How to Ripen Bananas

Green bananas will ripen more quickly if wrapped in a moist towel and kept in a paper bag.

Overripe Bananas

Overripe bananas can be mashed up, placed in a plastic bag, and stored in the freezer. Use them later for baking.

Baked Apples

To keep apples from bursting out of their skins, prick the skins before putting the fruit in to bake. For added flavor, drop a dried apricot or several raisins into the core area along with spices of choice.

Selecting Raspberries

When purchasing raspberries, look for deep-colored fruit that is still firm. Underripe raspberries will not possess that special raspberry flavor. Overripe fruit may end up having to be discarded.

Selecting a Ripe Cantaloupe

A ripe cantaloupe usually smells sweet, has a creamy background with golden streaks, and is soft to the touch at the blossom end.

Adding Life to Lemons

Whole lemons will stay fresh and provide more juice if stored in the refrigerator in a tightly capped jar filled with water.

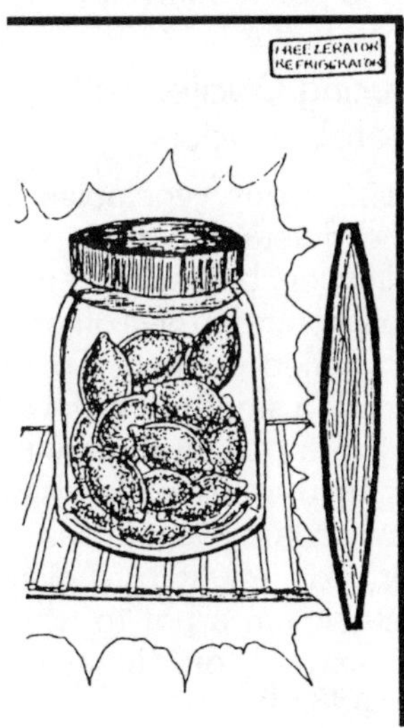

Increasing Lemon Output

Before cutting and squeezing a lemon, immerse it completely in a pan of hot water for ten to twenty minutes. The juice yield will be increased. Warming a lemon in a toaster oven for three minutes produces similar results.

Cooked Cranberries

The flavor of cooked cranberries can be improved by adding a slice of raw apple to each pint of berries before cooking.

Softening Hard Raisins

Place hard raisins in a glass jar and add thin slices of apple or lemon. The moisture from the apple or lemon will penetrate the raisins and soften them.

Preserving Flavor

The skin on fruits and vegetables provides fiber needed by the digestive system to function optimally. Therefore, do not peel unwaxed cucumber, potatoes, apples, pears, and other such fruits and vegetables before eating.

Vibrant Vegetable Colors

To keep the color of vegetables vibrant, add a bit of vinegar to the water being used for boiling or steaming. Cabbage will stay green and beets red. It is also advisable to leave the lid off the pot during the first few minutes of cooking.

If You Must . . .

It is better not to peel vegetables. But if you must, pare as close to the skin as possible. That is where the nutrients are.

Refreshing Leafy Vegetables

Lettuce, celery, or cabbage that has begun to wilt can be restored to a crisper state by sprinkling with cold water, wrapping in a towel, and refrigerating for a while.

Salad Bars Are Expensive

Save a great deal of money: rather than buying ingredients from a salad bar, buy individual ingredients and compose your own salads.

Restoring Canned Vegetables

To restore good flavor to canned vegetables, all you need is air. After opening the can, allow to stand for about 15 minutes. The vegetables will pick up oxygen from the atmosphere to replace that which was lost in the canning process—and your vegetables will taste much better.

Boiling Vegetables

Use a minimum amount of water when boiling fresh vegetables. One-half inch to one inch is adequate.

Cooking With a Low Flame

It is not necessary to boil vegetables over high heat. When vegetables begin to cook, turn the heat down a bit. You will be saving on fuel and preserving the nutrients.

Shorten Cooking Time

To shorten cooking time, cut vegetables into pieces: slice, dice, or shred coarsely.

Cooking in Salted Water

If you cook your vegetables in salted water, it will not be necessary to add as much salt later.

Mineral-rich Vegetable Water

Don't throw out the water in which vegetables have been cooked. It is rich in vitamins and minerals derived from the cooked vegetables. The liquid makes a nutritious substitute for water in recipes.

Microwaving Vegetables

Fresh or frozen vegetables cooked in a microwave hold more of their vitamin C than vegetables cooked conventionally.

Reducing Cruciferous Vegetable Odors

Cruciferous vegetables (those in the mustard family), such as cauliflower, brussel sprouts, and cabbage, tend to give off offensive odors when cooked. To reduce same, fill a small pot with vinegar, bring to a boil, and allow to simmer on the stove alongside the pot of cooking vegetables.

Or, you might try boiling the vegetables in a pot to which vanilla extract or cinnamon has been added.

Another old favorite way of reducing the odor of cooking vegetables is to add a few walnuts to the pot.

Steaming Vegetables

Vegetables lose nutrients when in prolonged, direct contact with water. By steaming vegetables, fewer vitamins are lost. Stainless steel steamers can be purchased for less than five dollars at variety and hardware stores—a worthwhile investment.

Grating Carrots

To make it easier to grate a carrot, leave on an inch or more of the green top for a handle. Also, remember that the last half-inch of carrot, just beneath the green top, is loaded with vitamins and should not be thrown away. Keep it for a snack for yourself or the children.

Keeping Cauliflower White

To prevent cauliflower from darkening, add a piece of lemon to the cooking water. Overcooking will darken the vegetable, so when it is tender, turn off the heat.

No Salt for Tender Kernels

Avoid adding salt to the water in which you are cooking corn. It toughens the kernels.

How to Get Whole Corn Kernels

After cooking, stand the ear of corn upright in a large soup dish

with pointed end up. Insert a fork close to the cob and work your way down, lifting the fork toward you as you proceed. The kernel will come off without a mess, neat and clean. Add butter and salt.

Corn Silk

To remove the silk from cobs of corn, stroke the strands downward, toward the stem, with a damp cloth.

How to Feel Garlic

When purchasing garlic, be sure the cloves are firm to the touch. They should feel solid rather than shriveled up.

Homemade Olive Oil

It may not taste exactly like *pure* olive oil, but you might like the taste even better. For one week, soak four large unstuffed olives in a jar of vegetable oil. Keep the jar tightly covered and refrigerated throughout the entire period—then taste.

Onion Juice

Rub an onion against the finest part of a vegetable grater to extract its juice. It won't take long to produce a teaspoonful. Catch the liquid in a saucer placed beneath the grater. Onion juice is a wonderful gravy and sauce enhancer.

Stop Crying Over Sliced Onions

- If you have a tendency to tear when slicing or dicing onions, keep the onions you are planning to use in the refrigerator for at least one hour. Cold onions will keep the tears back.
- A one-inch square of bread on the point of your paring knife

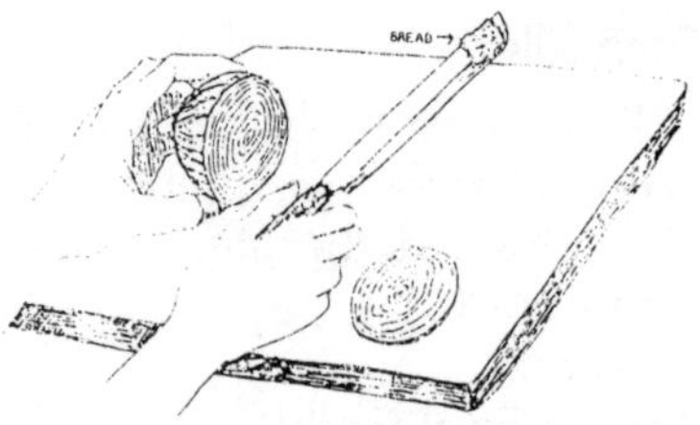

  as you dice or slice an onion will absorb the onion fumes that cause tearing.
- When peeling or dicing an onion, you will shed less tears if you cut the root end (stringy portion) of the onion last.

Onions in Foil

To prevent onions from sprouting and becoming soft, wrap them individually in aluminum foil.

Adding Life to an Onion

In order to keep a cut onion fresh, rub some cooking oil on the surface before storing it in the refrigerator. Or, place plastic wrap flush against the cut surface.

Onion Odors

Rubbing your hands with a thick slice of lemon will help eliminate onion odor.

Hot Pepper Caution

After working with fresh or dried hot peppers, make sure to wash your hands thoroughly. Otherwise, you may touch your eyes accidentally and suffer severe discomfort.

Hot Pepper Relief

If you burn your mouth by eating too much hot pepper at once, drinking water will not offer relief. Experts recommend consuming dairy products or liquor (small amounts) to offset the discomfort.

Keeping Peppers in Shape

Stuffed peppers will keep their

shape if baked in a muffin tin.

Preparing Potatoes for Cooking

No matter how potatoes are to be cooked, first remove sprouts and cut off green portions. If potatoes are pared, keep parings thin in order to preserve nutrients.

Potatoes slice more easily when the knife is dipped into boiling water first.

Keep Potatoes Uniform

If you plan to cook whole potatoes, keep the sizes uniform so that all will be done at the same time. Odd-sized pieces can be used for potato salad or other dishes where uniformity of pieces is not required.

Keeping Raw Potatoes White

Peeled potatoes will not discolor if kept covered with cold water to which a few drops of vinegar have been added. If refrigerated, potatoes can be held peeled for several days, although peeling immediately before use is preferred.

Keeping Cooked Potatoes White

Boiling potatoes in water, with a little milk added, will improve the taste. Milk keeps the potatoes from turning dark, as will a teaspoon of vinegar when added to the water.

Pared potatoes usually retain their whiteness better during boiling than do potatoes cooked in their skins.

Baked Potatoes

For tasty baked potatoes select medium-sized ones. Clean them and wrap in foil. Prick the foil with a fork to allow the steam to escape. Bake at 360 degrees Fahrenheit for an hour or until tender. Open foil and test with a fork from time to time. Serve with plenty of butter and a dash of black pepper.

Preserving Potato Nutrients

Keep the skins on while boiling potatoes to retain more of the nutrients. The skins of boiled or baked potatoes are very tasty when prepared with melted butter. They are a good source of potassium, which is essential to good health and which few other foods contain.

To get the greatest nutritional value from potatoes, boil in a minimum of water. Don't overcook. Potatoes lose their nutritional value if cooked too long.

Shucking Peas

Do not peel more peas than you intend to serve at the next meal. Store the remainder in their pods.

Softening Dried Peas

To soften dried whole peas, boil them in water for two minutes. Remove the pot from the stove and allow the peas to soak for one hour. They are now ready to cook.

Tasty Squash

Cut the squash lengthwise and take out the seeds. Put a teaspoon of butter in each half, then sprinkle on a dash of cinnamon and cloves. Bake the squash in a covered pan in an inch of hot water. Preheat the oven and bake for 25 minutes at 400 degrees Fahrenheit. Remove cover, then bake for ten minutes more, until brown and tender.

How to Ripen Tomatoes

To ripen tomatoes without softening them, allow the fruit to ripen in the shade rather than in direct sunlight. Place tomatoes with the stem end facing up.

An alternative way to ripen tomatoes is to store them in a closed paper bag at room temperature. The ethylene gas that is released by the fruit hastens the ripening process.

Tomato Care

Cold temperatures affect tomatoes adversely. Do not refrigerate them if you want to take advantage of their full flavor. However, the skin can be scraped off easily if the tomatoes are first refrigerated.

Fluffy Rice

Your rice will be fluffier if a teaspoon of lemon juice is added to the water in which it is cooked.

Also, a dash of olive oil added to the water will keep the rice grains from sticking to one another.

Overflowing Rice

Boiling rice tends to overflow the pot. A piece of butter added to the water will keep the rice from boiling over. It is important to keep the heat low after boiling has begun.

Softening Dried Beans With Baking Soda

For beans that take an hour or longer to boil, cooking time may be shortened by adding baking soda to the water. With most tap waters, adding one-eighth teaspoon of soda to the water allowed for one cup of dry beans will shorten cooking time by about one-fourth. Add to the water at the start. Too much soda will affect flavor and nutritive value, so measure carefully.

Enhancing Flavors

When using herbs to enhance any dish, it is important to remember that the herb should complement the dish rather than dominate it. Start with a small quantity and increase gradually, tasting as you do.

Dried vs. Fresh Herbs

The flavor of dried herbs is more concentrated than that of fresh herbs. When substituting dried herbs for fresh herbs in a recipe, use one-third of the amount called for.

Flavoring Beans

When soaking beans, peas, or lentils, introduce herbs for added flavor. Cumin, coriander, and garlic work well with black beans, and thyme goes well with lentils.

Mustard in Salad Dressings

Mustard, with its wonderfully pungent taste, can be substituted for mayonnaise as an emulsifier in salad dressing preparations. It can also serve as a thickening agent for sauces.

The Many Uses of Sorrel

In Europe, where sorrel grows as a weed in hayfields, farmers munch on it and find it to be a handy thirst-quencher. To tenderize tough meat, cooks wrap sorrel leaves around it.

Long ago, housewives discovered the stain-removing properties of this sour-tasting herb. Sorrel leaves are effective in removing rust, mold, and ink stains from linen and silver. The active ingredient in sorrel, as in rhubarb and spinach, is oxalic acid.

Herbs as an Air Freshener

After you have harvested your herbs, do not discard branches and leaves you think are of no use. Let the branches and leaves dry out. In winter, place the dried herbs in boiling water and simmer. This will give your kitchen—your entire home, in fact—a nice aroma.

6
Food Storage & Preservation

Introduction

The key to tasty, appetizing food is freshness and quality. The two are not the same. Fresh fruit—especially apples, peaches, oranges—are often picked before their prime because immature fruit ships more easily. So, the fruit you purchase in the market might be fresh, but it might also be of inferior quality. Quality is often difficult to determine except by tasting. Thus, if you are after the best in produce, do not be shy about asking the greengrocer if you can sample what you are about to purchase. Many stores permit this as a matter of policy.

Once any food product is purchased, much can be done to maintain its quality. With foods which deteriorate with time, this can be accomplished in two ways: by lowering the temperature of the food and by keeping it air-free. Though there are limitations and exceptions, the cooler the temperature at which a food is maintained, the slower will be its rate of deterioration. Freezing at temperatures below 0 degrees Fahrenheit will always retard deterioration better than ordinary refrigeration, but freezing often alters the texture of food, which is why fresh fruits and vegetables usually are not frozen.

Keeping air away from perishable food deprives it of oxygen; and without oxygen organisms and agents that cause food to deteriorate cannot function. Because plastic is largely impervious to air, placing food in a plastic bag and drawing out as much air as possible before closing the bag is the best way to store food in the refrigerator or freezer.

Unpleasant Freezer Odors

One or two pieces of charcoal placed in the freezer will absorb unpleasant odors and keep the interior smelling sweet and fresh.

Portable Freezer

Empty milk cartons filled with water and frozen make handy portable "freezers" to take on picnics for keeping salads and beverages cool and ice cream frozen.

Freezing Small Units

It is to your advantage to freeze foods in small packages. These will freeze and thaw more quickly than foods frozen in large containers or packages.

Freezer Efficiency

Full freezers work more efficiently than partially empty ones. Paper products can be used to

fill the empty spaces. Make sure, however, to allow enough space for air to circulate.

Self-defrosting Freezers

If you can spare the extra expense, purchase a self-defrosting freezer and save yourself a lot of manual labor.

Defrosting Your Freezer

Defrost your freezer when the food supply is low. Temporarily place the remaining frozen foods in the refrigerator. Fill a large pot with hot water. Place in the freezer and close the door, allowing the steam to soften the ice. Pry off as much as you can with a spatula. Never use a sharp implement to chisel off the ice; doing so may damage the appliance. Repeat the process if necessary.

You can also hasten the defrosting process by using a handheld hair dryer. Cover the floor with toweling before you start, and be careful that the hair dryer does not come in contact with water.

If the freezer is in the basement and you are not concerned about wetting the floor, throw bucket after bucket of very hot water into the freezer until the ice is loose, then pry off.

Freezer Temperature Check

To determine the temperature of the freezer, use an accurate thermometer and take the temperature in several locations. Adjust the temperature control knob so that the warmest spot in the freezer is no more than 0 degrees Fahrenheit.

Freezing Action

Freezing does not sterilize food; the extreme cold simply slows down all action that would normally affect the quality of the food or cause it to spoil. Therefore, keep all food to be frozen—and anything that touches it—clean.

Soft Packages of Frozen Food

Buy only packages that are frozen solid. Avoid packages that feel soft, indicating that they have started to thaw. Refreezing after thawing lowers quality and robs the taste.

Stained Packages of Frozen Food

Do not buy packages of frozen food that are stained. The stains are an indication that the package once defrosted and was then refrozen.

Freezer Foil

A special aluminum foil is made specifically for wrapping foods to be frozen. Extra heavy for freezer durability, it is available at most supermarkets.

Head Room for Freezer Jars

Liquids and semiliquids such as soups, juices, and cooked fruits freeze well. However, their water content expands upon freezing.

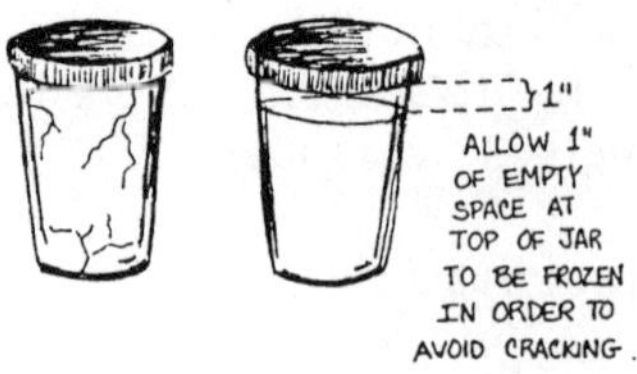

Allowing up to an inch of empty space at the top of a jar to be frozen will prevent the glass from cracking in the freezer.

Plastic Bags for Freezing

The best way to maintain the quality of frozen foods is to keep them moisture- and air-free. Placing the food in a plastic bag

and drawing the air out with the mouth before twist-tying it is the best way to achieve this. Plastic does a better job than freezer wrap.

Blender/Food Processor Warning

Do not place frozen food in a blender or food processor. It could break the blades.

Cutting Frozen Foods

There are knives specifically designed for cutting frozen foods. After cutting off as much of the frozen food as you expect to use (cut right through the package), place what remains in a plastic bag and seal well before returning the package to the freezer.

Labeling Frozen Foods

To keep your freezer orderly, take the trouble to mark on each package of frozen food what the package contains and the date it was frozen. And, keep a running inventory of the food inside the freezer, including the date it was put in. Though some foods will keep relatively well in the freezer for up to a year, quality does deteriorate with time.

Microbial Hazards

Meats, poultry, and fish are generally known to be susceptible to microbial hazards such as salmonella. If not properly refrigerated, these foods can spoil and cause serious illness. What is not as well known is that the same is true for egg products, potatoes, pasta salads, custards, and cream-filled desserts. Keep them refrigerated.

Refrigerating Raw Meat and Fish

Raw meat and fish should be refrigerated at 35 to 40 degrees Fahrenheit as soon as possible after purchase. Raw items that are not used within three to four days should be frozen. Cooked food items will hold longer in the refrigerator.

Power Failure

When you experience a power failure, the best response is to keep the refrigerator or freezer closed. Refrigeration units are well insulated and will retain much of their coldness for many hours, at which time most power failures are rectified.

Once the food in the freezer has begun to thaw out, it is safe to refreeze most of it as long as ice crystals are still in evidence. Some authorities warn against refreezing thawed fruit and juice concentrates because they have a tendency to ferment when left at room temperature after thawing.

Ice to the Rescue

If your refrigerator or freezer goes on the blink, pick up some dry ice (a local fish store may sell some to you) or fill a plastic bag with ice cubes and place in a food chest or box along with the food from the refrigerator or freezer. Store in the bathtub until repairs have been made.

Freezing Homemade TV Dinners

If your schedule is such that you can't prepare home-cooked meals everyday, consider making meals in advance and storing them in the freezer. These will be especially useful when unexpected guests show up at mealtime or when noncooks in the family must make their own meals.

Long-term Freezing of Meat

Frozen meat wrapped in moistureproof freezer paper can be stored for fairly long periods if kept in a home freezer set at 0 degrees Fahrenheit or lower. Don't store frozen meats for long periods in the freezer compartment of a refrigerator.

Wrap meat (and fish) to be frozen in moisture and vapor-resistant coverings. Place two layers of wax paper between individual chops, steaks, and fillets so that individual frozen pieces can be separated easily, then wrap in freezer paper. Make the packages airtight to prevent drying out.

Freezing Meat Patties

Meat patties and similar uncooked foods should be stacked in layers with two thicknesses of freezer wrap separating the layers. This will enable you to separate them easily after they are frozen.

Defrosting in a Microwave Oven

It can be dangerous to refreeze meat and poultry after defrosting it in a microwave. Foods so defrosted should be cooked immediately. Leftover cooked meat may be refrozen.

Cooking Frozen Meats and Fish

Most frozen meats and fish may be cooked either with or without previous thawing. But extra cooking time must be allowed for unthawed meats. Just how much will depend on the size and shape of the cut.

Large frozen roasts may take as much as one and one-half times as long to cook as unfrozen cuts of the same weight and shape. Small roasts and thin cuts, such as steaks and chops, require less time.

Frozen fish, fillets, and steaks may be cooked as if they were in the unfrozen form if additional cooking time is allowed. When fish is to be breaded and fried, or stuffed, it is more convenient to thaw first to make handling easier.

It is best to thaw frozen meats and fish in the refrigerator in their original wrappings.

For most satisfactory results, cook thawed meat and fish immediately.

Freezing Homemade Jam

Homemade jam is generally much superior to commercially prepared products, primarily because higher quality fruit is used. The best way to store homemade jam is in the freezer. Jam that undergoes canning loses some of its flavor during the canning process.

Vegetable Storage Guide

Ideally, vegetables should be used fresh from the garden. If they must be held a few days, follow this storage guide:

Refrigerate: corn (in husks), peas (in shells).

Refrigerate and keep covered: asparagus, beans (snap or wax), broccoli, cabbage, cauliflower, celery, corn (husked), cucumbers, greens, onions (green), peas (shelled), peppers (green), radishes.

Refrigerate or keep at room tem-

perature: beets, carrots, squash (summer).

Keep at room temperature (or slightly cooler): onions (dry), potatoes, squash (winter), sweet potatoes, turnips.

Longer Life for Vegetables

Fruits and vegetables will keep longer in the refrigerator if the basket or container holding them is lined with toweling (cloth or paper) that is absorbent. Dry sponges are also useful in that they absorb excess moisture.

Storing Leafy Vegetables

Leafy vegetables such as lettuce, cabbage, and celery will stay fresh longer if, before refrigerating, they are placed in paper bags or wrapped in cotton towels rather than in plastic or cellophane.

Storing Mushrooms

So that mushrooms will not discolor or become overly soft, place them in a paper bag in the refrigerator or in an open plastic bag stuffed with paper towels to absorb moisture. Store them in the fruit or vegetable bin of the refrigerator, where the mushrooms are able to breathe and will not accumulate excess moisture.

Storing Potatoes

Do not refrigerate potatoes. Temperatures below 45 degrees Fahrenheit cause a sugar buildup in tubers, giving them an unpleasant sweetness. It is best to store potatoes in a dark humid place that is well ventilated. Winter storage in an unheated garage or basement is often preferable, provided that suitable temperatures are maintained. For infrequent cold snaps, covering the potatoes with plastic, towels, or burlap is usually satisfactory

Storing Root Vegetables

Cut off the tops of carrots, beets, turnips, and parsnips before storing. If left on, the tops will draw moisture from the roots and cause the vegetables to soften. They can also be the source of rot.

Vegetables You Should Not Freeze

Some vegetables that are eaten raw don't take well to freezing. Lettuce, celery, cucumbers, and carrots, among others, lose their crispness when frozen. The same is true of the tomato (which is a fruit). If the vegetables are to be cooked, freezing might not matter, depending upon the effect that the altered texture will have on the dish being prepared.

Blanch Vegetables Before Freezing

Before freezing vegetables, blanch them first by plunging them into boiling water for one to several minutes. This will prevent deterioration and loss of flavor during freezing. The exact blanching time required will depend upon the maturity of the vegetable, its tenderness, and its size. Overblanching vegetables such as asparagus or broccoli will make them mushy.

Freezing Corn on the Cob

Although the thought of sinking your teeth into a plump, juicy, summer-grown ear of corn in the dead of winter is appealing, the freezer won't be of much help. Frozen corn on the cob invariably ends up soggy and unappetizing. So, be patient until summertime.

Storing Herbs and Spices

To keep herbs and spices fresh store them in a cool, dry place. Keep them in tightly closed jars in a cabinet, avoiding exposure to light.

Storing Garlic

To prevent garlic cloves from drying out, keep them in a jar

filled with cooking oil. The oil can then be used to give salads a garlicky flavor.

Preserving Herbs

Parsley, dill, and other such herbs can be preserved and kept fresh for future use by removing

TIMETABLE FOR COOKING FROZEN VEGETABLES IN A SMALL AMOUNT OF WATER[1]

Vegetable	Time to allow after water returns to boil[2]	Vegetable	Time to allow after water returns to boil[2]
	Minutes		*Minutes*
Asparagus	5-10	Chard	8-10
Beans, lima:		Corn:	
large type	6-10	whole-kernel	3-5
baby type	15-20	on-the-cob	3-4
Beans, snap, green, or wax:		Kale	8-12
1-inch pieces	12-18	Kohlrabi	8-10
julienne	5-10	Mustard greens	8-15
Beans, soybeans, green	10-20	Peas, green	5-10
Beet greens	6-12	Spinach	4-6
Broccoli	5-8	Squash, summer	10-12
Brussels sprouts	4-9	Turnip greens	15-20
Carrots	5-10	Turnips	8-12
Cauliflower	5-8		

[1] Use ½ cup of lightly salted water for each pint of vegetable with these exceptions: Lima beans, 1 cup; corn-on-the-cob, water to cover.

[2] Time required at sea level; slightly longer time is required at higher altitudes.

the stems and laying them out on paper towels in a sunny window to dry. Then, store the dried herbs in tightly closed jars.

Freezing Herbs

The leaves of parsley, basil, and other herbs can be frozen whole if they are thoroughly dry. Defrost small quantities as needed in cooking.

Another handy way to freeze herbs is to chop them then place in ice cube trays with water. When frozen, transfer the cubes to plastic bags to store. Take out a cube or two as needed.

Storing Citrus Fruits

Do not store high-acid foods such as oranges, lemons, and grapefruits in aluminum foil. The acid in the foods interacts with the aluminum and gives the food a foul odor. Store these fruits in the closed fruit bin on the lower shelf of the refrigerator. Place a paper towel under the fruit to absorb excess moisture.

Storing Delicate Berries

When storing raspberries, blackberries, blueberries, and other delicate berries, it is a good idea to line the container in which they are to be placed with paper toweling or another soft, porous material. This will prevent the fruit from being bruised.

Refrigerating Strawberries

Strawberries hold best at around 50 degrees Fahrenheit. Stored at lower temperatures, they tend to wilt. When storing strawberries in a household refrigerator, where the temperature is generally between 38 and 40 degrees, wrap the container of berries in a towel to raise the temperature of the fruit.

Freezing Strawberries

Whole strawberries will hold well in the freezer for up to a year. Hull, wash, and drain the whole berries, then place in a plastic bag. Before closing the bag and freezing, add four tablespoons or more of sugar per quart of berries and disperse within the bag by shaking. The sugar will help preserve the berries. After thawing, add sugar to taste and marinate the berries in the sugar syrup for one to two days, basting from time to time.

Storing Apples

Apples continue to ripen after they have been picked, even when refrigerated. To prolong their life, keep apples in a closed plastic bag from which the air has been drawn out. If the bag is free of holes and closed with a wire twist tie, the apples will be deprived of the oxygen they need to continue to ripen. If you have access to freshly picked apples, storing them in closed plastic bags at temperatures as close to 32 degrees as possible will enable you to hold the apples at near-picked quality for one or more months.

Avoid Storing Apples Without Stems

Removing the stem from an apple will hasten its ripening (which continues after picking). Such apples are likely to be mushy and will not hold up in storage.

Freezing Fruit Pies

Fruit pies that are to be wrapped for freezing will be easier to handle if placed in the freezer for a short time until frozen; then remove and wrap with freezer paper. The pies will not crumble if this procedure is followed.

Thawing Frozen Fruit

If set in a bowl of room-temperature water, a package of quick-frozen fruit will be ready for serving in a little less than half an hour.

Freezing Fried Foods

Although it is not unsafe, it is best not to freeze fried foods, which somtimes turn rancid when frozen even for very short periods of time.

Freezing Coffee Beans

If you grind your own coffee and purchase the beans in quantity, you can freeze the unground beans. In fact, coffee beans keep better frozen than on the cabinet shelf.

Storing Bread

The best place to store bread is in the freezer. Take out (or cut off) as much as is needed for each day. Heat it through in a 325-degree Fahrenheit oven before serving.

Storing Vegetable Oils

Vegetable oils should be kept in the refrigerator, especially in warm climates. Unrefrigerated, oils will become rancid in time. The cloudiness that you see in oil that has been chilled does not affect the taste of the oil. Cloudy oil left at room temperature for an hour will turn clear again.

7
Wines & Liquors

Introduction

A generation ago, except for upper social circles it was "beer or booze" and nothing more. With the popularization of wines in the United States over the last two decades, however, this has changed; and a wide selection of white, red, and rosé wines can be found at the dinner table of families without social yearnings. With the increased American interest in wines has come an expansion of the domestic wine industry, and today wine is produced countrywide in places far removed from California's Napa Valley.

Choosing a wine in a store or restaurant is overwhelming for many people. This chapter will introduce you to some wine basics and, we hope, thereby make wine purchasing less intimidating and more fun.

Although abstaining from alcoholic beverages seems to be very much in vogue nowadays, there are still many people who enjoy a good cocktail before dinner. And it is always nice to be able to offer guests a drink with hors d'oeuvres. So, with this in mind, we include in this chapter guidelines for setting up a home bar and mixing drinks successfully.

WINES

Buy by the Case

Usually, twelve bottles of wine are contained in a case. Many dealers offer a 10% discount on case lots of same or assorted varieties. Be sure to ask your wine merchant about the store's policy.

Chablis or Burgundy?

American winemakers have attempted to capitalize on the names of famous French wines by marketing their own products under French names. Among them are Chablis and Burgundy. As a result, in America any white wine is often loosely referred to as a Chablis and any red wine as a Burgundy. Because these American wines are not produced in the same soil as their French namesakes, and because they are blended from several grape varieties not used in these regions, the American wines for the most part bear little, if any, resemblance to the French wines for which they are named.

WINE LANGUAGE

There is nothing more intimidating than being a novice among experts. The following guide should help you become conversant with some of the terms surrounding the classification and description of wines and Champagne.

Acidity: The quality of tartness or sharpness in a wine.

Aroma: That part of a wine's fragrance originating from the grapes used to produce it.

Assertive: A term used to describe a wine of strong character; a wine with sharply defined characteristics.

Astringency: The "pucker ability" of wines, usually derived from tannin in the skins and seeds of the grapes. Moderate astringency is considered desirable in most red table wines.

Balance: A term that refers to a pleasing proportion of all the elements (particularly sugar, acid, tannin, and alcohol) in a wine.

Big: A term used to describe white wines that are complex and flavorful or red wines that are *robust* or assertive.

Body: The consistency or "thickness," also known as *substance,* of a wine. Usually used when describing a red wine.

Bouquet: The part of a wine's fragrance that originates from fermentation and aging; unlike *aroma.* Bouquet becomes more pronounced as a wine ages.

Brut: A term that refers to the driest of Champagnes.

Clear: A term used to describe wines that contain no suspended solids—that is, no cloudiness. A clear wine, is often described as "brilliant."

Dry: The absence of sweetness. Not to be confused with *sour.* However, when referring to Champagnes, *dry* means sweet (see *brut*).

Extra Dry: This term causes confusion, but it is used to designate Champagne that is less sweet than *dry* but sweeter than *brut.*

Fruity: Having the freshness, fragrance, and flavor of the fruit, but this should not be the actual taste of grapes, and in a good wine it will not be.

Heavy: A term used to describe wines with a "clinging" texture, one that one's taste buds can "hold on to." Wines of this type are usually very deep in color—gold for whites, purplish for reds.

Light: A term usually used when referring to young wines devoid of bold character.

Nose: A term for the total of aroma and bouquet of a wine.

Robust: A term that refers to wines that are full-bodied, extremely well-balanced, and with assertive character.

Rosé: A light pink wine made chiefly by removing the grape husks after partial fermentation.

Soft: A term used to describe wines that are pleasant and nonassertive.

Sour: A term used to describe a wine or Champagne that has "turned" or spoiled and should be returned to the place of purchase.

Vintage: A term that refers to the crop or yield of a particular vineyard or grape-growing region in a single season. A superior quality wine is sometimes called a *vintage wine.* The *vintage year* is the year in which the grapes are harvested and pressed. Vintage designations for Champagne appear on Champagne labels in good years only. Champagne from other years is blended and bottled as *nonvintage* Champagne. Vintage Champagnes are drier than their nonvintage counterparts.

Young: A term used to describe a wine that has not yet come to its peak of *balance.*

MOST POPULAR WINES

The following are among the most-consumed wines. It's a good idea to become familiar with them.

RED WINES

Amarone: Just coming into its own popularity, Amarone is a big, sometimes sweet, mellow red wine.

Barbera: This very rich, very full-bodied red is grown in different parts of Italy.

Bardolino: A light, dry red from Venetia, Bardolino is best when young. Although made from the same grape as Valpolicella, Bardolino is lighter.

Barolo: This dry, full-bodied, velvety red wine is from Piedmont.

Beaujolais: One of the most popular red Burgundy wines, Beaujolais is the lightest of all red Burgundies.

Cabernet-Sauvignon: This Bordeaux wine is astringent when young, and full-bodied, rich, and smooth when aged. The best Cabernets are from France and California.

Châteauneuf-du-Pape: This well-known Rhône wine is made from a mixture of grape varieties. It is lovely deep red in color and has the highest alcohol content of all French wines.

Chianti: The best known of Italian reds, this wine is dry and well-balanced when aged. Regular Chianti is sold in round, sometimes straw-covered, bottles. Aged Chiantis come in long, slender bottles.

Côtes-du-Rhône: This Rhône wine is lighter, more fruity, and more subtle than Côte Rotie and Châteauneuf-du-Pape.

Côte Rotie: A first class Rhône wine, Côte Rotie has full flavor and an agreeable perfume.

Hermitage: Red Hermitage is a vigorous Rhône wine with full body and bouquet.

Médoc: A light-bodied, velvety, medium-colored Bordeaux wine, Médoc is prized particularly for its delicate fragrance and taste.

Pinot Noir: Pinot Noir is the name of the red grape principally used in French red Burgundies.

Porto: Porto is the most renowned red wine produced in Portugal. Labels that bear its true name, Porto, indicate that the wine is Portuguese. Other wines of this type, called Port, are made in California and New York State. *Ruby Port* is rich and mellow. *Tawny Port,* aged in wooden barrels, is less rich and drier.

Sherry: The name Sherry is actually the anglicized version of Xeres, the name of the Spanish city from which the wine comes. There are several types of Spanish Sherry, ranging from *fino* and *manzanilla,* which are very dry, to *cream,* which is very sweet.

Spanna: This very full-bodied wine, similar to an aged Chianti, has a slight sharpness. It is best when allowed to mature for several years and is often compared to a Rhône wine.

Valpolicella: A deep ruby-colored medium-bodied wine from Venetia, Valpolicella has a very delicate bouquet and very dry aftertaste.

Zinfandel: This excellent American red is zesty and well-balanced and has an intriguing bouquet. Depending on the year and the maker, some Zinfandels are lighter than others. There is also a Zinfandel rosé available, which is light and dry.

WHITE WINES

Chablis: A fine pale green wine that is delicate and flinty; by French law Chablis can be made only from Chardonnay grapes.

Corvo Bianco: This dry, light- to medium-bodied white wine is produced in Sicily. Corvo is also available in a red version.

Frascati: The Frascati most available in the United States is a pale, extremely light, very dry wine. A sweet version is also produced.

Gewürztraminer: A spicy Alsatian wine with a flowery perfume, Gewürztraminer is recommended to be served throughout a meal, even with dessert. Gewürztraminer is very full-bodied.

Montrachet: This expensive dry white Burgundy has roundness of body and is best when drunk young.

Orvieto: The best known and choicest of Italian whites, Orvieto, from Umbria, is light yellow in color and has a delicate bouquet. It is available in two types: *secco* (dry) and *abboccato* (sweet).

Pinot Chardonnay: The Pinot Chardonnay grape produces a dry, full-bodied wine that is said to be the best dry white in America. Pinot Chardonnay is sometimes called Chardonnay.

Pouilly-Fuissé: An excellent, medium-bodied white Burgundy, Pouilly-Fuissé is very pale and sometimes greenish in color. It should be drunk young.

Pouilly-Fumé: This soft, medium-bodied, perfumed white wine from the Loire Valley has a refreshingly earthy taste.

Riesling: Riesling is a fruity, excellent, and refreshing wine made in Alsace. It is most satisfying with a rich meal.

Sauternes: The greatest of sweet white French wines, Sauternes is fruity, rich, and deep gold in color. It has a high alcohol content. Because of its sweetness, Sauternes is usually served as a dessert wine.

Soave: This excellent Italian white wine made from grapes grown near Verona is light and dry.

Verdicchio: A gold-colored full-bodied, dry white wine, Verdicchio is becoming increasingly popular in the United States.

Vouvray: This soft, fruity wine produced in the Loire Valley ranges from dry to very sweet.

ROSÉ WINES

Anjou: This Loire rose is light and ranges from medium-dry to medium-sweet, depending on the year and the maker.

Lirac: A good Rhône rose, Lirac is pleasant, dry, and fruity in bouquet.

Tavel: The best of the Rhône rosés, Tavel is at its peak when young and fresh. Produced from the Grenache grape, it is dry, fruity, deep pink in color, and very refreshing.

SPARKLING WINES

Asti Spumante: From Piedmont, this popular Italian Sparkling Muscatel has a delicate flavor and fresh, sweet taste.

Champagne: The French produce the best of this most famous of all Sparkling Wines, of which there are different grades produced even by one company. Some are big, full, and even heavy; others are elegant and light. French Champagnes are made with extreme care from either the Pinot Chardonnay or the Pinot Noir grape. Unlike California Champagnes, French Champagnes are fermented in the bottles in which they are sold. For this and other reasons French Champagnes are highly regarded by connoisseurs.

Sparkling Burgundy: Although it may be made from a white, red, or rosé wine, the Sparkling Burgundy made from red is best known in the United States and has become synonymous with the name. Sparkling Burgundy is pleasant, pretty, rich, and heavier than Champagne because the wine from which it is made is more full-bodied.

Guidelines for Serving Wines

The proper serving temperature for different wines varies. Aperitifs, white table wines, rosés, and sparkling wines generally are served chilled. About an hour in the refrigerator will make them delightfully chilled. Red wines should be served at cool room temperature. It is important to uncork full-bodied red wines about two hours before serving to allow the wine sufficient time "to breathe" and gain depth of flavor. This practice will help improve wines that are not well aged. When air enters the bottle, it aids in oxidizing the unpleasant taste of the tannin. It is therefore even recommended that all or half of the wine be poured into a decanter to maximize contact with the air.

Ideal serving temperatures for wines are:

Dry whites:	47° to 54° F.
Sweet whites:	44° to 47° F.
Young dry reds:	54° to 60° F.
Vintage reds:	59° to 65° F.

Preferred Wine Glassware

Long-stemmed glassware is preferred for wine because it serves to keep the hand from warming chilled wines.

Choosing Cheese and Wine Partners

Cheese and wine mating has been discussed by connoisseurs for centuries, and while differences in opinion exist, there is a consensus on general guidelines that ought to be followed:

- Very soft and creamy cheeses, such as Cream cheese and the French Neufchâtel, take on added flavor when enjoyed with a dessert wine such as Port, cream Sherry, or Sauternes. Mild and creamy cheeses are excellent in combination with a Sparkling Wine or a wine punch as well.
- Cheddar and Cheddar-type cheeses, which offer a wide flavor range, go well with any rosé wine-except for the very sharp Cheddars. For those select a Burgundy, a Beaujolais, or a sturdy Italian Chianti.
- Dutch and Dutch-type cheeses, notably Gouda and Edam, are delectable with practically all wines—ranging from a sweet dessert wine such as Sauternes, to the dry reds, dry whites, or rosés.
- Swiss and Swiss-type cheeses, such as Gruyère, have sweetish nutlike flavors; those flavors are heightened by almost any white table wine. The Swiss-type cheeses also go well with reds, rosés, or Champagne.

- Soft-Ripening cheeses, such as Brie and Camembert, are delicious with the fruity white wines—Vouvray, for example—and most reds, especially the light ones such as Beaujolais.
- Ultramild cheeses, such as domestic Muenster and Monterey (Jack), are best with Rhine wines, rosés, or light red wines.
- Ultrastrong-tasting and strong-smelling cheeses, such as Liederkranz and Limburger, are usually paired with robust, fruity German wines, a red Burgundy, or one of the Alsatian whites. However, these cheeses go *best* with ale or beer.

Save Empty Wine Bottles

Save small empty wine bottles. Store leftover wines from larger bottles in them. The less empty space in a bottle, the less will be the air-wine contact and the greater the staying power of the leftover wine.

Storing Wine

Wine that has been aged should be stored lying on its side in order to keep the cork moist and prevent air from penetrating. Wines sold in bottles with screw-on tops can be stored standing up.

Getting Rid of Wine Sediment

To get rid of sediment in very old red wines, uncork the bottle slowly and hold the neck of the bottle over a bright light. As you pour the wine into a clean bottle, you will be able to see when the wine flowing through contains particles of sediment. At that point discard the old bottle.

Recorking Leftover Wine

If some wine in a bottle is left over, recork the bottle tightly and store it on its side in a cool place. If the cork has been pierced through and wine might dribble out, store the bottle upright in the refrigerator.

Experimenting With Leftover Wines

Experiment with leftover wines by mixing reds and whites to get a nice rosé, or make up a punch by adding fruit juice and/or soda.

Red Wine Spills

If you act immediately, a freshly made red wine stain can be removed by pouring salt or white wine, liquor, or rubbing alcohol over it. Rub with a clean cloth and send through the washing machine.

Opening Champagne

When opening a bottle of Champagne, hold the bottle slightly inclined. In this way no froth will be lost. A wet bottle may be wrapped in a cloth napkin to prevent possible slippage. Keep warm hands away from the neck of the bottle: the warmth may cause the Champagne to foam

out of the bottle when the cork is popped.

Serving Champagne

Champagne should be cooled but not iced—that is, it should be served at about 44 degrees F. to 48 degrees F. Below that temperature, Champagne loses all its fragrance. Warmer, it becomes heavy and loses its sparkle. Cool the bottle slowly by placing it in a mixture of ice and water. If you must chill it in a refrigerator, avoid leaving it there too long because the flavor dissipates quickly.

How to Pour Champagne

Hold the bottle at the base, not around the neck. Incline it over the glass, which should itself be tilted slightly, and pour very slowly against the inside of the Champagne glass until the glass is half full. Pour a little Champagne into each glass at first and replenish when necessary.

Champagne Glassware

Although the appearance of a wide and shallow glass to serve Champagne may be appealing, the tulip-shaped goblet is preferable. The Champagne bubbles do

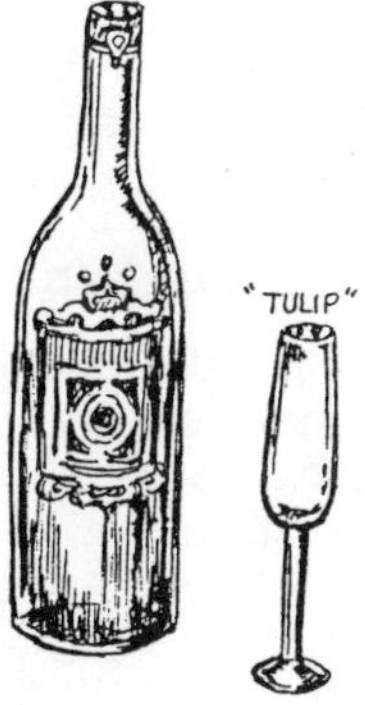

not dissipate as quickly in its deeper, narrower bowl, and the bouquet itself is more concentrated. The best tulip glasses are very sleek and narrow and begin to turn in at the top.

LIQUORS

Setting Up a Bar

Whether you live in a mansion or a small apartment, if you plan to entertain it is important to have on hand the proper equipment for preparing and serving drinks. Here are the basics:

- cocktail shaker
- blender
- mixing glass and spoon
- liquor measuring utensils
- corkscrew
- can opener
- bottle opener
- swizzle sticks
- ice bucket and tongs
- shot glasses
- wine glasses
- Champagne glasses
- assorted cocktail glasses
- beer glasses
- brandy snifters
- cocktail napkins

Stocking the Bar

In addition to the basic bar equipment, it is of course necessary to purchase a sufficient assortment of liquors and mixers to be able to prepare a wide variety of cocktails. Don't forget these essentials:

- Scotch
- gin
- vodka
- bourbon
- rye
- tequila
- rum
- cognac
- brandy
- dry vermouth
- sweet vermouth
- crème de menthe
- Kahlua
- triple sac
- Grand Marnier
- Drambuie
- Amaretto

Mixers and enhancers:

- Angostura bitters
- Grenadine
- tonic water
- dry ginger ale
- soda water
- cola
- bitter lemon
- water
- an assortment of juices: lemon, lime, orange, tomato, etc.

DRINK MIXING GUIDELINES

- Serve cocktails in chilled glasses, unless your guests request otherwise.
- Use only freshly squeezed fruit juices if at all possible.
- When a drink calls for lemon, lime, or orange peel, be sure to use only the colored portion of the rind. The white part beneath it will be bitter.
- Don't fill the shaker to the point where there will be no room left for shaking.
- Use only clean glasses that are crack-free.
- When handling glasses, make sure not to touch any part other than the stem or the base.
- When mixing clear drinks, such as Martinis, should be stirred with ice.
- Drinks containing fruit juices or cream—Brandy Alexanders or Daquiris, for example—should be shaken vigorously by hand

or mixed in an electric blender so that the ingredients are thoroughly combined.

- Serve the cocktails as soon after mixing as possible. And let your guests enjoy!

Fruit-flavored Vodka

Surprise your guests with a special vodka drink. Flavor your bottles of vodka by adding to it the seasonal fruits of your choice. Excellent results have been achieved by adding a cup of red raspberries, strawberries, or cherries to the vodka and allowing it to sit untouched for two weeks. By then the liquor will take on a hint of fruit flavor and color. Strain and serve over ice, straight or mixed with fruit juice.

Protect Your Guests!

A good host will be aware of how much his guests are drinking. Stop serving a guest who has already imbibed too much. And don't let an intoxicated person drive a car until he has sobered up.

8
Treating Your Body Well

Introduction

We live in perplexing, contradictory times regarding health care. On the one hand, miraculous drugs and electronic-aided procedures have pushed average life expectancy to the point where reaching the age of 80 is no longer considered extraordinary. On the other hand, the cost of good health care has escalated to the point where it is outside the reach of major segments of the population. In the absence of any considered national health care policy, a third or more of the population now finds itself without health insurance.

Nowadays, most people are thirsty for information relating to health. Reflecting this wide interest in the subject, the media literally overflow with health information as never before. And this is certainly to the good. But in our world of media hype the prudent will note that the quality of all information is not the same. Very often an item presented in depth in a medical journal will be sensationalized soon thereafter in the tabloids. A wise consumer will therefore weigh the sources of his or her information. If you are concerned about a particular health condition, it makes good sense to clip out articles on the subject and save them in a folder. If you consider the information urgent, immediately call your doctor—even if he or she is a noted specialist—and ask about it. Otherwise, discuss it during your next appointment. It is wise practice, when visiting doctors, to inquire as a matter of routine whether there have been any noteworthy advances in the area of concern since your last visit. The media are not an adequate source of this type of potentially crucial information.

There was a time when patients feared to ask a doctor anything. With current patient awareness, this phenomenon has diminished. There are, nevertheless, many people who continue to stand in awe of medical personnel, to the detriment of their health. Make it a practice to ask your doctor, dentist, or other health care professional as many questions as you have. Write them down to avoid being intimidated in the doctor's office and forgetting to ask them. *If your doctor is reluctant to answer your concerns, you probably have the wrong doctor.* Also, be aware that not all doctors are quick to embrace positive change. Though new and better methods have emerged to treat certain conditions, some doctors stick with outdated procedures simply because they are familiar with them or because they don't want to invest in costly, new equipment. It is true that an older treatment in the hands of a seasoned practitioner is preferable to a newer treatment performed by less experienced hands. Your obligation to yourself is to understand that, in medicine as elsewhere, vested interests sometimes conflict with your own interests.

The information presented in this chapter has been followed with success by many people. However, it is always wise to check with a medical authority before adopting an unfamiliar procedure whose compatibility with your personal physical condition is in question.

HEALTH AND NUTRITION

High Heels and Sore Backs

Doctors recommend that women suffering from back pain avoid wearing shoes with high heels. High heels increase the arch in the lower back and thus throw the body out of alignment. Flat shoes with crepe soles are recommended for people with sore backs.

Back Pain Relief

If you suffer from lower back pain and you drive, help yourself by making sure that you do not have to stretch your legs to brake and accelerate. Keep your seat sufficiently far forward that your knees remain bent even when you have to apply pressure to the brake or accelerator. When getting out of the car, inch your way out slowly gradually straightening your back if it has stiffened during the journey.

Easier on the Back

If you suffer from back pain, avoid standing on hard tile floors for extended periods. Lessen such discomfort by placing rugs with nonslip backs in areas where you stand the most.

Sudden Back Injury

Severe back pain can develop suddenly from something as insignificant as twisting or bending to pick up something, or even from sneezing and coughing. Often, the sudden injury will be accompanied by a "pop." Some experts advise that the best thing to do when that happens is to lie down in a comfortable position and have someone drop five or ten ice cubes into a plastic bag, wrap the bag in a towel, and hold the cold compress against the area of pain for at least ten minutes.

Whether or not you apply ice to a sudden back injury, lying on your back and slowly extending your legs might prevent the back muscles from tightening. If you sense serious injury when you attempt to get up, do not force yourself through the pain unless absolutely unavoidable. Find someone to help you home, and keep pressure off the back. Further taxing an already injured back can extend an injury for days or even months.

Lifting Heavy Loads

If you try to lift a heavy object improperly, you may hurt your back. Whenever possible, move heavy objects on rollers (you can improvise with pipes and poles), or use a dolly. When lifting an object, always start with a straight back, then bend the knees so as to take the pressure off the back.

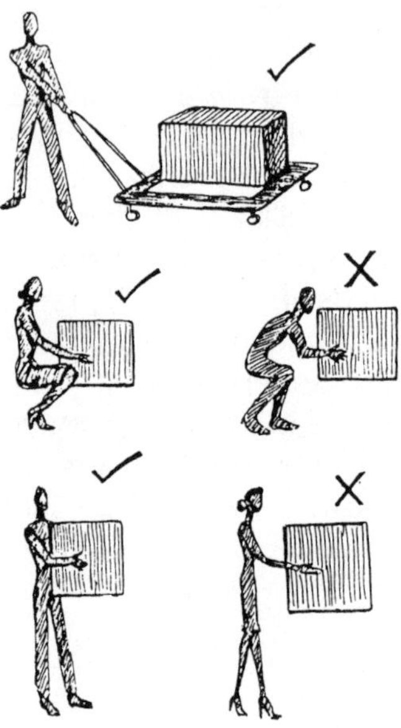

The power should come from the legs, not the back. Keeping a heavy object cradled to your chest rather than holding it with arms extended will substantially reduce stress on your back.

Aerobic Exercises

Doctors advise that aerobic exercises strengthen the heart muscle, making it work more efficiently. Aerobic exercises include brisk walking, jogging, swimming, and bicycling.

Sauna Caution

Before using a sauna, do not eat. The digestive process does not work well when the body is very hot. Wait about one hour after a meal before putting yourself into a very hot environment, and drink fluids to restore what your body loses through perspiration.

Cold Compress for Puffy Eyes

To reduce puffiness and redness around the eyes, try applying a cold compress (or a fresh slice of cold cucumber) to the area.

Long Walks to Ease Arthritis and Back Pain

Some people suffering from lower back trouble and arthritis find that long, brisk walks and swimming help to alleviate the aches and pains. For many people, exercise is one of the best remedies for arthritis.

Painless Hours

Scientists point out that people are less sensitive to pain in the morning than in the afternoon. So, be advised to schedule dental and medical appointments for the morning hours.

Salt Substitutes

The Senate Select Committee on Nutrition and Human Needs has reported that high salt intake leads to high blood pressure. To reduce salt intake, try seasoning foods with oregano, thyme, or other herbs or spices that appeal to your family.

GOVERNMENT RECOMMENDATIONS

The U.S. Senate Select Committee on Nutrition and Human Needs recommends that Americans

- eat more fruits, vegetables, whole grains, poultry, and fish.
- eat less meat and foods high in fat and partially substitute polyunsaturated fat for saturated fat.
- decrease consumption of salt and foods with a high salt content.

UNDESIRABLE FOODS

The American Chiropractic Association Council on Nutrition suggests that the following popular foods be avoided:

- foods containing refined sugar
- alcoholic beverages
- coffee and artificially-colored and -flavored drinks
- junk foods and snacks
- foods containing chemical preservatives

Margarine in Nondairy Diets

Not all margarines are dairy-free. If you are on a regimen that excludes dairy products, it is important that you read the ingredient list on margarine products before buying.

Safe Drinking Water

If you have any doubts as to whether your drinking water is pure, boil it for ten minutes to be on the safe side.

Bottled Water

Government studies have shown that bottled water is not necessarily safer or more healthful than tap water.

Advantages of a Sugarless Diet

It has been well established that sugar is full of empty calories—calories without vitamins, minerals, protein, or fat. Eating food high in sugar has been known to cause tooth decay, diabetes, and heart disease.

Sugar Substitutes

Instead of sugar in desserts, health-minded cooks have experimented using dried fruits (raisins, dates, apricots) and fruit juice concentrates as a sweetener.

Nutritious Snacks

To satisfy a craving for sweets, snack on raisins, dried pineapple, strawberries, and other such fruits rather than candy.

Bread Grains

Whole wheat and rye breads have very high nutritional value. Nutritionally they are a much better buy than white breads, including "enriched" white breads.

Soya Bread

Soya flour adds valuable protein to bread. When baking, use one part soya flour to nine parts of whole wheat flour.

Cholesterol Testing

It is unwise to have one's cholesterol level tested in shopping malls and similar places. Such screenings are not regulated and are often inaccurate. The testing must be done by a health-care professional who can interpret the results properly.

Saturated Fats and Cholesterol

When too much food containing saturated fats is eaten, the amount of cholesterol circulating in the blood increases. Saturated fats are contained in butter, cheese, chocolate, coconut, coconut oil, palm oil, and red meats.

Note that all fats have the same calorie content.

Fat and Milk

To reduce fat intake, substitute skim milk, 1% milk or 2% milk for whole milk or buttermilk. Whereas a cup of whole milk has 150 calories, a cup of skim milk has 90 calories, a cup of 1% milk has 100 calories, and a cup of 2% milk has 120 calories. Note that whole milk contains 3½% butterfat, so 1% milk represents a fat reduction of about 75%.

Reduce Fat Intake

Fat intake can be reduced—and weight loss effected—by substituting low-fat dairy products for whole-milk products, by trimming excess fat from meats, and by using nonstick pans and vegetable-oil sprays in cooking in place of heavier concentrations of oil or fat.

Low-calorie "Dip" Substitutes

You can make your own low-calorie substitute for sour cream or cream cheese dips by puréeing low-fat cottage cheese or ricotta cheese in a blender. The end result is a delicious blend, a wonderful topping for steamed vegetables or baked potatoes.

Working Off Calories

Studies have shown that exercising within an hour after mealtime helps burn off a significant portion of the calories taken in. A brisk 20-minute walk will do the trick.

Lose Weight

You can help curb your desire for postmeal sweets or salty nuts by brushing your teeth immediately after the meal. Also, rinsing your mouth with mouthwash helps curb the appetite.

PERSONAL HYGIENE, HOME REMEDIES, AND RELATED MATTERS

Sensitive Skin

To protect sensitive skin, always use gloves when doing household chores, especially when using cleaning solutions containing bleach. After each handwashing, use a hand lotion or moisturizer to keep the skin soft.

Good Skin Care

Dermatologists tell us that good skin is, for the most part, inherited. Nutrition also plays a role. Overexposure to the sun is the skin's greatest enemy. Wear a hat during outdoor activity, and cover exposed parts of the body with sunblock. When purchasing a sunblock lotion, be aware that the larger the number on the package, the more of the sun's rays that will be screened out.

Oatmeal as a Hand Cleanser

Hands can be cleaned of grease, oil, and grime by moistening a small amount of oatmeal flakes with water. Rub the paste on your hands, then wash off with plenty of water. If you prefer, commercially prepared Gresolvent is an effective cleanser available in most hardware stores.

Dry, Cracked Skin

If you are among those who suffer from cracked skin near the fingernails in cold weather, you might find that covering them with Finger Cots—thin, plastic finger covers shaped like condoms—will help diminish the discomfort. Finger Cots come in small, medium, and large sizes, and are available from Medi-Source, Inc., See the Appendix for the address.

Pumice Stone

Use a pumice stone to remove dead skin cells from elbows, hands, and the bottom of the feet. Doing this after a bath or shower will keep the areas soft.

Makeup Removers

To remove makeup it is much more economical to use mineral oil or baby oil than the more expensive commercial preparations.

Skin Softeners

Government analyses show that the face creams of various companies are basically similar in chemical composition, and that vegetable oil can be just as effective as the most expensive face cream in keeping the skin soft. To help you make an informed purchase without wasting money, the FDA has a free reprint available from its magazine, the *FDA Consumer*. For your free copy of "Cosmetics—the Substances Beneath the Form," just send a postcard to the Consumer Information Center, Dept. 684E, Pueblo, Colorado 81009.

Proper Eye Makeup Removal

Use care when removing eye makeup. Saturate a cotton ball with makeup remover or baby oil. Wipe gently (never rub) in an out-

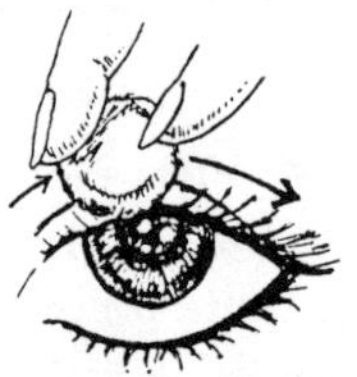

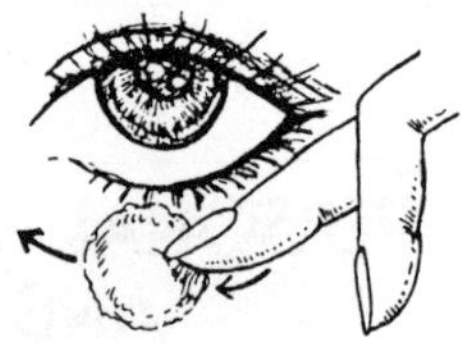

ward motion on the eyelids and an inward motion under the eye. Repeat this process until all traces of makeup are gone.

Proper Care of Makeup Brushes

To clean and refreshen make-up brushes, soak them in a solution of equal parts rubbing alcohol and water. After ten minutes, work a small amount of shampoo into the bristles and rinse. Shake off excess water and allow to air-dry. Follow this procedure at least once a month.

Homemade Shampoo

If you want to save on shampoo, try using unscented dishwashing liquid in its place. If you find the dishwashing soap too concentrated, dilute as required by adding water to the bottle.

Natural vs. Synthetic Hairbrushes

Use natural bristle brushes as opposed to synthetic bristle brushes. The natural bristles distribute hair oil evenly, giving the hair a healthier look.

Don't Brush Wet Hair

Don't brush or comb your hair while it is still wet, as this pulling action stretches and weakens the hair and may lead to breakage.

Chewing Gum in Hair

Try rubbing cold cream, peanut butter, or an ice cube in your hair to remove stuck chewing gum. After most of the gum has been removed, a regular shampooing will wash away remaining gum.

Hairpieces

To clean hairpieces or wigs, use benzene rather than the more expensive hairpiece and wig cleaners on the market. It does an excellent job.

Oral Surgery Carries Risks

With a small percentage of patients, oral surgery on the lower teeth, and particularly on the wisdom teeth, carries the risk of damage to the lingual nerve, resulting in temporary or permanent numbness to the tongue and lips. Such injury can also injure the taste buds adjacent to the lingual nerve. Understand the chances of such injury before agreeing to oral surgery.

Homemade Toothpaste

Make your own toothpaste by adding a pinch of salt to a tablespoon of baking soda. Add water to make a paste.

Frequency of Teeth Cleanings

Periodic teeth cleanings by competent hygienists remove plaque from the teeth and gum areas and prevent tooth and gum disorders. They also alert the dentist to developing problems before they become major. There are nevertheless dental practitioners who encourage cleanings at excessively frequent intervals because they are an important source of income. Unless there are compelling reasons, six months is considered a satisfactory interval for teeth cleanings.

Silver Fillings

In recent years it has been suggested that silver amalgam fillings be avoided because of the danger of mercury poisoning. Recent research, however, has concluded that the use of amalgam fillings carries no danger of mercury poisoning, and any suggestion that old silver fillings be replaced in wholesale fashion because of mercury poisoning should be viewed with skepticism.

Teeth Cleaner

If you find yourself without a toothbrush and toothpaste, use baking soda to clean your teeth. Place a bit in a handkerchief and rub the teeth.

Unwaxed Dental Floss

Dentists advise that unwaxed dental floss is more effective than the waxed variety in removing food particles.

Removing Food Particles

If you've run out of dental floss, use a small piece of celluloid or thin plastic wrap, slightly bunched up, to remove stubborn food particles from between teeth.

Brush Your Tongue

When brushing your teeth, take a moment to brush your tongue. This will both clean the tongue and stimulate the taste buds. Use a soft brush and rub gently.

Teeth Brightener

To brighten teeth use a wedge of lemon or a rag saturated with lemon juice.

Eyeglass cleaning

Eyeglasses should be washed regularly in sudsy water to remove accumulated grease and grime derived from oils in the skin. To dry, use a soft tissue or lintless cloth. Pat dry—do not wipe or rub—until the water is absorbed.

The Durasol Corporation has recently put on the market a small penlike dispenser with a solution that can be dabbed on lenses for easy cleaning. Check with your local pharmacy.

Cleaning Plastic Eyeglass Lenses

Plastic eyeglass lenses are more difficult to clean than glass lenses because they retain greasy deposits more tenaciously. Fantastik is an effective cleanser for plastic lenses provided that the cleanser is rinsed off thirty seconds or so after it is applied. Leaving Fantastik on for longer periods can harm the lenses. Never dry plastic lenses with a rubbing action; instead, pat the water with a tissue until it is absorbed. Rubbing plastic lenses with a dry towel, tissue, or handkerchief will scratch them.

Pay Less for Sunglasses

According to consumer organizations, the prices of sunglasses bear little relationship to their practical performance. Pay more for sunglasses only if you think they are so attractive that the higher price is worth it.

Avoid Misshapen Eyeglasses

To avoid misshaping your eyeglasses, avoid folding them unnecessarily. By leaving the temples open, you will minimize the need for adjustments. To further avoid the distortion, obtain an optical screwdriver and tighten the eyeglass screws (do not supertighten) periodically.

Replacement Eyeglass Screws and Bolts

It is a good idea to keep spare eyeglass screws on hand. If replacements are not available or if the screw threads are worn, obtain tiny bolts for the screws.

If a screw falls out of your eyeglasses and a replacement is not available, a toothpick can be inserted into the screw hole as a temporary remedy.

Importance of Clean Contact Lenses

It is extremely important to wash the hands thoroughly before handling a contact lens. The slightest particle on a lens can cause irritation to the eye. Lenses that are torn or that have nicks should be discarded immediately, as severe eye injury could result.

Contact Lens Caveat

Avoid inserting contact lenses over a sink unless you first close the drain and cover it with a washcloth.

Contact Lens Search

If your contact lens falls into a deep-piled carpet and you can't find it, cover the nozzle of your vacuum cleaner with a nylon

stocking and tie it. The lens will be sucked up into the stocking.

An alternative way to locate a dropped lens is to turn off all the lights and use a flashlight. Light will be reflected off the lens, making it easier to find.

Razor Blade Preferences

According to a recent survey, men prefer the cartridge-razor system, with Trac II blades as the most effective. Women prefer disposable razor systems, and Flicker was found to be the primary choice.

Replacing Blades on Foil-type Electric Shavers

The cutting mechanism in foil-type electric shavers consists of cutting blades (a cutting block) and a screen. Since the screen only serves as a guide, the only time that it needs to be replaced is when it tears. The cutting block should be replaced periodically. Change cutters when you notice that you are getting a less efficient shave. One test is to replace the blade and compare the results. If there is no discernible difference, put back the old blade and continue to use it until it is no longer effective. Cutter blades are expensive, so replacing them unnecessarily should be avoided.

Baking Soda as a Deodorant

Baking soda (sodium bicarbonate) has proven to be effective as an underarm deodorant.

Vaginal Douche

White vinegar mixed with warm water (two tablespoons to one quart of water) has been recommended by doctors when an acidic vaginal douche is needed.

Clipping Baby's Nails

Use small, specially designed clippers when cutting a baby's nails. They are usually sold in pharmacies. The best time to clip a baby's nails is when he or she is asleep.

Nosebleeds

The nose blood vessels of some people tend to rupture quite easily. This is often caused by nose picking, violent sneezing or coughing, and sometimes by exposure to high altitudes.

The first step in treating a nosebleed is to sit down and angle the head slightly downward so the blood will not run down your throat. Then, if bleeding from only one nostril, press the side of that nostril firmly toward the center. If bleeding from both nostrils, pinch both nostrils closed and hold for at least five minutes. If the bleeding continues, press the nostrils for another five minutes. Breathe through the mouth only.

If the bleeding cannot be controlled in ten more minutes, insert sterile gauze in the nostrils and put pressure on both nostrils. If the bleeding doesn't stop within ten more minutes, see your doctor.

First-degree Burns

First-degree burns caused by overexposure to the sun or by exposure to a hot object can be treated by applying very cold water or an ice pack to the affected area. By cooling the area, the pain is lessened and the healing process enhanced. For more severe burns, consult a physician.

Removing Band-Aids

If you find that a band-aid does not come off the skin easily, dab on a generous quantity of cooking oil or baby oil. Wait a minute, then pull. The band-Aid should come off painlessly.

Healing Minor Bruises

If you have been struck by a blunt instrument and there is no break in the skin, a first step is to wrap ice in a towel and apply it to the area that is turning black and blue. This will usually reduce the swelling and the pain.

Leg Cramps

When a muscle that is not used often is suddenly exercised vigorously, a painful cramp can result.

THE HEIMLICH MANEUVER

The Heimlich Maneuver is a creation of Dr. Henry J. Heimlich. In 1974, *Emergency Medicine* magazine published his proposed method for saving the life of a person whose windpipe is obstructed by food or some other foreign body.

When you see that a person is choking and unable to breathe, remember that a great deal of air is still in the lungs, and if the lungs are properly compressed, the air will drive the obstruction out of the throat. Perform the Heimlich Maneuver as follows:

1. Stand behind the victim and wrap your arms around his or her waist.
2. Form a fist and place your thumb against the victim's abdomen, above the navel and below the rib cage.
3. Hold the fist tight with your other hand and push upward with a hard, quick motion, thus forcing the air out of the lungs.
4. Repeat several times if necessary, until the obstruction is dislodged.

To relax a muscle that has tightened up, apply a heating pad or take a warm bath and massage the muscle gently. If necessary, take two aspirins every four hours to relieve the tension.

Medicinal Uses of Tea

Because tea contains tannic acid, a compress saturated with tea will soothe mild burns and itching. A wet tea bag might be even easier to use.

Preventing Poison Ivy

If you suspect that you have been in contact with poison ivy (or poison sumac or poison oak), remove contaminated clothing and wash all areas of the body that have been exposed. Use a strong soap, then rub on alcohol and rinse with a lot of water, under a shower if possible.

Soothing Poison Ivy

Baking soda mixed with water and made into a thin paste can soothe irritating poison ivy, sumac, and oak. The baking soda will help absorb the contents of the blisters.

Don't Burst Blisters

Don't burst blisters or you may end up with an infection. Doctors advise that blisters should be kept clean and dry. If they appear to be inflamed, apply an ice pack. If they break open naturally, keep clean with soap and water, apply antibacterial ointment (your pharmacist can advise you), cover with a sterile bandage, and allow nature to take its course. If in doubt, see a doctor.

Removing Splinters

When you have trouble removing a splinter from a finger, soak it in cooking oil for a few minutes and you will probably have better luck.

Skeeter Stik

Skeeter Stik, sold in pharmacies, offers effective temporary relief of pain, itching, and swelling due to insect bites and minor skin irritations. When rubbed on the affected area, this product, sold in stick form, will reduce itchiness considerably.

Insect Bite Protection

If you are one of those individuals who seem to attract insects, apply Muskol (available in pharmacies) before going outdoors. This lotion is often quite effective in repelling chiggers, ticks, and other insects.

Taking the Itch Out of Bites

To take the sting and itch out of bites from mosquitos, gnats, fleas, and other insects, many people are helped by washing the area with soap and water and then applying a cold compress. This should be followed up with an application of calamine lotion or a homemade paste made from water and baking soda. Many effective over-the-counter medications are also available.

Itchy Skin

Add one tablespoon of ammonia to about one glass of water. Apply it to insect bites and the itching will be relieved.

Animal Bites

If your household pet bites you, even superficially, wash the area with soap and water and apply a hydrogen peroxide solution or some other antiseptic. If the skin has been punctured even slightly, see a doctor.

Baking Soda Bath

If you suffer from severe burn, sprinkle a generous amount of baking soda into a lukewarm bath and soak in it for five or ten minutes. Or, make a paste of baking soda and water and apply the paste to the sunburned area for relief.

Sunburn Soothing

A cold bath will greatly help reduce the pain that results from overexposure to the sun. Add a little Aveeno powder (sold in most pharmacies) to the bath water. It will help soothe and soften parched skin.

Loose Crowns

If a temporary cap or crown on a tooth falls off and you cannot get to the dentist immediately, use an adhesive for false teeth, such as Polygrip, to secure it temporarily. Dental adhesives are available in drug stores.

Sleep Problems

Doctors have suggested that if you have a problem falling asleep, you might want to

- avoid taking naps during the day or eating big meals before bedtime.
- avoid caffeinated drinks in the evening. This includes coffee, tea, and many soft drinks.
- do some light exercise in the early evening.

Dizziness Antidote

If you suffer from dizziness or lightheadedness when getting up from a sitting or reclining position, make it a habit of getting up slowly. This may solve your problem.

Heartburn Remedies

Heartburn is caused by stomach acid backing up and entering the esophagus. Over-the-counter antacids are effective in neutralizing excess stomach acid. Or, if you prefer, ease the discomfort by drinking a cup of water into which one-half teaspoon of baking soda has been mixed.

If the heartburn persists, ask your doctor about drugs such as Pepsid.

Stroke Warning

Doctors advise that one act quickly and get to a hospital when the first symptoms of a stroke appear. The most common symptoms are inability to move an arm or a leg for a minute or two, difficulty in speaking clearly, and inability to understand what someone else is saying.

Foreign Body in Eye

If a foreign object is lodged inside the lower lid of the eye, pull the lower lid down and look towards the ceiling while someone tries to remove it with the corner of a clean handkerchief or a moistened cotton swab. If the object is lodged behind the upper lid, take hold of the upper lid and pull it down over the lower one. Tearing will develop and the object in all likelihood will be washed out. Flush the eye with lukewarm water.

Sore Throat Treatment

For an ordinary sore throat a good remedy is salt-water gargling. An effective solution consists of one-quarter teaspoon of salt to one cup of water. Gargle several times a day.

Hot Tea for Sore Throats

An old but effective remedy for sore throat discomfort is hot tea with honey and lemon added.

Frostbite Treatment

If you are out in the snow and get frostbite, do not follow the home remedy advocated by many. Doctors warn not to rub snow on frostbite. That will only serve to add coldness to the area and aggravate the condition. Also, do not try to warm the area by rubbing or massaging it. That will only further damage the frozen tissue. The best remedy is to wrap the affected area in a blanket or dry clothing or several layers of newspaper. Severe frostbite should be shown to a doctor as soon as possible.

Chicken Soup

Despite all the jokes about chicken soup, doctors believe it to be a nutritious and beneficial food. Because its taste is appealing and it is easy to swallow, ill people with little appetite are willing to accept it. Chicken soup is also soothing to sore throats.

Hiccups Remedies

To stop hiccups some doctors recommend reaching into the back of the throat with a cotton swab and touching the pear-shaped piece of flesh that hangs down from the middle of the soft palate (the uvula).

Alcohol Ear Drops

If you cannot get water out of your ear in any other way, doctors suggest that, with an eye-dropper, a few drops of rubbing alcohol be placed in the affected ear. After a few minutes, tilt your head so that the clogged ear is facing the ground. The alcohol will cause some of the water to evaporate and the balance will ooze out slowly.

Water-clogged Ears

If your ears are clogged with

water after swimming, try jumping up and down on your left foot to get the water out of the left ear and on your right foot to relieve the right ear. If this doesn't work, try tilting the head so that the clogged ear is facing the ground. Then, with the palm, tap the side of the head facing the ground.

WHAT YOU SHOULD KNOW ABOUT MEDICATIONS

HOW TO READ A PRESCRIPTION

If the prescription you receive from a doctor reads

Ampicillin 250 mg
20
Sig: 1 tid

it means that the bottle you receive from your pharmacist should have in it twenty 250-milligram pills of the ampicillin drug. TID means that the pill is to be taken three times a day.

COMMON ABBREVIATIONS ON PRESCRIPTIONS

mg = milligrams
sig = indicate on the label
qd = every day
qh = every hour
BID = twice a day
TID = three times a day
QID = four times a day
q—h = every—hours
ac = before meals
pc = after meals
prn = when needed

Brand Names and Generic Drugs

The generic name of a drug is the official name given to it by the federal government, while the brand name is the name given to it by the manufacturer. Generic drugs are often less expensive than brand name products.

Not All Drugs Available as Generics

The original manufacturer of a drug holds a seventeen-year

patent and has exclusive rights to produce the drug during that time. For this reason many medications are not yet available as generic products. Your pharmacist can advise you as to which generics are available.

Make sure the prescription given to you by the doctor permits the pharmacist to substitute a generic drug, if available, for the brand name specified on the prescription.

Prescription Refills

The doctors always indicate on the prescription whether the pharmacist is permitted to refill the prescription and, if so, how many times. After that you will have to get a new prescription from your doctor. If you ask, very often your pharmacist will call the doctor for permission to refill the prescription.

Federal Refill Laws

Regulations on refilling prescriptions differ from state to state. However, there are federal laws that apply to all states, such as the one that specifies that controlled drugs such as narcotics may not be refilled.

Count Your Pills

Pharmacists make mistakes when dispensing pills. It is a good idea to count them as soon as you get home and to notify the pharmacy if there is a discrepancy. It is, after all, not unusual today for pills to cost from $2.00 to $5.00 each.

Illegible Prescriptions

To avoid serious mishaps, do not leave the doctor's office with an illegible prescription. Have the doctor or nurse print or type the words of the prescription right under the chicken scratches.

Pill Swallowing

If your child (or you yourself) has trouble swallowing a pill, bury it in a teaspoonful of applesauce and it will slide down easily.

Over-the-counter Nasal Drops

Do not ignore the warnings on over-the-counter nasal drops such as Neosynephrine or Afrin. If used for long periods, these preparations become addictive, counterproductive, and even harmful.

Over-the-counter Sleeping Pills

Doctors specializing in sleep disorders report that nonprescription over-the-counter sleeping pills are, for the most part, useless.

Sleeping Pills

Doctors generally do not prescribe sleeping pills for more than one or two weeks at a stretch. Expect to have difficulty falling asleep for one or two nights after you have stopped taking such medication.

Aspirin and Heart Attacks

Since aspirin is known to prevent blood from clotting, many doctors suggest that an aspirin be taken every day or every other day to reduce the chance of heart attack. Consult your doctor regarding your own situation.

Aspirin for Pain

For minor aches and pains, particularly dental pain and pain caused by arthritis, aspirin often provides welcomed relief.

Aspirin on an Empty Stomach

Nausea, vomiting, and stomach pain is often a side effect of aspirin. Therefore, it is wise to take aspirin at mealtime, with a snack, or with a full eight-ounce glass of water.

Aspirin With Other Drugs

Some people become ill when taking aspirin along with other medications. It is advisable to check with your doctor or pharmacist on the compatibility of aspirin and your other medications.

Vitamin C and Aspirin

Vitamin C and aspirin don't mix and, when combined in heavy doses, can cause severe stomach irritation leading to ulcers.

Aspirin and Pregnant Women

Doctors advise that pregnant women use aspirin sparingly, and that it be avoided completely in the last trimester.

Allergies and Aspirin

If you have a medical problem and have been advised by a doctor to stay away from aspirin, be sure to check the list of ingredients on the label of any nonprescription medicine you are considering purchasing.

Breastfeeding Mothers

Breastfeeding mothers are advised by doctors to avoid taking aspirin without prior consultation.

Drugs and Pregnancy

The first trimester (90 days) of a pregnancy are the most precarious, for it is during this time that malformations may occur. Do not take any drugs during this period without first checking with your doctor.

Aspirin Dosage for Children

Children, particularly those under age 12, should not be given the same dosage of aspirin as adults. Overdosing is possible, especially in young children, so consult your doctor before giving a child aspirin. (Note that aspirin is available in children's doses.)

Incidentally, aspirin causes more accidental poisoning of children than any other drug.

Deteriorating Drugs

Drugs lose potency even before their expiration date if exposed to light for prolonged periods. This is true even for medications stored in amber-colored vials. Medicines will keep significantly longer if kept in a dark cool place in an airtight bottle.

Lightheadedness and Dizziness

Medications such as Demerol (Meperidine is its generic name) are narcotics that make some people lightheaded, dizzy, and drowsy. Do not drive a car when on such medications.

When to Discontinue a Drug

If after you take a new medication, unusual symptoms (such as rashes, high fever, or loss of appetite) begin to develop, discontinue the drug and advise your doctor immediately.

9
Appliances

Introduction

One of the phenomena that differentiates today's households from those of previous years is the abundance of appliances to be found in them: VCRs, compact vacuums, microwaves, garage door openers, self-cleaning ovens, computers, cordless drills. If you think back to your youth, you will probably recall the neighborhood TV repairman. He was a specialist who did a thriving business. Nowadays, the television repairman has become a disappearing species. Household appliances break down less frequently and, when they do, it is often not worth the expense to repair them.

Today, a consumer's interest lies in selecting the best appliance for his needs, in using as little electricity as possible, and in using each appliance to maximum advantage. The best advice to any purchaser of a household appliance is to carefully read the manual provided and then to reread it when there is greater familiarity with the various features and adjustments. When points about a product remain unclear, additional information is often available toll-free through the 800 telephone numbers now provided by many large companies.

Life Expectancy of Electric Appliances

More often than not, it is wiser to discard than to bear the expense of repairing an old appliance. The chart below gives a rough idea of the point at which certain electric appliances are considered old. If used regularly.

air conditioners	8 years
electric can opener	4 years
clock	3 years
dishwasher	10 years
microwave	10 years
toaster	4 years
typewriter	6 years
television	7 years
washing machine and dryer	12 years

Labeling Appliances

It is a good idea to keep labels on appliances that you acquire. The information on the label might prove valuable at some later date. To keep the information legible, coat the label with shellac right after buying the appliance. This applies also to electric tools. The information on the label will save you time, money, and effort when it is necessary to call for service or replace a part.

Taking Accurate Measurements

Before purchasing a major appliance, it is very important to take accurate measurements of the appliance and of the space where the appliance is to be placed. When measuring the appliance, do not neglect to consider lips and other protrusions. When measuring the space into which the appliance is to fit, consider that slanting floors and walls that are not plumb require additional tolerances. Also be sure to measure doorways leading into your home to be certain the appliance will fit through without a problem.

Swing Space for Appliance Doors

Before going refrigerator shopping, measure how much clearance is available for the refrigerator door to open. If the refrigerator cannot be opened fully, it might be impossible to pull out the bins and shelves fully. Also be sure to consider whether you want the doors to be hinged on the right side or the left side.

Leveling Appliances

Make sure your stove and refrigerator are level. If not, the doors will not close properly. Major appliances sometimes have leveling screws; shims of wood can also be used.

Refrigerator Efficiency

The air inside a refrigerator must circulate freely, so it is a bad idea to line shelves with aluminum foil or shelf liner of any kind.

For obtaining maximum cooling power with a minimum use of electric power, the cold air must be able to circulate freely in the refrigerator. It is therefore wise to keep items stored uncrowded on the shelves.

Side-by-Side or Top-Bottom?

Before purchasing a refrigerator-freezer with side-by-side doors, keep in mind that the

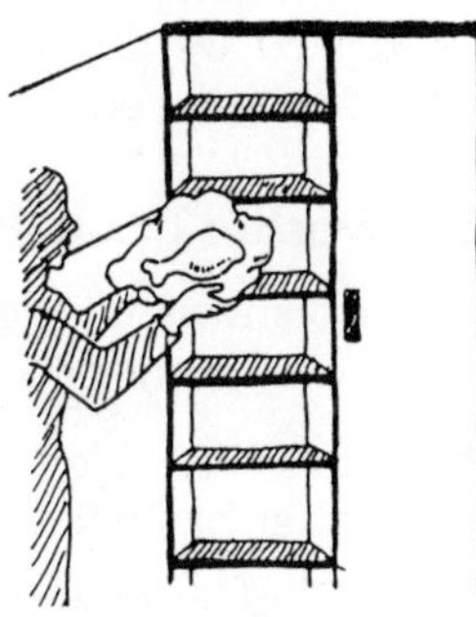

shelves in this style appliance tend to be narrow and that certain items, such as turkeys, large cakes, and watermelons, might not fit. The shelving in top-bottom models is almost always wider.

Keep the Refrigerator Stocked

Refrigerators work most efficiently when they are three-fourths or more full (assuming there is space between the items to allow air circulation). The mass of the products stores the cold, prevents wide swings in temperature within the refrigerator, and increases the on-off interval of the compressor. If your refrigerator is commonly half or more empty, you might want to add canned products to increase the mass.

Refrigerator Location

Never place a stove next to a refrigerator. The heat emitted from the stove will strain the refrigerator's cooling system. Locate the refrigerator near the coolest kitchen wall where space is available.

Before Refrigerating

Never place something hot, or even warm, in the refrigerator to cool. Doing this makes the refrigerator work excessively. Save on power by bringing hot foods to room temperature before storing in the refrigerator.

Total Refrigerator Care

Do not neglect to reach under the refrigerator regularly to clean out accumulated dirt, which disturbs necessary air circulation and will eventually cause damage to the condenser coils. The space under the refrigerator is sparse, so be careful not to cause damage as you clean.

Defrosting Refrigerators

Although many refrigerator and freezer models are now self-defrosting, others still require periodic manual defrosting. This procedure can be expedited by placing rags soaked in hot water or pans filled with hot water on the ice that has built up inside the unit. It is essential that heat not be applied directly to bare metal, for this might warp the cooling element.

Appliance Bulbs

Special lightbulbs that can withstand extreme cold and heat are made for use in refrigerators and stoves.

Replace burned-out oven bulbs with specially-designed 40-watt *appliance* bulbs only.

Stove Positioning

If at all possible, try to position the stove so that there is enough "elbow room" on each side. This is particularly helpful when stirring pots on the back burners.

Is the Oven Temperature Correct?

When purchasing an oven, also purchase an oven thermometer to make sure the oven thermostat is correct. Oven thermostats can sometimes be adjusted quite easily, without the assistance of a serviceman.

Continuous-cleaning vs. Self-cleaning Ovens

Although continuous-cleaning ovens are supposed to remove dirt gradually as normal cooking is in progress, research has shown that major spills must be wiped up as they occur; they are not dissipated under normal cooking temperatures.

Continuous-cleaning ovens are not to be confused with the self-cleaning type. Self-cleaning ovens, which are considerably more expensive, are equipped with a special high-heat cleaning cycle, during which oven grime is literally burned up.

Gas vs. Electric Stoves

Heat can be controlled better with a gas stove than with an electric stove. Whereas an overflowing pot can be controlled instantly by reducing the gas flow, reducing the setting on an electric range does not cool the element immediately. An overflowing pot on an electric range is best controlled by physically lifting it off the heating element.

Dishwasher Troubleshooting

If a dishwasher won't start or runs poorly, check to see if

- a fuse has blown or circuit breaker has been tripped;
- the plug is securely in the outlet;
- foreign objects are caught in the strainer;
- the faucets supplying water are turned on;
- the hot water temperature is set properly.

Dishwasher Shelving

In order to accommodate large dishes, pots, and pans, it is helpful to purchase a dishwasher with adjustable shelving.

Appliance Surfaces

The baked enamel surfaces on many kitchen and laundry appliances scratch easily. They do not have the hard porcelain enamel finishes found on some stoves and washing machines. Therefore, it is advisable not to use an abrasive cleaner on baked enamel surfaces. Use soap and water or a liquid all-purpose cleaner.

Hot Water Preservation

Appliances such as dishwashers and washing machines require a steady stream of hot water to operate efficiently. Therefore, do not use more than one appliance at a time, and do not use hot water from the sink or shower while these appliances are in operation.

Save Appliance Energy

Reduce the amount of energy required to run a dishwasher or washing machine by running these appliances only when full and thus less often. Some washing machines allow you to regulate the amount of water used according to the size of the clothes load.

Troubleshooting a Washing Machine

Check the following before calling a repairman. If you cannot make the repair yourself, ask the serviceman to check out these probable causes of your problem.

1. Motor does not run
   a) fuse blown or circuit breaker off
   b) loose or broken wiring

2. Motor runs, but agitator does not move
   a) belt off pulleys
   b) broken belt
   c) loose pulleys

3. Motor runs, but cylinder does not (tumbler washers)
   a) belt off pulleys
   b) belt broken
   c) loose pulleys
   d) broken spring

4. Washes, but does not spin
   a) heavy load
   b) loose basket

5. Water does not drain, or drains slowly
   a) pump belt loose or broken
   b) pulleys loose

6. Noisy operation
   a) motor pulley
   b) drive pulley
   c) pump pulley
   d) unbalanced load
   e) cracked belt

7. Leaks water
   a) door or lid gasket loose or dried out
   b) hose connections loose
   c) machine overloaded with detergent
   d) door or lid out of alignment

8. Excessive vibration
   a) worn belt
   b) motor shaft bent
   c) floor weak
   d) washer not even on floor
   e) unbalanced load

9. Clothes get torn
   a) agitator is loose.

Cost-efficient Washing Machines

Front-loading washing machines have been proven to be

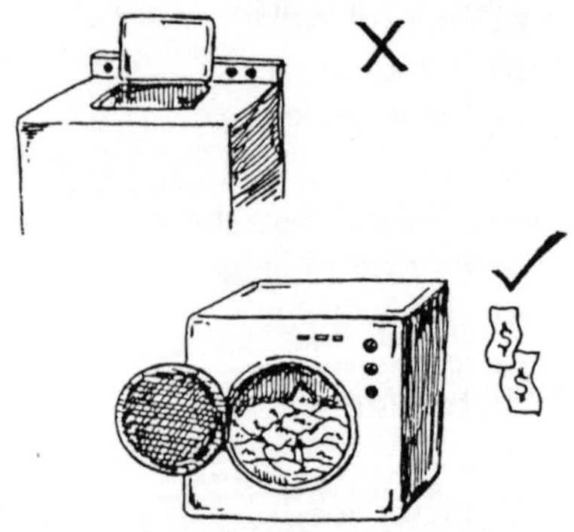

40 percent more energy-efficient than the top-loading type. The initial cost is higher, but in the long run this is offset by reduced electric bills.

Washing Machine Cleaning

From time to time it is advisable to pour a gallon of distilled vinegar into your washing machine and run it through the cycles. Grime that has accumulated in hoses will be cleansed, and the machine will operate more efficiently.

Overflowing Suds

If your washing machine is overflowing with suds, sprinkle salt on the suds and they will fade away. A small dash of liquid fabric softener will also do the trick.

Overloading Washing Machines

Packing too many pieces of clothing into a washing machine is harmful to the appliance and will produce inferior results. Particularly, one must avoid packing tightly the area around the agitator.

Premix Detergent

Many soap manufacturers suggest that a washing machine be partially filled with water and detergent be stirred into the water before clothing is added. This allows for more uniform cleaning.

EER Rating

To get the most for your money, purchase an air conditioner with the highest EER (energy efficiency ratio). The EER is applied to some other major appliances as well.

BTU FORMULA

To determine how many BTUs an air conditioner should have to cool a specific room, use the following formula:

length x width x 35 = number of BTU's required

For example, a 10 x 12-foot room would need a 4,200 BTU unit.

Other factors to consider are:

- the number and size of the windows in the room;
- the amount of direct sun exposure to the room;
- whether the room is on the top floor of the building;
- the height of the ceiling.

Vacuum Troubleshooting

If your vacuum cleaner doesn't run at all or does not pick up dirt effectively, the problem may be one of the following. Check each out yourself before calling a repairman.

Tank (Canister) Type

- Is the nozzle clogged?
- Is there an obstruction in the hose?
- Is the bag full?
- Is the bag broken?
- Is the filter old or clogged?
- Is air leaking from the hose?

Upright Cleaner

- Is the nozzle clogged?
- Does the brush need cleaning?
- Is there an obstruction in the bag?
- Is the bag old?
- Is the belt broken?
- Is the belt weak or loose?

Movable Microwave Oven

If you have no space in your kitchen for a microwave oven, you might find it convenient to place the oven on a movable cart. Microwave ovens generally can be plugged into any average house outlet (110 volts).

Microwave Carousel

It might be wise to invest the extra money and buy a microwave oven equipped with a carousel. The slow spinning motion of the carousel insures the even cooking of the foods placed therein.

Microwave Cooking Utensils

Do not use metal cooking utensils in a microwave oven. Only glass, wood, paper, or plastic are recommended. Utensils suitable for microwave use will be so labeled.

TV Troubleshooting

If your television is malfunctioning, see if you can solve the problem yourself before calling a repairman. Try one of the following:

1. No picture or sound
   a) check if cord is connected
   b) check if plug is in outlet
   c) check fine tuning control
   d) check antenna connections

2. Weak or snowy picture
   a) check fine tuning control
   b) check antenna connection
   c) check contrast or brightness control

3. Picture too high or low
   a) adjust vertical height control (located in back of or under picture tube)

4. Bars in picture
   a) adjust horizontal and vertical controls.

Cassette Caveat

Beware of leaving a tape cassette on top of a TV. It is quite possible that when you turn on the television, its magnetic field will erase the tape.

Tape-cleaning Tapes

Cassette players will work better if you clean the heads periodically. Most department stores sell tape cleaning and demagnetizing kits that are effective in eliminating tape noise and distortion.

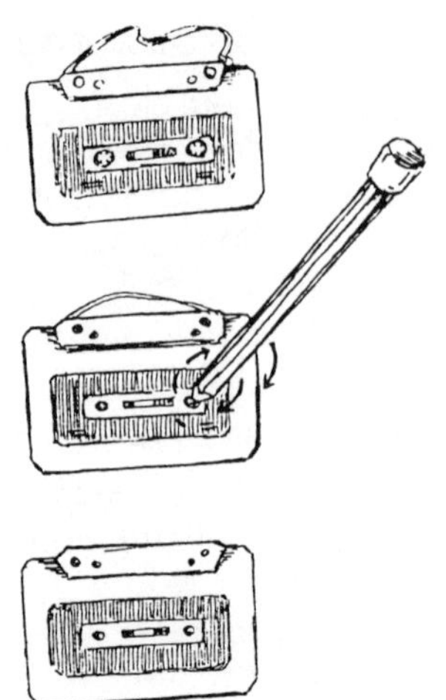

Tape Deck Warning

When purchasing a tape deck, don't assume that it will allow you to record with a microphone. Some models do not have this feature.

Taking the Slack Out of Tapes

Before playing a tape, it is wise to wind it with a pencil or your finger until it is tight. Leaving it slack when starting to play may cause the ribbon to become entangled.

10
In the Bathroom

Introduction

For most of us, who are several generations removed from outdoor plumbing, it takes a trip to rural Latin America or an extended stint in the military to appreciate the blessings of our convenience. Today, the bathroom has become a room to be decorated and pampered as any other room. Carpeting, telephones, subdued lighting, pastel colors, designer shower curtains, and towels are all commonplace. What makes the contemporary bathroom different from its predecessors, however, is the ease with which it can be maintained. Tile cleaners, bowl sanitizers, rust removers, caulkings, and sealants all contribute to turning normal sanitary and periodic restorative tasks into routine undertakings. With a bit more enterprise, faucet aerators, shower heads, leaky washers, and malfunctioning water tanks can all be cleaned, replaced, or adjusted, eliminating the need for costly plumber service calls and providing a satisfactory sense of self-sufficiency.

KEEPING THE BATHROOM CLEAN AND FRESH

Bathroom Cleaners

To clean chrome, tile, porcelain, mirrors, and windows, commercial products such as Windex and Sprayway are effective.

Adding Life to a Bathtub

Dull bathtub surfaces can be enlivened by rubbing with a solution made of one tablespoon of salt dissolved in one-quarter cup of turpentine.

Cleaning the Bathtub

Since a bathtub must be cleaned each time it is used, which in a large family can be several times a day, it is a good idea not to use abrasive scouring powders. When used repeatedly, cleansers tend to dull porcelain finishes.

Instead of abrasives, use a plastic sponge and a mild detergent. This will remove the film left around the tub. A mild scouring powder may be used occasionally, and a solution of ammonia and water may be used about once a week.

Cleaning Shower Walls

Add one-half cup of chlorine bleach to a cup of warm water. Pour the solution into a spray bottle. Dry off the shower walls, then spray the tiles with the chlorine solution. When completely covered, wash the walls down with an old towel or with a sponge mop wrapped in toweling material. Repeat once each month to keep your shower mildew-free and sweet-smelling.

Cleaning Shower Doors

Clean shower doors with a cloth or sponge dampened with white vinegar. Dry with paper toweling.

Cleaning the Toilet

Although there are bathroom brushes of various shapes and sizes on the market, it is best to choose one with bristles set at a 45-degree angle to the handle. This type of brush makes it easier to clean the area beneath the toilet bowl rim.

Silent Bathrooms

Silent valves are now available to replace the older style rubber bulbs, which often produce loud flushing sounds. Your hardware dealer can show you the products available.

Mildew on Bathroom Ceilings

If mildew is marring your bathroom ceiling, a good scrubbing with a strong solution of chlorine bleach will produce good results. If the ceiling is seriously mildewed, buy a small amount of trisodium phosphate (also called Beetsall) at a paint or hardware store and add it to the bleach solution. To avoid having to repeat the process in a year or two, it may be wise to repaint the ceiling after cleaning it.

Bathroom Curtain Mildew

Because of constant moisture in the room, bathroom curtains are subject to mildew. To relieve this problem, scrub the surfaces first with clean warm water and then with chlorine bleach: one-half cup to a gallon of water. Maintain cleanliness by occasionally spraying the surfaces with mildew germicides such as Lysol or Listerine.

Bathroom Tile Joints

The mortar used to join bathroom tiles usually darkens with age. You can slow down the darkening process by giving the joints a good scrubbing with a stiff brush. Try removing grout stains with cotton or fabric that has been dipped in chlorine bleach. Follow this by covering the areas that remain soiled with a paste made by mixing white tile cement with water. Keep the mixture loose so it will go on easily.

If this process fails to cover the joints properly, a mixture of muriatic acid and water will usually remove the remaining stains. Your hardware dealer can supply the acid. Flush the muriatic acid with water immediately after use.

Rust Stains

Most rust stains caused by faucets dripping on porcelain sinks and bathtubs can be cleaned with any mild cleanser containing chlorine as an ingredient. Rub lightly and rinse with cold water. Rust stains can also be removed by treating them with a paste made of borax and lemon juice. Whisk-Away is a commercial product that has been recommended as effective in this regard.

Removing Stubborn Stains

To remove stubborn staining from a toilet bowl, apply a liberal amount of liquid bleach (or powdered bleach) to the toilet brush and rub lightly. Do not flush for one-half hour. Repeat if necessary. If this doesn't do the job, try a paste made of borax and lemon juice or vinegar. Place on a sponge and rub vigorously.

Toilet Bowl Cleansers

Plumbers advise that some commercial toilet-bowl cleaners that are placed in the tank contain strong chemicals that can erode parts of the flushing mechanism. Check the product label before making a purchase.

Toilet Bowl Cleaners—Brush and Flush

Aside from the commercial toilet bowl cleaning preparations, try using ordinary liquid bleach as a bowl cleaner and sterilizer. Simply pour three-quarters of a cup of liquid bleach into the bowl. Brush, let stand for ten minutes, then flush.

Toilet cleaner and liquid bleach should never be used at the same time, as the two together may combine to emit poisonous fumes. When using potent bathroom cleansers, always make sure there is adequate ventilation.

BATHROOM MAINTENANCE AND REPAIR

Toilet Flush Bowl

If the water in a toilet tank is less than two inches from the top of the overflow tube, there will probably not be enough water in it to flush the toilet. Bend up the float, raising the large bulb at the end, so that more water will enter the tank. When the water fills to about one and one-half inches from the top, there will be an adequate amount of water to flush the toilet.

Toilet Tanks

If a toilet tank runs constantly, the float arm in the tank might not be closing the water valve and might need adjustment. Try bending it down slightly. This will probably stop the flow of water.

Constantly Running Tanks

A common cause of constantly running water in a toilet tank is a defective flush ball—the rubber or plastic ball that comes up when you press the outside flush lever down. This permits the water in the tank to flow into the bowl and to flush it.

To check the flush ball for proper operation, take off the top of the tank and flush the toilet.

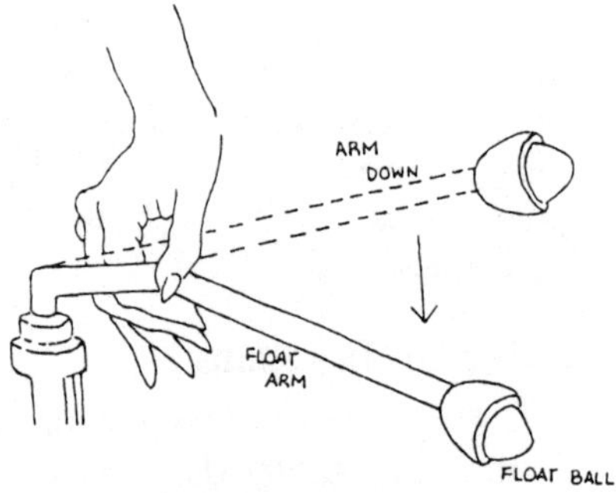

If the ball fails to drop down and completely cover the opening below it, the guide arm is slightly out of place. If so, move the arm until the ball drops down properly. If this does not solve the problem, press down on the rubber ball with your fingers. If this stops the noise of running water, the ball is worn out and needs to be replaced.

Unclogging a Toilet Using a Plunger

To clear a clogged toilet, use a toilet bowl plunger—a rubber cup with a curved skirt that fits

into the throat of the bowl. Be sure there is enough water in the bowl to cover the rubber cup (to the point where it joins the wooden handle). Force the cup down and up with vigorous motions until the clogged section appears to be free. Try again if the clogged material has not been dislodged. If the process does not work, use a snake.

Unclogging a Toilet Using a Snake

Clogged toilets that cannot be cleared by the ordinary use of a plunger can usually be cleared with a snake. The snake must be forced up the curve through

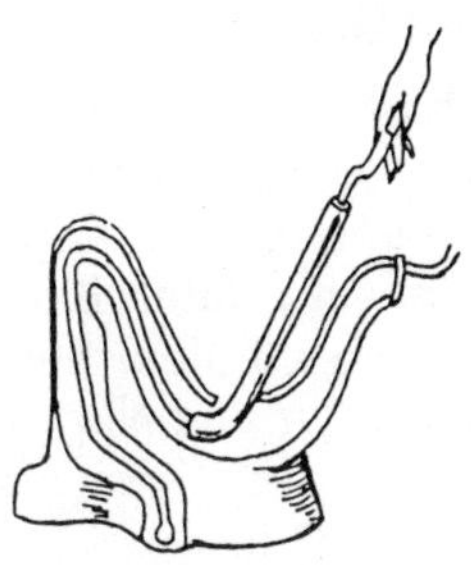

which the water drains. Getting around the top of the curve and down the other isn't easy, but it can be accomplished by pushing and turning the handle at the same time. When you buy a snake, get the type known as a closet auger. It works better than other types on the market.

Bathroom Sealants

Silicone sealants developed by the aerospace industry are sold in tubes at hardware stores. These are excellent for filling in cracks and the space where the bathtub meets the tile floor and tile wall. In preparing the area, remove all loose grout, and clean the area thoroughly. Then, press the grout out through the tube nozzle that is provided, and run the sealant around the edge of the tub against the tiles. Wet your finger and smooth the grout to get neat results. Wash your hands immediately with soap and water.

Replacing a Broken Bathroom Tile

After removing all particles remaining from the old, damaged tile, apply beads of silicone tub and tile sealer to the back of the new tile and position it. After the adhesive is fully cured and firm, fill the open joints with grout.

Chipped Porcelain

An enamel made specifically for covering chipped porcelain in sinks and bathtubs is available at hardware stores. Although the area treated might be noticeable after application, covering the chipped porcelain will prevent spread of the deterioration.

Faucet Aerators

If water squirts from a faucet when it is turned on, the aerator is probably clogged. Remove it carefully without allowing the various washers to fall out. Turn over the aerator and flush with water to dislodge sediment that has collected. If it is necessary to separate the components of the aerator, first note the assembly pattern carefully.

Shower Spray Nozzle

Shower nozzles become clogged with sand and other impurities from time to time. Push a needle or pin into the nozzle holes to free the sediment, or remove the nozzle and flush with a strong stream of water.

GENERAL BATHROOM HINTS

Sundry Toothpaste Uses

Toothpaste has been found to be an effective cleanser for jewelry, piano keys, and precious stones. Rub well with a small amount, then buff with a clean, dry cloth.

Toothpaste Tubes

If your toothpaste tube springs a leak, clean and dry the spot where the toothpaste has oozed through the tube. Then, wrap the area with several turns of adhesive tape.

Removing Water Stains With Toothpaste

Water rings and spots can be removed by wiping with a bit of toothpaste applied to a damp cloth or sponge.

Toothpaste will also clean plastic tabletops and will remove small scratches in glass.

Toothbrushes as Tools

An old toothbrush is useful for cleaning those hard-to-get-at spots on windows, carved furniture, baseboards, etc. A toothbrush can be used to clean the grout between tiles and around the bathtub. You will also find a toothbrush a good tool for cleaning kitchen appliances.

Bathroom Drinking Cups

Keep bathroom drinking cups germ-free by dropping in two tablespoons of bleach and filling to the brim with water. Let stand for one or two minutes, then rinse with fresh water and allow to air-dry.

Toothbrush Conditioning

Before using a new toothbrush for the first time, soak it in cold water for 24 hours to strengthen the bristles.

Shower Curtain Magnets

Shower curtains often billow away from the sides of the tub when warm air currents generated by hot water get under them. Curtains can be kept firmly in place by sealing small magnets in the bottom hem. The magnets will be attracted to the cast iron or steel under the porcelain of the bathtub.

Antislip Bathtubs

If you are prone to slip in a bathtub, you may want to try End Slip, a relatively new antislip spray available at pharmacies and supermarkets. Produced by the Durasol Corporation, it is an inexpensive, invisible spray that will help prevent bathtub accidents.

Bathtub Grab Handles

Older people especially should install a soap dish with a grab handle to help them stand up after a bath.

Mounting Fixtures

It's easy to mount bathroom fixtures (toothbrush holders, soap dishes, etc.) with a number of cements made specifically for the purpose. The old practice of removing a tile in order to affix the fixture to the wall is no longer necessary. A hardware dealer can suggest the proper adhesive.

Cloudy Mirrors

If you do not want the bathroom mirror to cloud up when drawing a hot bath or taking a hot shower, fill the sink with a couple of inches of cold water drawn from the tap.

Sweating Commodes

Beads of water that form on toilet tanks and drip onto the floor in hot weather can be avoided. In many cases, applying a coat of floor wax to the tank will prevent the condensation from forming. Apply the wax at two-month intervals and the sweating problem may be solved.

If the problem persists, your plumber might be able to install a mixing valve which will introduce warmer water into the tank and thereby prevent condensation.

Bathing Pets

When bathing dogs and cats, place steel wool in the drain opening to catch hairs and prevent clogging of the drain.

11
The Home Interior

Introduction

As the exterior of the home sets the initial tone for those who live in it as well as for visitors, the interior of the home carries through on that impression. As a slovenly exterior diminishes infinitely the warmth of the interior, a poorly conceived interior quickly undoes the harmonious invitation of even the most exquisite exterior. The need to maintain this balance is something that is grasped intuitively by all who strive to attain truly inviting homes.

Aesthetics are, of course, assumed. A garrish color scheme; clashing textures in furniture, floor coverings, and window appointments; and careless distribution of bric-a-brac all diminish the appearance of the most elegant furnishings. Equally crucial, however, are the mundane. A cavalier mirror left unpolished, smoke stains on the brickwork of a traditionally sculptured fireplace, peeling paint peeking out from behind window drapes are not products of a homey, lived-in philosophy, but of neglect. With a marvelous range of cleansers and restorers so widely available, maintaining a residence at its very best falls within the grasp of all who seek it.

For specific stain removal techniques and additional cleaning advice, see Chapter 14, Cleaning and Stain Removal.

GENERAL HOUSEHOLD HINTS

Rough Measurement Equivalents

one meter = about 1.1 yards (3.28 feet)
one liter = about 1.06 quarts
one gram = about the weight of a small paper clip
one ounce = 28 grams
one kilogram = 2.2 pounds
one pound = .45 kilograms
one inch = 2.54 centimeters
one foot = .305 meters
one centimeter = .39 inches
one mile = 1.6 kilometers

See-through Shelves

When articles are stored on the top shelves of a closet, it is practically impossible to see the articles unless you are over 6′6″ in height. One way to overcome the difficulty is to replace the wood shelves with see-through shelves of glass or plastic. In this way, you will be able to see from below what is stored above.

Prevent Rust Rings

Save the plastic lids on peanut cans, coffee cans, and the like, because they can be put to good use as holders for cans of scouring powder and similar items. The plastic will keep dampness away and prevent the metal bottoms from rusting and leaving unsightly rings.

Curtain Rods

Before inserting curtains on rods, wax the rods with a candle or some other wax product. The curtains will pass through the rods with less likelihood of getting stuck.

BUYING LUMBER

When buying lumber, remember that a certain amount is planed off by the mill in the finishing process. If you order boards

1″ x 2″ you will get $1\frac{3}{4}$″ x $1\frac{1}{2}$″
1″ x 6″ you will get $\frac{3}{4}$″ x $5\frac{1}{2}$″
1″ x 12″ you will get $\frac{3}{4}$ x $11\frac{1}{2}$″
2″ x 2″ you will get $1\frac{1}{2}$″ x $1\frac{1}{2}$″
2″ x 6″ you will get $1\frac{1}{2}$″ x $5\frac{1}{2}$″
2″ x 12″ you will get $1\frac{1}{2}$″ x $11\frac{1}{4}$″

Drapery Weights

To keep drapes hanging straight, insert thick washers, nuts, or large treated nonrust nails into the hems.

Shrinking Drapes

The more loose the weave of the fabric, the more likely that the material will shrink when washed. When buying drapes, look for those with hems that have extra material which can be pressed out in case of shrinkage. Also, try to purchase drapes that are even longer than the size actually needed, so that if they do shrink, it will not be noticed. Of course, it is best to buy material that is guaranteed not to shrink.

Piano Care

Extreme temperatures will hurt a piano. Keep the instrument away from open windows in the winter, and away from radiators and steampipes. The piano will stay in tune longer.

A piano must be used periodically to stay in good condition. It should be played once a week, or at least the keys should be exercised, even if only through the act of dusting them.

Cabinet Nailing

When doing fine woodwork, to avoid marring the wood, do not drive the nails all the way into the wood. Allow them to protrude about one-eighth of an inch and use a nail-set (or another nail) to drive them in the balance of the way.

Adding Life to a Mattress

Keep a mattress from wearing out unevenly by turning it over as well as reversing the head-toe positions regularly. Turn an innerspring mattress once a month. turn a mattress without springs once a week. The mattress will stay in better shape, and you will always enjoy a good night's rest.

Protecting Your Mattress

To keep your mattress as sweet-smelling as possible, do not place a bedsheet directly on the mattress. First, cover the mattress surface with a mattress pad or with an old, clean sheet.

Squeaky Beds

Spray liquid wax directly on bedsprings to take the squeak out of them. Also avoid rolling up innerspring mattresses, which are weakened by such repeated action.

Umbrella Stands

When an umbrella stand gathers the drippings from wet umbrellas, the bottom of the umbrella stand might take a long time to dry out. One way of avoiding the problem is to line the stand with a sponge cut to size. Squeeze the sponge dry from time to time.

KEEPING YOUR HOME CLEAN AND FRESH

Musts for Every Household

Ammonia

Useful for cleaning ovens, loosening wax, and washing windows and mirrors.

Vinegar and Lemon Juice

Both products are useful agents in removing hard-water spots. They are also helpful in removing rust stains from sinks.

Bleach

Bleach can be helpful in removing some stains, but test it first. It can mar the shiny finish of sinks, bathtubs, and kitchen appliances. Use with caution.

Steel Wool and Soap Pads

Especially useful on aluminum articles, these products can help remove hard-to-get-off foods from pots, pans, and oven racks.

Dustpans

Dustpans with long handles spare the user from having to bend over to pick up dirt.

Dry Mops and Dust Mops

Use mops with removable heads. These can be washed and dried more easily.

Sponge and String Mops

Like the dry mop, the sponge and string mop should have a removable head. When making your purchase, be sure the handle is long enough to be comfortable for your height.

Vacuum Cleaners

Lightweight vacuums are best for use on wood floors. The canister (tank) type is a good all-purpose cleaner. If the vacuum is to be used mainly on rugs and carpets, the upright type is preferred. Hand-held rechargeable portable vacuums are useful for spot work.

Pails

Two pails, one for washing and one for rinsing, makes work easier. Be sure the size is right to accommodate your mops.

Reaching Aids

Every household should have a sturdy stool or a short stepladder (about three feet high) to reach hard-to-get-at spots. Aluminum ladders are easiest to handle because of their light weight.

Chlorine Bleach

Chlorine bleach in liquid form is effective in the cleaning and sanitizing of refrigerators and other household products and appliances. Among the popular commercial bleaches available in supermarkets are Clorox, Fyne-Tex, Fleecy White, Purex, Action, and Stardust.

Ammonia on Glassware

Being a good grease-cutter, ammonia is effective in cleaning mirrors, windows, auto windshields, and all types of glassware. Use a mixture of one tablespoon of ammonia to one quart of water.

New Brooms

Soak a new broom in hot, heavily salted water to give it longer life. In the winter, clean it with a few sweeps to the snow.

Broom Handles

Wooden handles that attach to brushes and brooms are worthless when their threads are spent. But you can add new life to them by wrapping the worn threads with one or more turns of adhesive tape. Twist the handle back into the socket, and the fit will be secure again. If the handle is still loose, add another turn of tape.

Sliding Brooms

A rubber tip (like that used on the bottom of crutches) put on a broom handle will prevent the broom from sliding down when propped up against a wall.

Storing Brooms

Brooms should be hung up or rested on their handles, not on the bristles, when not in use.

Broom Care

Keep brooms cleaned by washing them regularly in warm sudsy water. Always hang brooms with the straw-end down.

Brooms on Rough Surfaces

The rough surfaces of sidewalks, driveways, and basements are tough on brooms. To keep brooms from wearing out quickly, dip the ends of the bristles into a shallow pan of thinned shellac, and allow to dry thoroughly.

Add Life to Sponges

If you will squeeze rather than twist the liquid out of sponges, they will last much longer.

Stale Sponges

Sponges that are fresh are more pleasant to use, and they do a better job. Freshen up sponges by soaking them in cold salt water.

Slimy Sponges

Refurbish slimy sponges by soaking them overnight in a mixture of one part vinegar to two parts water. Rinse thoroughly in hot water in the morning.

Sponges as Soap Dishes

Sponges that are no longer useful for wiping surfaces can be used as soap-savers. A bar of soap placed on a sponge won't get soft and gooey on the bottom as it does in a soap dish, making a mess and wasting soap. Place the sponge in the soap dish. When the sponge becomes saturated with soap drippings, use it for cleaning up around sinks and wash basins.

Dusting Techniques

It is wise, when starting to dust, to begin at the top. Dust the higher areas and objects first. The dust that falls will land on the lower areas, which will be cleaned later. Moisten the dusting cloth with the tiniest bit of furniture cleaner, and the dust will stay on the cloth rather than the furniture.

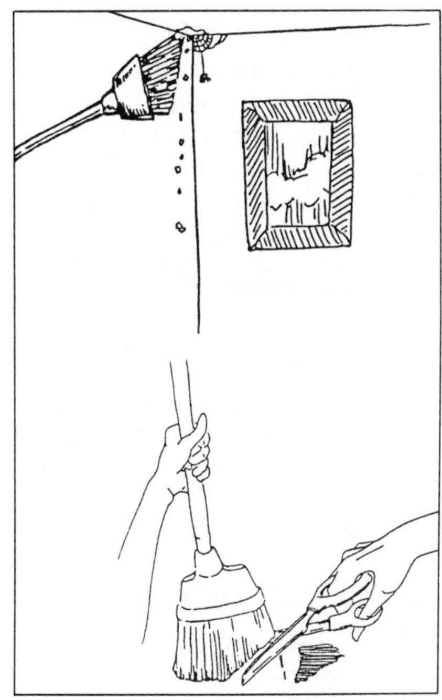

To get at dust and dirt in corners, cut an old whisk broom on a 45-degree angle, using a scissor or a razor blade. The tapered point will help you do a thorough job.

Floating Dust

To keep the dust from floating out of your dustpan, dampen the inside of the dustpan before using.

Chamois

Pronounced "shamee," chamois is soft leather made from the skin of a chamois (a small goatlike antelope) or deer. It makes an ideal polishing cloth because it leaves no lint, as well as an excellent drying cloth because it can absorb a great deal of water.

Chamois Treatment

A chamois should be rinsed in clean water after use. If soiled, use a mild soap. Do not use a detergent, which would draw out the natural oil in the cloth. After washing, squeeze out the water and stretch out to dry in the open air.

Stiff Chamois

Soften a stiff chamois by soaking it in a pot filled with a quart of hot water to which two spoonfuls of cooking oil or linseed oil have been added.

Sweeping With a Broom

If possible, save your sweeping chores for rainy or humid days. The dampness keeps the dust from rising, making it much easier to gather the dirt.

Cleaning Under Radiators

To clean hard-to-reach areas—such as under radiators, refrigerators, stoves, and dressers—wrap an old sock around a yardstick or a long wooden spoon and sweep the area clean.

Venetian Blind Mittens

An old cotton mitten or glove will make the job of cleaning venetian blinds a lot easier. You can make your own mitten out of old towels by simply tracing the outline of your hand with a marking pencil. Make the tracing one inch larger than your hand. Lay this piece of toweling on a second piece, and cut both pieces at one time. Sew together, leaving one end open to receive your hand. Turn the sewn mitten inside out and you are ready to clean the blinds.

Washing Ceilings and Walls

To wash ceilings and walls, use a wall detergent such as Mr. Clean or Pine Sol in a bucket of hot water. When washing walls, start at the top of the wall and rub down with a sponge soaked in the solution. Rinse off with clean water. Dry off with a clean cloth.

Reaching Cobwebs

Hard-to-reach cobwebs that develop where the wall meets the ceiling can be easily reached and removed using an old sock tied around the handle-end of a broomstick. Use a wire twist'em or rubber band to secure the sock.

Windowsills

Windowsills will be easier to clean if you protect them with a coating of floor wax. Wax prevents dirt from adhering and generally protects the painted surface. When time for repainting arrives, make sure to remove the wax buildup.

Cleaning Ashtrays

Ashtrays should be cleaned extra well from time to time to remove the clinging foul odor that does not always disappear with normal washing. You can accomplish this by soaking the ashtrays in denatured alcohol diluted with water. One cup of alcohol to one cup of water will make up an effective solution.

Preventing Brass From Tarnishing

Brass doorknockers, doorknobs, and nameplates can be protected by coating with a thin layer of paste wax. Clean with metal polish first and buff after waxing. Rewax once or twice yearly.

Clean, polished brass that is given a thin coat of shellac will not need to be polished again. A second coat will give still better protection. The only cleaning needed thereafter will be an occasional dusting.

Cleaning and Preserving Brass

There are a variety of methods for restoring tarnished brass to its original luster:

To clean a tarnished brass object, use a product such as Mr. Clean. Place the cleaning agent in a plastic pail, then add water and a piece of aluminum foil. Leave the brass object in the solution for 15 minutes. Rinse, then dry and polish. Alternate method: Dip a lemon peel in salt and rub it on the brass object.

To clean discolored brass, rub with a rag soaked in a mixture of vinegar and salt.

Brass Polish "Recipe"

To make your own brass polish, start with a cup of vinegar; add two tablespoons of salt and enough flour to make a smooth paste. Apply the paste to brass with a damp cloth to remove stains. Rub hard, rinse with cold water, and dry with a soft cloth.

Cleaning Books

To remove stains from the edges of book pages, first blow off loose dirt, then press the pages tightly together and sand with very fine sandpaper. Blow off dirt and continue to sand as necessary. The dirt will disappear without damaging the pages.

Book Bindings

Leatherbound books can be kept in good condition by applying a thin coat of vaseline or saddle soap containing lanolin.

Cleaning Chrome and Stainless Steel

Chrome utensils and fixtures can be cleaned easily by wiping them with a cloth moistened with a solution of one part ammonia or vinegar to one part water. Toothpaste is also effective in cleaning stained chrome, as is rubbing alcohol and baking soda. Avoid using abrasive cleansers.

Mirror Cleaning

Keep mirrors clean by rubbing with a soft, damp cloth dipped into a solution of water plus a small amount of ammonia or vinegar. Dry off with a lintless cloth or paper toweling. Of course, preparations such as Windex and Glass Wax are available for mirror cleaning. Bon Ami is another old favorite.

Cleaning Pewter

To clean articles made of pewter, use only hot, sudsy water. Rinse, dry off, then apply a coating of silver polish.

Piano Key Whiteness

Ivory piano keys can be kept clean by wiping them with a cloth dampened with a solution of salt and lemon juice and then wiped dry. Alcohol may also be used for this purpose.

For piano keys to retain their whiteness, avoid keeping them covered constantly. Keys will stay white longer if exposed to the light of day, particularly sunlight.

Cleaning Windows on Sunny Days

Avoid cleaning windows when the sun is shining on them. The window washing liquid sometimes dries before they can be wiped clean.

Cleaning Windows to Perfection

When wiping the inside of windows, use vertical strokes; and when cleaning the outside, use horizontal strokes. This will enable you to tell at a glance on which side smudges remain.

Avoid Streaking on Windows

To avoid streaking, use water to which a few tablespoons of ammonia or vinegar have been added. Dry off with a chamois, paper toweling, or newspaper.

Homemade Window-cleaning Solution

You can save money by making your own window-cleaning solution. Simply fill a bucket with warm water and add to it one-half cup of white vinegar, one-half cup of ammonia, and two tablespoons of cornstarch. Divide into two or three parts. Use as much as needed and save the remainder for future cleanings. Apply with an old spray atomizer.

Cleaning Glass Fixtures

Hard-to-reach glass fixtures, such as chandeliers, can be cleaned by dipping a cloth or sponge in ammonia diluted with water (one part ammonia to three parts water) and applying generously. Keep some toweling under the fixture to absorb any liquid that drips.

Use a long-handled mop with a sponge at the end (rather than strings) to clean hard-to-reach windows.

Preventing Steaming and Icing Up of Glass

To prevent glass from steaming or icing up, add a teaspoon of glycerin or alcohol to a pint of water and apply with a soft tissue or cloth. After the surface has been cleaned with the solution and is allowed to dry, the film that remains will prevent steam and ice from forming for a few hours.

Mirror Back Repair

Place a smooth piece of tinfoil over the bare spots that have developed on the back of a mirror. Secure the tinfoil in place with a coat of shellac.

Cleaning Framed Mirrors

In order to prevent water from getting inside a mirror frame as

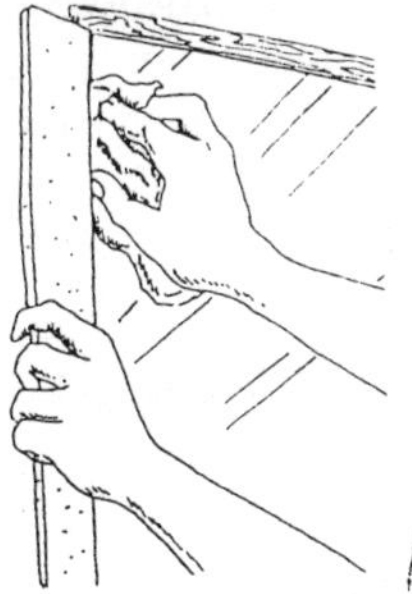

you are cleaning it, hold a piece of cardboard against the inside edge of the mirror.

Cloudy Mirrors

To keep mirrors from becoming cloudy, position them in your home in spots where the sun will not shine directly on them.

Eliminating Gasoline Odors

Reduce the odor of gasoline and kerosene that may have gotten on your hands (or clothing) by rubbing them with vinegar or a strong salt solution.

Grease Stains on Wallpaper

Place a piece of blotting paper over the stained wallpaper as soon as you notice it. Press an iron at medium heat (wool setting) against the blotting paper. The grease will be liquefied by the heat and absorbed by the blotting paper. You may have to make several tries to get up all the stain. Use a clean section of the blotting paper each time. If you have acted quickly enough, the soil will disappear.

Glue Stains on Furniture

If a glue stain on furniture cannot be removed by soaking the area in hot water, apply a dry-cleaning solvent. Acetone will usually do the trick.

Cleaning Acrylic Plastics

Acrylic plastics are used to protect many objects in the home, including tabletops, desktops, drawer fronts, and trays. To remove stains and sticky spots from such articles, avoid using abrasive cleansers containing acetone, benzene, or alcohol, which might mar the finish. Instead, use liquid cleansers containing vinegar or ammonia.

Aerosol Cleaners

Aerosol glass cleaners are available commercially from many manufacturers. Besides cleaning glass and mirrors, most will clean formica, tile, and porcelain. Sprayway, Inc. (see Appendix for address) produces a cleaner (#50) that is environmentally safe.

Removing Grease From Wood

To remove grease spots from wooden cabinets, rub with a rag

moistened with a bit of vinegar. Dry with a clean cloth.

Cleaning Stained Woodwork

The woodwork in kitchens is often stained by grease and dirtied by smoke. Rectify this by spreading a solution of starch and water on the woodwork and letting it dry. Then, rub with a soft brush or cloth. The stain will usually come off with the starch.

Washing Woodwork

If painted woodwork has become discolored, clean it off with a solution made up of one gallon of water to which one-quarter cup of ammonia and two tablespoons of detergent have been added. Wash, then rinse with clear water.

Cleaning Metal Furniture

After washing metal furniture with detergent and water, rinse and dry with a soft cloth. If the finish appears dull, polish with a white cream wax made for kitchen appliances.

Protecting Marble Surfaces

Marble countertops are quite likely to become stained from spilled liquid and food. Protect the surfaces by applying hard, automobile-type paste wax and polishing to a shine.

Marble Tabletop Stains

A small amount of lemon juice to which a sprinkle of salt has been added will remove stains from marble tabletops. Apply lightly with a soft cloth, dry, then buff gently with a soft towel.

White Ring Stains

Unsightly white rings need not mar the surfaces of tabletops permanently. Rub the area lightly with a chemically pure petroleum (such as Vaseline) and let it soak in overnight. Remove in the morning with a clean cloth. The mark will at least be lighter and in many cases will have disappeared altogether.

Spots and Rings on Furniture

Many spots or rings can be removed by rubbing with a piece of soft cotton dampened with spirits of camphor or with a solution of one part ammonia (or turpentine) mixed with one part linseed oil.

Black spots, usually caused by water penetrating a polished surface, cannot be removed superficially. You might try to remove the finish with steel wool soaked in methylated spirits, and follow this by bleaching the spot. Refinish with the appropriate color stain, then varnish.

Tobacco Odors

An old favorite way of getting rid of tobacco odors is to leave one or two uncovered bowls of vinegar in the room.

Litterbox Odors

To rid a litterbox of odors, wash it with a solution of one gallon water to three-quarters cup of liquid bleach. Allow the solution to stand in the box for five minutes, then rinse thoroughly with water.

Cleaning Plaster Ornaments

Dip into liquid starch the plaster ornaments you would like to clean, then let them dry. Brush off the dry starch and you will find that new luster has been added to your decorative pieces.

Removing Decals

To remove a decal without damaging the surface beneath, cover the decoration with a wet washcloth and press a hot iron to the cloth. In a few minutes steam will loosen the decal.

To ease the removal of vehicle inspection and registration stickers, press a hot, moist towel against the decal for ten minutes before removing.

Picking Up Pins and Tacks

Picking up pins and tacks with a magnet is not always efficient. A piece of paper placed over the

magnet before picking up the pieces will make it easier to handle them once you've got them.

Keeping Cockroaches Out

Before using commercial pesticides, try to eliminate cockroaches by pouring boric acid under sinks and into crevices.

Preventing Mildew on Wicker

To prevent mildew from forming on hampers and baskets made of straw or wicker, coat the surface with two coats of shellac.

Protecting Leather

Leather items should not be stored in sealed plastic bags. They should be kept in places that are cool, dry, and have ample air circulation.

Preserving Leather Furniture

Before soil has a chance to work its way into leather furniture, clean it with saddle or castile soap. Work up a good lather, then remove it with a damp cloth. Follow this by wiping the leather dry.

Also, you might want to try one of the specially manufactured leather dressings available. It will help keep the leather pliable and prevent it from cracking. Sporting goods stores and department stores stock a variety of preparations.

Mildew on Leather Goods

Mildew can sometimes be removed from leather by wiping the object with a cloth moistened with vinegar. Dry off, then repeat the process several times, as needed.

Saddle soap is often effective in removing mildew odors.

Cleaning Leather Furniture

A quick, usually effective way of cleaning leather furniture is to dip a sponge in water to which the juice of half a lemon has been added.

Homemade Leather Polish

Make your own leather polishing agent by adding one part vinegar to two parts linseed oil.

Leather Conditioning

Leather becomes brittle and cracks when it loses its oil. To recondition such articles, apply saddle soap, which contains lanolin (derived from sheep's wool); neat's-foot oil; castor oil; or cod-liver oil. Rub in vigorously with your fingers and allow the oil to settle in for at least one hour before cleaning off excess. This procedure will keep the leather pliable.

Darkening Leather Goods

Light-tan leather shoes and belts can be darkened by rubbing them with a cloth dipped in ammonia. Apply the ammonia uniformly for an even finish.

Wet Leather

Before storing away wet leather garments or shoes, or luggage, allow the articles to dry out in the open air. This will prevent mildew from forming. Ring marks that remain can be cleaned with saddle soap.

Lemon Juice to Shine Leather

An effective way of giving leather a high shine is to place a few drops of lemon juice on a rag and to rub well into the leather.

Washing Fake Suede

When washing synthetic suede by hand, do not squeeze or wring out the garments. To remove excess moisture, roll the clothing in a towel. Then, lay flat or hang to dry.

Mildew Prevention

A piece of charcoal placed in a cup and left in the corner of a room where mildew has a tendency to gather will usually serve as an effective preventative.

Cellar Dampness

Cellar dampness caused by condensation rather than direct leaks through the walls can be relieved by improving ventilation. An easy way to solve the problem is to keep an ordinary fan running in the basement. Position the fan so that the stream of air is directed toward the cellar window, which should be kept partially open.

Testing for Cellar Dampness

There are two tests to determine whether cellar dampness is caused by condensation. One test is to attach a small mirror to one of the walls with adhesive tape. In eight hours or less tiny drops of water will gather on the mirror if condensation is causing the dampness. The other test is to lay a rubber mat on the bare concrete floor and to remove it 24 hours later. If the floor is damp, it indicates that moisture has penetrated the concrete from below.

Waterproofing Paint

Special cellar waterproofing paint that will solve many dampness and moisture problems is available at paint stores. Check with your local dealer. Such products will only alleviate marginal moisture problems, however; serious leakage must be stemmed from outside.

RESTORING, REPAIRING, AND REMODELING

Unfinished Furniture

Finishing unfinished furniture can be pleasurable, provided that the wood is of reasonably good quality. Furniture made of kiln-dried wood is less likely to shrink or warp. If the wood selected has knots, make certain they are firm and tight and are not likely to fall out. Avoid furniture with too many knots. Watch out for blue-gray streaks, which indicate the presence of mildew or some other fungus. These streaks cannot be bleached out easily, if at all, and may show through even after several coats of paint have been applied.

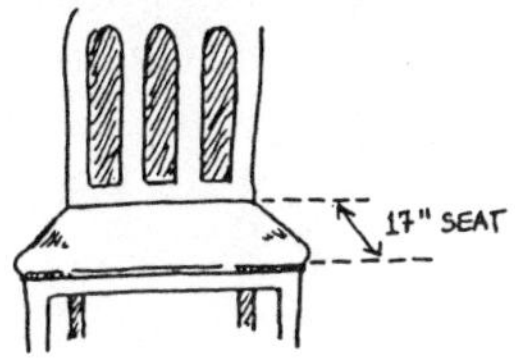

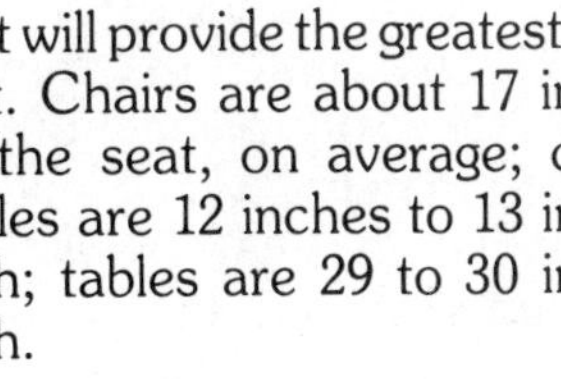

Building Furniture

If you are planning to make your own furniture—tables, chairs, cabinets, chests—follow the standard measurements that have been tested and proven, and that will provide the greatest comfort. Chairs are about 17 inches to the seat, on average; coffee tables are 12 inches to 13 inches high; tables are 29 to 30 inches high.

Furniture Polish

For polishing pieces of furniture with sharp corners and fancy molding, use a clean shoe buffer. The soft pad can get to uneven, hard-to-reach spaces.

Homemade Furniture Restorer

If your furniture lacks luster, one of the ready-made finishes available in hardware and paint stores may rectify the situation. If you have no luck with the standard products available, make your own. Here is a recipe which will provide you with a sufficient amount for testing:

¼ cup turpentine
¼ cup linseed oil
¼ cup white vinegar
1 tablespoon denatured alcohol

Rub onto a small area, and polish with a soft cloth. If the restorer works to your satisfaction, make a larger amount by increasing the ingredients proportionately. Whatever is leftover can be safely stored in a glass jar for future use.

Deep Gouges in Furniture

The best way to fill holes and deep gouges in a furniture surface is with a stick of solid shellac, available in the usual furniture colors. Soften one end of the stick by applying a lighted match to it. Then, slice off pieces of the softened material with a knife or a flexible spatula. Apply the softened shellac to the hole and smooth over with the blade. The repaired area can be covered with fresh varnish, lacquer, or the same material as was there originally.

Paper Stuck to Wood

Paper that has stuck to wooden surfaces will come off if a few drops of olive oil are allowed to soak into it. Rub the paper off gently with a soft cloth. Do not use a sharp object for removal.

Homemade Filler

To create a patch filler that will stain well and match the surrounding wood, combine sawdust of the type of wood to be patched with a plastic resin glue that has been thinned. Mix the ingredients to form a match. Coat the hole with full-strength glue, then fill the hole with the mixture. Press firmly. When the filler has dried, sand and stain.

Wood Filler

Another type of wood filler can be made by mixing glue, torn-up tissue paper, linseed oil, and chalk. If the mixture appears too light, add a dark tinting pigment, which is available in paint stores. Apply the filling with a putty knife, and after it has dried, sand the area if necessary.

Plastic Wood Filler

Plastic wood is a synthetic filler that does a good job in filling holes and drying to form a hard finish. It will not absorb a water-based stain well but will be effective with an oil-based stain.

Minor Furniture Scratches

Liquid Gold, available in hardware stores and supermarkets, does a good job removing minor scratches on furniture.

Toothpaste for Scratches

Because toothpaste contains a very mild abrasive, it can be used successfully to remove small scratches and blemishes from furniture.

Shoe Polish as Stain

If you want to darken a scratched furniture surface, select a shoe polish of the same approximate color and buff the area.

Scratched Walnut

Shallow scratches in walnut furniture can be concealed by rubbing the scratches with the meat or kernel of a walnut. The natural oil in the walnut will darken the scratches, and they will become almost invisible to the naked eye. After rubbing with the kernel, dry off with a clean cloth.

Burns in Furniture

To remove burns like those caused by cigarettes, obtain powdered pumice from your hardware or paint store. Wrap a piece of felt around a wooden block and tack it down. Dip it in water and squeeze almost dry. Sprinkle the powdered pumice on the burned area and rub lightly. If the area that has the burn is very small, wrap the felt around your fingertip and rub the pumice in gently.

Scratched Mahogany

You can hide scratches on your mahogany furniture by using ordinary iodine as a touch-up. Apply with the end of a match or toothpick. Polish when dry. If the iodine is darker than the mahogany, lighten it with a drop or two of rubbing alcohol.

Dented Wood

A small indentation in furniture can be evened out by placing a damp cloth over the area and pressing an electric iron set at

medium heat on it. This will cause the compressed fibers to swell. The procedure might have to be repeated several times.

Another alternative is to pour hot water into the hollow area and allow it to stand.

Holes in Wood Paneling

Nail holes, small cracks, and other minor imperfections in wood paneling can be made almost invisible with the aid of colored putty sticks, available wherever wall paneling is sold. The sticks consist of a soft waxy material that can be applied directly to the hole or crack.

Nailing Down Paneling

To protect paneling when hammering nails into it, drill a small hole into a thin piece of wood and slide it over the nail. If you miss the nail, you won't hit the paneling. When the nail is flush with the wood strip, remove the wood and drive in the nail with a nail-set.

Wall Paneling Edges

Before installing tongue-and-groove wall paneling, check the color of the tongue-and-groove edges. If they are lighter than the panel surface, darken them with stain or paint. By so doing, if the panels shrink, the tongue-and-groove edges will not show.

Precise Cutting of Paneling

It is very difficult to figure exactly where to cut a hole in wood paneling in order to be able to gain access to an electrical outlet or switch. One mistake and an entire panel could be ruined.

One way of proceeding is to coat the edges of the outlet or switch with lipstick or chalk and to place the panel in the proper position with its back against the outlet. Tap the panel against the outlet with a rubber mallet or an ordinary hammer, using a block of wood to protect the panel surface. The outline of the outlet will then appear on the back of the panel and serve as an accurate guide for cutting the opening.

Loose Dresser or Cabinet Knobs

When a dresser or cabinet knob is loose, tighten it as follows: open the drawer, insert a screwdriver into the slot on the head of the screw that holds the knob, hold the screwdriver firmly with one hand, and with the other hand tighten the knob. Sometimes the threads of the knob itself are worn out, in which case remove the knob and insert one or two short lengths of a flat toothpick (or any flat piece of wood or cardboard) into the hole of the knob. Then, while holding the screw with the screwdriver inside the drawer, replace and tighten the knob.

Loose Doorknobs

The old-fashioned doorknobs that come loose in your hand are

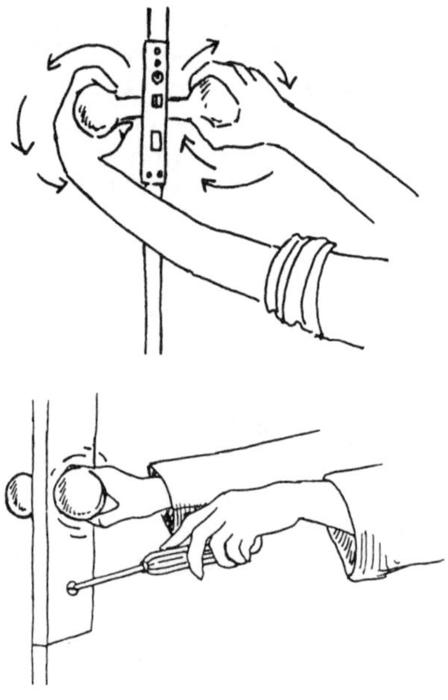

easily fixed. Put the loose knob back on the square, threaded shaft that holds both knobs together. Hold one knob and turn the other until both are tight. Tighten the setscrew at the base of each knob and jiggle the knob as you tighten so the screw will stay in the groove.

If this doesn't work, the threads on either the shaft or the knob are probably worn, and you will have to replace the knob or the shaft. Your local hardware store should have the necessary parts.

Warped Doors

Moisture causes the warping of doors, and removing the dampness will often rectify the warping. A heat lamp directed at the bulging side should dissipate the dampness. As soon as the warp disappears, remove the heat and cover both sides and all edges of the door with sealer to prevent further absorption of moisture.

Sagging Doors

Old wooden doors have a tendency to sag because the screws in the hinges have become loose. If the lower corner of the door touches the floor and the upper corner sticks to the frame, try tightening the screws of the upper hinge by putting a thin piece of cardboard or wood under the door jamb and tightening the hinge screws.

Resetting Hinges

Sometimes the wood in which a hinge is set was mortised too deeply and will prevent the door from closing properly. You can correct this by cutting out a cardboard shim the size of the hinge and placing it under the hinge before replacing the screws.

Squeaky Hinges

Hinges on old doors should be oiled from time to time to prevent squeaking. Vaseline is a good lubricant for this purpose, as are silicone sprays. Periodically check that hinge pins have not risen. If they have, tap down with a hammer.

Modernizing Old Doors

Old doors can be modernized by simply gluing or nailing panels of plywood to the old surface. Plywood that is one-quarter inch thick will do the job. When attaching the plywood with glue, remove the paint from the old door first so the glue will stick. After the paint has been removed, wash the surface with alcohol.

Easy-sliding Cabinet Doors

Cabinet doors that slide in ordinary grooves routed into the wooden frames (not using the special hardware that is available) can be made to move more smoothly by applying some shellac to the surface and then adding wax. Apply a thin coat of shellac to the inside of the groove and the bottom of the door. When dry, apply ordinary polishing wax. Even a candle will do the trick.

Removing Sliding Doors

The slotted wood, metal, or plastic channels in which sliding doors ride are deeper on top than on bottom. This also applies to sliding shower doors. Therefore, when you want to remove them, push up as much as you can so the doors clear the bottom track, then pull out at the bottom.

Fiberglass Screens

You can mend a tear or hole in fiberglass window screening by laying a patch of fiberglass over the tear and applying a hot iron to it. Cover the patch with aluminum foil when applying the iron.

Balancing Furniture Legs

A perfectly balanced table or chair, when moved to a new spot, may rock and be unsteady. The fault is not in the chair but in the floor. Nevertheless, you will have to adjust the chair leg lengths to solve your problem. One way is to pack plastic wood or ordinary glazing putty under the "short" leg. Before applying, place a piece of waxed paper between the leg and the floor to prevent the putty or plastic wood from sticking to the floor. If the table or chair is later moved to a spot where the shim is not needed, it can be cut loose with a sharp knife.

Another solution is to attach a piece of wood of the correct thickness and size to the bottom of the leg. Nail it in place with thin brads, which can be easily removed.

Still another cure for a wobbly chair is to force a thumbtack into the short leg.

Tightening Loose Casters

Casters will wobble when they fit loosely in their sockets. You can easily correct this by removing the casters from the sockets and wrapping the stems with aluminum foil or Scotch tape. Crinkle the foil or tape a bit to create a rougher surface. Use several turns of foil if necessary.

Sagging Cane Chairs

To take the sag out of the seat of a chair made of cane, allow a cloth that has been thoroughly dampened with hot water to remain on the seat for ten to fifteen minutes. Then, place the chair outdoors in the sun to dry.

Squeaky Chairs

The same silicone lubricant recommended to take the creak out of door hinges can be used to take the squeak out of chairs. The lubricant is packaged in aerosol cans and is available at hardware stores. Spray a small amount directly at the point where the tops of the legs meet the seat of the chair—and also on the spots where the crossbars meet the legs. A light coating of Vaseline might also be effective.

Fixing Furniture Joints

When glued furniture joints begin to loosen, it is time to reglue. It is not necessary to disassemble the piece to do the job.

Pull the joint slightly apart and apply the glue with an eye-dropper. Warm the glue beforehand for easier spreading by placing the container in hot water for a few minutes. Clamp or tie rope at proper points, and tie a strong knot to hold the furniture together until the glue has dried.

Tightening Loose Furniture

Chair-Loc, available at hardware stores, has proven effective in swelling wood fibers. It can be used to help make wooden handles for tools and loose rungs on chairs expand and fit tighter.

Blistered Veneer

To repair blistered veneer, make an incision around the blister with a razor blade. Next cover the area with a cloth moistened with hot water, and leave the cloth in place until the veneer softens. Quickly, apply stainproof glue to the area beneath the raised blister, using the blade of a knife. Then cover the blister with wax paper and press flat with a heavy weight to hold the blister down until the glue dries. Scrape off the glue that oozes out and apply a fresh coat of furniture polish or wax.

Swelled Drawers

Drawers sometimes swell in damp weather and become difficult to open. When the weather is dry, remove them, and sandpaper the runners to reduce the size a bit, then cover all sides of each drawer with a coat of shellac. This will prevent future swelling. Keep the drawer tracks clean by wiping with a cloth dampened with ammonia.

Locating Studs

If you have tried other methods and failed, a good way to locate studs is to remove the molding at the bottom of the wall. There you will probably see where the sheets or plasterboard have been joined, which would indicate the

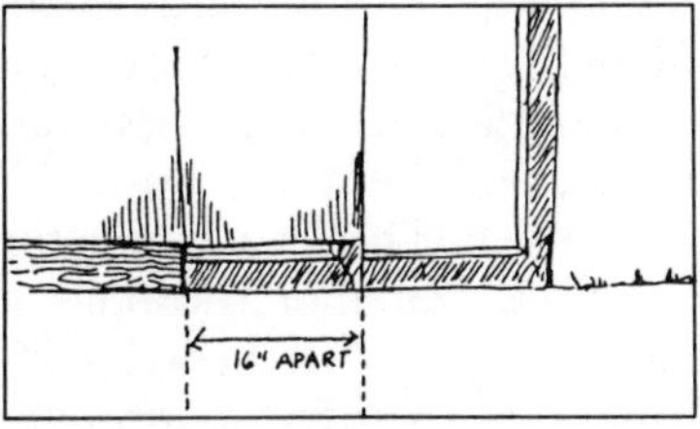

location of a stud. If, for some reason, stud location is still not clear, drive in nails every few inches along the area that was covered by the molding until a nail hits a stud. All marks and nail heads will be covered by the molding.

Once you have located one stud, in a properly built house the next stud will be 16 inches away, measuring from the center of one stud to the center of the next one.

Prybars on Molding

It is very easy to ruin a wall when attempting to remove a molding. The best tool for this purpose is a flat prybar. Insert the curved end behind the molding, preferably at a spot where there is a two-by-four behind the plaster. To be extra safe, place a large quarter-inch piece of plywood (at least 5 inches by 18 inches) against the wall before using the prybar. Pry up slowly until the molding is loose. Then, move to the next section until all the nails holding the molding have been loosened.

Popping Nails

The seasonal contraction and expansion of house studs often pushes out the nails that are holding the plasterboard to the stud. If the nails begin to protrude through the wallpaper or painted surface, pull them out if possible and fill the nail holes with plaster. Otherwise, hammer the nails in so that they are slightly below the surface. Then drive a threaded nail with a flat top (not a finishing nail) about one inch above or below the old nail and recess it slightly. Then, cover both dimpled areas with spackle or any standard patching compound. Use plasterboard screws available at any hardware store in different sizes.

Driving Nails into Plaster

When nails are driven into plaster, it often will crack. Here are a few suggestions that should be helpful:

- Heat the nail first and it will go in smoothly—and without dislodging a chunk of plaster in the process.
- Hit the nail into the wall at approximately a 45-degree angle.
- Apply a small piece of Scotch tape or electrical tape and drive in the nail at an angle. The tape can be removed immediately and the wall will remain unblemished.

Slow-drying Plaster

When preparing plaster for wall-patching, you will be able to work more slowly if you add a small amount of vinegar to the water that is being added to the plaster mix. The vinegar will retard hardening of the plaster.

Plaster Drippings

Plaster that has dripped and fallen on painted surfaces can be removed by rubbing very lightly with steel wool. Light rubbing will prevent damage to the underlying surface. Traces of plaster that still remain can be dissolved by rubbing with a solution of lemon juice and water: one part lemon juice to three parts water.

Holes in Plasterboard

A large hole in a plasterboard wall can be repaired by cutting out a rectangular portion of the plasterboard tall enough to include the entire hole and wide enough to reach from the middle of one stud to the middle of the next one. (If your contractor followed building-code rules, studs should be 16 inches from the center of one stud to the center of the next.) A new piece of plasterboard exactly the same size and thickness as the broken portion that was removed is placed over the new opening and nailed at the ends to the partially exposed studs. Secure the new section with plasterboard nail-heads driven in sufficiently so they do not protrude. Use a nail-set to be sure they are below the surface of the plasterboard. Fill in the edges of the newly inserted piece with a prepared plaster mixture (such as Spackle) available in all hardware stores. Then cover the mix with two-inch paper tape and smooth it out with a three-inch scraper. When dry, sand the area and paint. If the wall is not smooth, add more plaster and smooth out as above.

Quick Plaster Repair

To quickly patch a hole that goes clear through plasterboard, stuff the hole with a generous amount of crumpled newspaper that has been moistened. After being pushed into the hole, the paper will expand and stay in place. Fill the hole with plaster. After it has hardened, apply a second coat and smooth out.

Plastering Corner Cracks

Deep corner cracks are quite common in older houses. The best way to repair these cracks is to remove all loose plaster and then cover the area with a thin film of plaster. Fold a length of perforated tape in the center and lay it into the plaster. Press it into the plaster with your fingers. Next, spread more plaster over the tape until it is fully covered by plaster. Smooth with a corner trowel. In a few hours, after the plaster has dried, sand the area

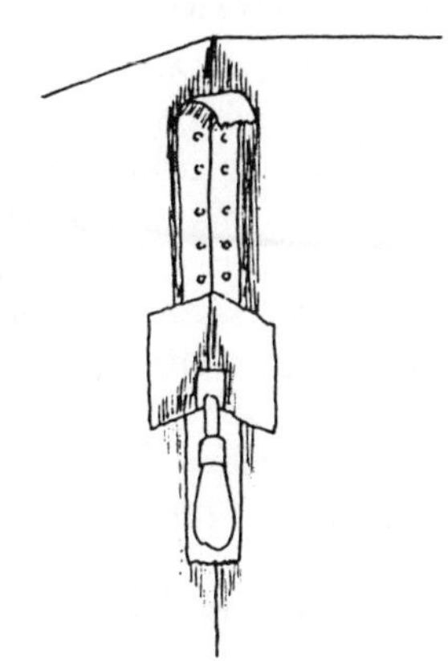

until the outer edges of the plaster blend in smoothly with the rest of the wall surface. You are now ready to paint or repaper the area.

Cracked Ceilings and Walls

Ceilings and walls may be so badly cracked that a great deal of patching is required before you can start painting. You can avoid all that work by using a textured plaster-like material that hides cracks and other blemishes. It is a heavy vinyl-compound mix that rolls on easily (with a deep-nap roller) and produces a surface that diffuses light pleasantly. The surface can be painted. Your paint dealer will be able to advise you.

Protecting Wallpaper

If you have wallpaper in your kitchen or bathroom, protect the corners from lifting or peeling by covering them with a coat of varnish.

Removing Wallpaper

To remove wallpaper make a solution of equal parts vinegar and hot water. Saturate the wall using a sponge or a paint roller. Two applications may be needed. The paper should come off easily. Electric steamers that will do a good job are also available for purchase or rental. Check with your hardware or paint store.

Wallpaper Blisters

You can cure blistered wallpaper by cutting through the length of the blister with a new razor blade to release the air. Then, with a very small brush or the edge of a piece of paper, apply wallpaper paste underneath the exposed material and press down for a minute or more until the glue sets. Wipe off the excess with a damp cloth.

Wallpaper Patches

If a small area of wallpaper has to be replaced, do as follows: From the original roll, cut off a piece of paper that will match in design. The patch should be approximately two inches larger all around than the area to be covered. Apply paste to the patch and position over the damaged area. Take a sharp razor blade and, one inch from the outer edge of the patch, cut through the patch and the damaged paper underneath it. Remove the patch, then remove the old, damaged paper. Discard the damaged paper and position the new paper in its place.

Leftover Wallpaper

Leftover wallpaper can be used to decorate some of the accessories in the same room. Remnants can be used to cover a wastebasket, a tissue box holder, or a window shade.

Cleaning Upholstery

To clean upholstery, first vacuum to remove as much loose dirt as possible, then shampoo with a mixture of one- quarter cup bleach-free powdered detergent dissolved in one cup warm water. Whip the detergent into a foamy lather and apply it to small areas of the furniture at one time. When moving on to the next area, be sure to go back over the edges of the area you have just washed so overlapping areas will not appear when the upholstery has dried. After shampooing, wipe the area several times with a damp sponge to remove all traces of soap. Take an extra moment to dry off with a clean soft cloth to hasten drying.

Fraying Rope

If the ends of a rope or cord within your home show signs of fraying, dip them in shellac and allow to harden.

Cigarette Burns in Upholstery

Use a yarn in a color that closely matches the upholstery. Darn over the burned area with small, close-together stitches. Then iron the patched area through a damp cloth.

Wax Removal From Candleholders

Pour very hot water in the candleholders in order to soften the wax. Remove the wax with a screwdriver. Caution: Hot water may affect the shellac finish that is sometimes applied to candlesticks.

Broken Windowpane

You may not have the time to replace a pane of glass the moment it cracks. If that is the case, paint over the crack on the inside of the window with fresh white shellac. The shellac will hold the glass together temporarily and will keep out the wind and rain. Being clear, the shellac will not interfere with your vision. If the crack is too wide for this procedure, cover it with heavy-duty (6 mil) polyethylene tape, which is available in hardware stores.

Charred Surfaces

Charred wood surfaces can be treated by rubbing the scorched area with an oxalic acid solution after having sanded the area with fine sandpaper or steel wool. (Borax powder will neutralize the acidity of oxalic acid.)

Fireplace Stains

Stains on the stone slab in front of the fireplace caused by charred wood can be removed by using an abrasive such as sandpaper.

Smoke-stained Bricks

Fireplace brickwork that has been tarnished by smoke stains can sometimes be cleaned with scouring powder and a good scrub brush. Occasionally that will not work effectively, in which case prepare a stiff paste made of talc mixed with trichloroethylene (available in hardware and paint stores). Spread this over the stains. In order to prevent the paste from drying out rapidly, tape a piece of plastic over the area, and secure the edges with masking tape. After the paste beneath the plastic has dried, remove the covering and scrape, sand, or brush off the paste. The stains should be totally gone.

Stained Brickwork

Whether the brickwork is indoors or outdoors, stains need never mar its surface permanently. Clean brick or stonework first with regular household detergent and warm water, then allow to dry. When thoroughly dry, apply a thin coat of wood sealer and turpentine mixed in equal parts.

Contact Paper

Contact paper accidentally sticking to a surface as you're trying to position it can be frustrating. Avoid the problem by rubbing the sticky side very lightly with a damp, sudsy sponge. The paper will slide into place easily as you position it, and the slight moisture applied to it will not affect the holding power of the adhesive.

Porcelain Repair

To repair nicks in a porcelain sink, refrigerator, range, or bathtub use the commercial product Porcelain Repair, available at most hardware stores. The product is easy to apply and quick-drying.

Sink Stains

To remove stains and to make your sink sparkle, close the drain and pour in enough household bleach to cover the bottom of the sink to a depth of about one-eighth inch. Allow to sit for 20 or 30 minutes, then rinse with cool water.

Shiny Faucets

To clean faucets effectively, wash down with detergent and rinse with water. Do not use scouring powder, which may wear off the chrome-plated finish. Remove brown stains around faucets with a one-to-one mixture of vinegar (or lemon juice) and water. Rinse with clear water.

Stains on Porcelain

Light stains can be removed from porcelain surfaces such as sinks and bathtubs by rubbing the stained area with a cut lemon. Dark stains can be removed by rubbing the area with a paste made of borax and lemon juice, or by dabbing on liquid bleach and letting it stand for a few hours.

Leaky Vases

Leaky vases or other glass containers that are used with only cold water can be saved by dripping some hot candle wax on the hole or by coating it with paraffin and allowing the paraffin to harden.

Loose Window Shade Springs

If you have a window shade that will not go up when tugged at, you will have to build up tension in the inner spring. This is done by taking the shade and roller down and inserting a fork in the flat slot at the end of the roller. Turn the fork clockwise until the spring feels taut, then replace the shade.

Bookmending Tape

A tough, thin, easy-to-use transparent tape that mends book bindings and torn pages is produced by the 3M Company. This product is available at stationery and department stores.

Book Care

To preserve bindings, do not allow books to lay at an angle. If a bookshelf is not full, use bookends or lay a few books horizontally as a prop for the other books, which will then be forced to stand vertically.

FLOORS AND FLOOR COVERINGS

Selecting Carpeting

Carpeting is available in a variety of fibers. Here are some facts worth remembering about the more common fibers:

- Nylon is durable, colorfast, and soil-resistant. It cleans easily and wears well under heavy traffic.
- Polyester has low static buildup, is soft, easily cleaned, and takes heavy traffic.
- Wool is warm, soil-resistant, easily cleaned, supports heavy traffic, and is usually the most expensive.
- Acrylic, which is harder to clean, is light in weight, fluffy, feels more like wool, and can stand heavy use.
- Olefin is soil-resistant, durable, has low static buildup, and is good for outdoors and bathrooms.
- Rayon can stand only light use.

Quiet Carpeting

When buying carpeting, consider its noise-absorbing qualities. Cut pile carpets absorb more noise than loop pile. The higher the pile, the more noise it absorbs. Backings also help to reduce noise. The more porous the backing, the more it reduces noise. If you have a choice, select cushions and backings of hair and jute because they absorb more noise than rubber and sponge.

Cleaning Rugs and Carpets

When preparing to shampoo a rug or carpet, first vacuum thoroughly to remove as much surface dirt as possible, then use one of the many rug shampoos on the market. If you prefer, make your own rug shampoo by mixing one-half cup powdered detergent with two cups of warm water. Beat the mixture to a stiff foam. It should look like whipped cream. (An eggbeater can be used.) Beat the mixture again when the foam disappears.

It is important when shampooing to remember that the foam, not the water, does the work. Apply with a sponge or long-handled sponge mop, using circular movements. Rinse well with a wet sponge until all the soap has been removed from the rug, and allow to dry.

A note of caution: It is recommended that you test an inconspicuous area of the rug or carpet with the shampoo before doing the entire job.

Carpet Odors

An hour or two before vacuuming, sprinkle a goodly amount of salt and crushed dried herbs over the carpet. It will give the carpet a fresh smell.

Club Soda on Carpet Stains

When a carpet has been stained, if you have club soda

handy, pour some on the spot immediately and allow it to sit for a half-minute or so. Often, it will do the trick. Use a sponge or toweling to blot up until dry.

Removing Stains From Carpets

Spot stains can be removed from carpets most successfully if treated immediately. First, wipe the surface with a cloth or blot with a paper towel. Apply dry cleaning fluid, working from the edge of the stain toward the center. Use a gentle blotting motion. If this is ineffective, mix one teaspoon of detergent and one teaspoon of white vinegar with one quart of water, and apply to the stain. Allow to dry, then brush the pile.

Stubborn Carpet Stains

Old or stubborn stains on rugs or carpets often can be removed by brushing vigorously with a tablespoon of a laundry detergent dissolved in a gallon of warm water.

Scorched Carpeting

If a carpet is scorched from cigarette or fireplace sparks, snip the burned edges with a sharp scissor. If fiber edges are still stiff, rub with fine steel wool.

Holes in Carpets

Scraps of carpeting left over after laying a new carpet will come in handy at a later date when you have to repair holes, especially those made by flying sparks from the fireplace or from dropped cigarettes. When preparing to fill a hole, shave off some of the nap from the carpet scrap, mix it with transparent glue, then carefully fill in the hole.

Pet Stains on Carpets

Spread salt over the damp spot where a pet has soiled the carpet. If the spot has already dried, add water to the salt. Leave a thick paste of salt on the spot for a day, then remove by vacuuming. Be sure to empty the vacuum bag immediately and clean any of the vacuum parts that may have come in contact with the salt.

Frayed Rugs

If you do not want to go to the trouble or expense of rebinding a rug that has frayed edges, trim off the straggly threads with a shear or razor. Select a glue that is transparent and place a bead of glue along the entire edge. When it hardens, the rug will hold up well for a good while and the glue will not be noticeable.

Slippery Rugs

To prevent a rug from sliding around on hardwood floors, sew or glue a rubber ring to each corner of the rug.

Curling Throw-rugs

Throw-rugs lose their attractiveness when the edges begin to curl, and they can also be a source of accidents. Avoid the problem by dipping the ends of freshly washed rugs in weak starch. Dry them thoroughly before placing them back on the floor.

Removing Old Floor Wax

To remove old floor wax, special wax remover is not required. Powdered detergent and ammonia will work just as well. Use ¾ cup of detergent and ⅓ cup of household ammonia per gallon of warm water. Spread the solution on the floor for three to five minutes, then rub it off with a coarse-textured cleaning cloth. You may have to use a scrub brush to get at stubborn spots. Rinse with clean warm water.

Built-up Floor Wax

Stubborn patches of built-up floor wax or dirt can be removed by rubbing with fine steel wool moistened with a little turpentine.

Fitting Vinyl Tiles Around Obstructions

To fit a vinyl tile around an obstruction, first lay a piece of paper the same size as the tile along the edge of the tile already

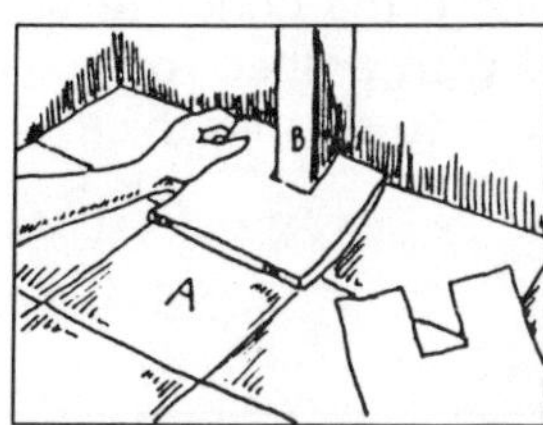

in place in the next row (figure A). Slide the paper to the edge of the obstruction (figure B) and mark the width of the obstruction on the paper with a pencil. Then, mark the depth of the obstruction against the far sides of the paper. Mark a point on each side of the paper indicating the depth, and draw a line joining the two points. Extend the width lines of the paper model until they meet the depth line. Cut away the enclosed area representing the obstruction. Fit the paper model against the obstruction to be sure it fits perfectly, then the tile will also fit. Trace the outline of the pattern on a loose tile and cut out the tile accordingly.

Fitting Border Tiles

When fitting the last row of floor tiles against the wall, the best method of measuring the size to which the tile should be cut is to place a loose tile (figure

A) over a tile already set in the next row. Place a second loose tile (figure B) against the wall, the outer edge overlapping tile A. Where the outer edge of tile B ends, draw a line against tile A with a pencil. Cut with scissors or a knife along the line. Remove the cut-off and slide tile A against the wall.

Holes in Linoleum

Small holes in linoleum can be mended with a thick paste made

of finely chopped-up cork mixed with shellac. As soon as the mixture has hardened in the hole, sandpaper the surface smooth. Touch up with a closely matching paint.

Replacing a Damaged Floor Tile

If you have a damaged vinyl or asphalt floor tile and want to remove it, lay a piece of wax paper over it and heat with an electric iron. The glue under the tile will soften, and you will be able to pry the tile with the tip of a knife.

Painting Linoleum

Worn-out linoleum can be given a new lease on life. Special linoleum paint is available and requires ordinary application. After the paint has dried, cover the area with a coat of wax.

Cutting a Ceramic Tile

To cut a ceramic tile in half, score the face side with a glass cutter, using heavy strokes. Then, place a dowel or pencil under the tile (still face up) lining it up directly under the score. Then press both sides of the tile down, thus snapping the tile in two. If you have a radial saw, the cutting can be done quickly and cleanly with the proper blade.

Caring for Wood Floors

Do not wash wood floors with water or water-based cleaners and waxes. Use a solvent-based cleaner-wax to dissolve the old wax, then apply a new coat.

Soiled Wood Floors

Soil that clings to waxed wooden floors can be removed by using very fine steel wool moistened with turpentine.

Holes in Floors

Holes in wooden floors can be filled with wood putty or plastic wood. Either filler can be sanded then stained to match the floor.

Protecting Concrete Floors

Concrete to be poured for garage floors, basements, patios, or fireplace bases can be protected against water vapor from the ground below by covering the area where the concrete will be poured with a sheet of polyethylene four to six mils thick.

DISPLAYING AND CARING FOR ARTWORK

Hanging Pictures

Standard picture hooks are safe and efficient. The smallest size available will hold a picture weighing up to 15 pounds; the largest will support 50 pounds.

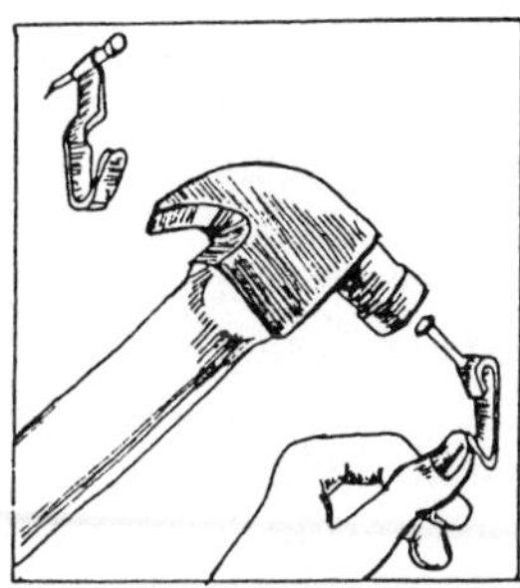

Before hammering the nail into the wall, place a small piece of tape on the spot where the nail is to enter the wall. The tape will prevent the wall from cracking. Place the hook (with the nail in position in the slot) flat against the wall, tap the head of the nail with your hammer, and drive the nail all the way in.

Picture Knot

The kind of knot you tie when putting the cord or wire through the rings on the back of a picture

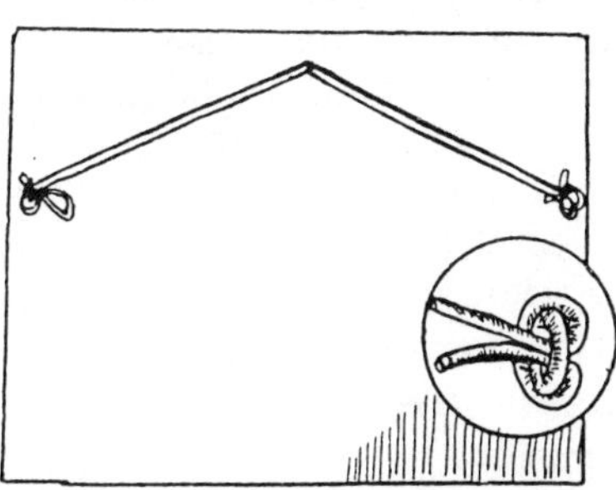

frame is important. The proper kind of knot will keep the picture from falling suddenly. You should have no trouble making the type of knot shown here.

Hanging Pictures

When hanging several framed pictures of the same size on a wall, you can make sure they will end up in a straight line if, after driving in the nail on which to hang the first picture, you use a level and draw a line or make a mark where the other nails are to be inserted.

Hanging Pictures Straight

To test whether a picture is truly straight, suspend a weight, such as a nut or bolt, from one end of a string and hold it against

the wall, allowing it to hang freely. The string will form a true straight line, and you can adjust the picture accordingly.

Rehanging Pictures

To avoid having to figure out where to place pictures which were removed before a paint job, insert a small nail with a head into the hole in the wall. Paint over the nail and then, when the paint is dry, pull out the nail and hang the picture.

Shifty Pictures

If the pictures on your wall keep shifting and end up hanging uneven, see if your hardware store carries Holdit, a puttylike, plastic adhesive manufactured by Faber-Castell Corp., of Lewisburg, TN. Just a tiny bit will hold your pictures in place indefinitely. A second way of solving the problem is to drive two nails into the wall about two inches apart and hang the wire over both.

Loose Picture Nails

If the nail holding your picture has become loose, wrap a thin strip of adhesive tape around the nail shaft and dip it in glue. Force the taped nail into the enlarged hole and allow the nail to dry in the hole for a day before rehanging the picture. Or, if you have plaster handy, you can simply refill the hole with new plaster, allow it to harden, then hammer the nail into the wall. Needless to say, before hanging a picture on any nail, make sure it is firmly secured in the wall.

Painting Picture Frames

It is easy to paint picture frames without getting finger marks on them and without getting paint on your hands. Simply attach a slim piece of wood to the back of the frame with small, thin nails (brads). The wood pieces should extend three or four inches beyond the frame on each side. The extended wood will serve as a handle by which you can move the frame around as you proceed with the painting. After you finish painting one part, you can turn the frame in any direction to reach the next part without touching the freshly painted portions.

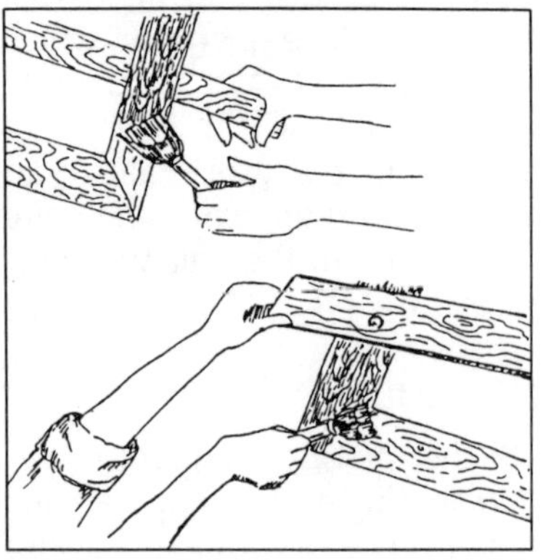

Cleaning Paintings

It is wise to dust oil paintings regularly and to brush them every few months with a clean, soft brush. Do not use a cloth on the painting. The glass covering the picture can be wiped with a cloth dampened with window cleaner, but do not spray the cleaning agent directly on the glass. Droplets might run down and get into the picture itself. When cleaning acrylic covers, use a cloth dampened slightly with a solution of mild detergent and water.

Pastel Drawings

Drawings executed with crayon, chalk, charcoal, and the like should be kept under glass, separated from direct contact with the glass by a mat or strip. Do not use an acrylic cover, as its static electricity may actually lift the medium from the picture. Handle pastels gently. Sudden movement can shock the colors right off their background. Since pastels are tricky to clean, leave this task to an expert.

Fading Pictures

Retard the fading of framed pictures by making sure that air circulates behind the picture. You can accomplish this by seeing to it that the lower corners of the frame are held away from the wall through the use of carpet tacks or similar devices.

Oil Paintings

Whether an oil painting has been executed on canvas or on wood, handle it with care. If the painting is on wood, be extremely careful about transferring it to a new location because changes in the atmosphere will cause wood to expand or contract. When an oil painting needs a cleaning, it is best to leave the task to a professional.

Watercolors

To preserve watercolor paintings, place them between pieces of glass, but do not varnish or spray-coat them. Watercolors are especially vulnerable to light and moisture. Should a valuable watercolor become soiled or damaged, take it to a restorer instead of trying to remedy the problem yourself.

Artwork Restoration

Restorers of damaged artwork, sometimes called "conservators," can work miracles in fixing damaged and deteriorated art. They can remove brown spots or foxing, clean watercolors and prints, repair cracks and checks (hairline splits which may be only in the varnish on an oil painting). They can prevent further cracking and can also disguise actual stains that cannot be removed. For a recommendation of a good restorer contact a university art department or a museum curator.

Picture Frame Repairs

Chipped sections of a wooden frame can usually be successfully repaired with one of the many fillers sold in powder form at hardware stores. Mix the powder with a small amount of water to make a heavy paste. Fill the chipped portion of the frame, shaping as required. The filled area will dry quickly and be ready for sanding, carving, and staining within two hours.

Art and Insects

Some insects are attracted to the ingredients in works of art. Silverfish, termites, cockroaches, and woodworms are particularly fond of paste, glue sizing, and wood pulp paper. Inspect the backs of frames occasionally for insect damage, even if you have not seen evidence of their presence. When attack by insects becomes a persistent problem, call in a commercial exterminator, and be sure to tell him to use insecticides that will not stain paper, reminding him that your works of art are valuable.

Two-faced Tape

Pictures with lightweight frames, as well as mounted but unframed photographs and pictures, can be attached to metal, wood, or plaster walls with double-faced tape, which has adhesive on both sides. Strips of tape placed around the edges of the back will hold the picture if it is pressed firmly against the wall. Larger pictures may require additional strips in the shape of an X from corner to opposite corner.

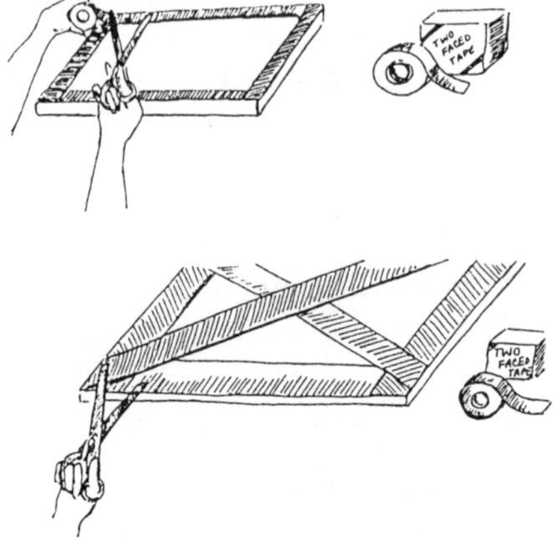

Handling Unframed Pictures

If you have valuable unframed pieces of art, make sure your hands are clean before handling them. Smudges can often be difficult to remove. When lifting unframed artwork, use both hands to avoid tearing it and be sure nothing rubs across the surface.

HOME SAFETY

Emergency Stoves

Keep a propane camp stove along with some fuel cylinders in a handy place in your cellar for those emergency situations when the electric power goes out, rendering your electric range inoperable. A propane camp stove can do everything that can be done on a bottled gas stove: the fuel is the same; the only difference is that the camp stove has room for only two pots.

Another good emergency standby is a Sterno-type stove. Cooking devices of this type are inexpensive and easy to store because they fold flat. Their solid alcohol-type fuel, which is safely stored in cans, burns with a clean blue flame. With a two-pot Sterno and two cans of fuel, one can easily cook a meal for four people in one and one-half hours.

Main Gas Valve

Be prepared for an emergency: learn how to shut off the main gas valve. It is located near the gas meter in your cellar or utility room. Usually, the shut-off valve is on a pipe leading to or from the meter. The valve that controls the meter is usually a square flat metal tab with a hole in it. The valve is open when the metal tab is in line with the pipe. It is closed when the tab is projecting at right angles to the pipe. You cannot release the valve with your fingers, so take a wrench along when you look for it.

Burglar Alarms

If you do not have a burglar alarm system, you can discourage burglars by leaving the impression that your house is occupied. This can be done by using timers with several settings to turn lights and radios and TVs on and off in various rooms at different times.

Home Security Code

If you have a home security system and fear that you might forget the code number, use all or part of a telephone number or an address that is very familiar to you.

Window Security

In addition to the normal window lock on all windows, you may want extra protection for those windows that burglars may use as entry points. Drill a hole through the upper and lower halves of a window that will accommodate a nail at least three inches long. Select a drill that is the same diameter as the nail to be inserted. The nail is easily withdrawn.

Burglarproof Screws

One-way screws are recommended for locks on windows and doors with glass panes. By breaking or cutting the glass, a burglar can reach in with a screwdriver and turn the ordinary screws that fasten a window or door lock. On a one-way screw, the top left and bottom right quarters on either side of the slot are missing. This makes it possible to turn it from left to right to screw it in but impossible to turn from right to left to unscrew it.

Glass Doors

Avoid accidents by placing a decal or colored tape at eye level on glass doors leading out to the patio.

Nonskid Chairs

Chairs, stools, and tables need not slide around on kitchen floors, even if the floors are waxed. Rubber tips, available in various sizes, can be attached to the bottom of each leg. Most hardware and variety stores sell them.

Christmas Tree Caveats

Christmas trees that are dry and brittle catch fire easily. Minimize chances of accidental fires in your home by observing the following:

- Purchase a fresh tree.
- Store the tree in a cool place, and keep its base submerged in warm water. Warm water is absorbed by the tree more easily than cold water.
- Make a fresh cut in the base of the tree as soon as you bring it home. The cut should be about one inch from the old one. The fresh cut will allow the tree to absorb water more easily.
- Keep the tree away from furnaces and fireplaces.
- Do not allow lightbulbs to touch branches or their needles.

12
The Home Exterior

Introduction

The outside of a home not only contributes much to its aesthetic tone and monetary value, it also protects the home from the elements and from intruders. The outside of a home should be at once beautiful and functional.

No matter the size or circumstance, all homes should be landscaped. For city-center residences or brownstones, which are paved up to the building, landscaping might be limited to window boxes of flowers or small trees or shrubs planted in stone or wooden tubs. But even these touches will add warmth, elegance, and cheer to the house. Houses with land will usually have a portion of it dedicated to lawn. Nothing is as impressive as a well-manicured lawn or as depressing as a neglected one. To keep a lawn at its best, it must be watered, fed, weeded, and cut regularly. If your best efforts are meeting with small return, consider replacing existing grass with sod. Shrubs and trees should suit the property. In residental areas, keep them small and make sure that there is adequate sunlight to meet growth requirements.

The wood trim of a house should be kept well painted. Oil-based paint is best for wood exteriors because it repels moisture. For stucco and brick exteriors, however, water-soluble latex paints are sometimes recommended because they allow moisture to pass through the stone instead of trapping it inside, where it might cause wood members to decay. Though they lack the elegance of wood or stone, if you are seeking a minimum-maintenance exterior, consider aluminum or asbestos siding.

In building or renovating your home, do not ignore security considerations. Windows and doors should provide more than token resistance to thieves. And, if your neighborhood warrants it, consider steel grating in front of ground-floor windows and an alarm system.

Loose Windowpanes

A loose windowpane not only rattles in the wind but also allows cold air to enter in the winter and hot air in the summer. To stop the rattle and cut down on heating and air conditioning bills, apply additional putty to secure the loose pane against the window frame. Before puttying, glazier points can be forced into the wood frame for a tighter fit.

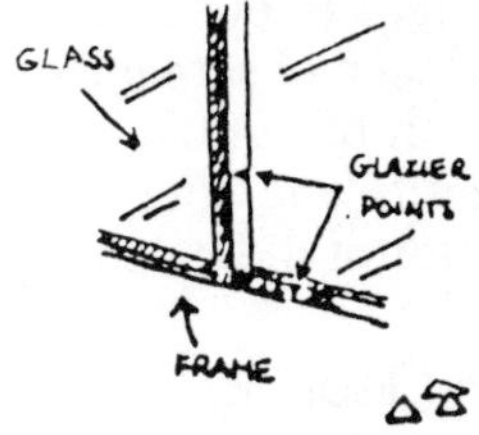

Replacing Broken Windows

When removing broken glass from a window, start by using pliers to remove glazier points. When inserting the new pane, first place a thin ribbon of putty along the inside of the frame, then press the glass firmly against the putty. Insert glazier points, first near the corners, then every four inches along the pane. Add more putty or glazing compound as needed, and smooth the surface with a putty knife. Moisten the putty knife with linseed or regular lubricating oil.

Removing Putty From a Glass Pane

In replacing a pane of glass, hardened putty is sometimes difficult to dig out. You can accomplish this by heating the tip of a long screwdriver on a gas range and pushing it into the putty. Repeat the heating as necessary.

Loose Wood-framed Window Screens

Weatherstripping can make loose wood-framed window screens fit snugly again. Tack the weatherstripping along the edge of any screen that fits loosely. It may be necessary to use the weatherstripping on more than one side and test the fit.

Caulking Out Drafts

Drafts are not only uncomfortable but add to fuel and electricity costs. The best way to avoid this

unnecessary expense is to do a good caulking job. Places most often in need of caulking are around windows where the siding butts up against the window frame and next to the door trim where two walls of different materials, such as brick and wood, meet.

Before adding new caulking, remove the old, dried-out caulking and clean the gap with a stiff brush. Then, place a cartridge of acrylic latex caulking in a caulking gun and apply the caulking to the gaps. Make a slanted cut in the plastic nozzle of the cartridge so that you get a bead of about ⅜ of an inch. As you work the gun, push it away from you along the edge to be filled. Choose a caulking color that matches the trim of the siding.

Aluminum Window Corrosion

After several years of exposure to the elements, aluminum windows become pitted and unsightly. To restore the windows, rub the frame with coarse steel wool and then complete the job with fine steel wool. A coating of zinc chromate primer followed by a good exterior enamel will prevent the return of the gray oxide.

Rust Removal

Naval jelly, sold in hardware and paint supply stores, is recommended to dissolve rust. The rusted part should be covered with the gel and allowed to stand for 24 hours. Then wash with warm water.

A coat of Rust-Oleum paint applied to roof gutters and outside furniture will cover existing rust spots and prevent the formation of new ones.

Screen Repairs

Use fast-drying model airplane glue or clear nail polish to patch small holes in nylon window screening. Only a few drops are needed to seal a hole.

To patch a hole in window screening, cut out a section from an old piece of screening. Attach the patch by running fast-drying model airplane glue around the perimeter of the patch.

Screen Cleaning

After brushing both sides with a soft brush or cloth, rub on kerosene with a clean cloth. Hose down, then allow to dry.

Patching Fiberglass Screening

A tear in fiberglass screening can be repaired with a patch of fiberglass screening a bit larger than the tear. Join the patch to the screen with heat. Have someone hold an iron frying pan to the outside of the screen while you lay the patch on the inside of the screen. Then, press a hot iron against the edges of the patch until the patch and screen fuse.

Another way to do the patching is to run a thin bead of transparent glue (like Elmer's) along the edges of the patch before applying the heat. Protect the iron from the glue by placing a piece of cloth over the patch before applying the heat.

Aluminum and Copper Screening

Do not discard an aluminum or copper screen because there is a hole in it. Mend it with squares of screen patching available in various sizes in most hardware stores. Trim the torn area with metal-cutting scissors so it is square, then select a patch larger than the new opening. Lay the patch over the hole so that the bent wires stick out on the reverse side of the screen. Then bend the protruding wires flat against the reverse side of the screen.

Metal Screens

Carpet scraps nailed to wood blocks are good for scrubbing metal screens. This is also a good way of applying varnish or shellac to screening in order to retard future corrosion. Use different blocks for the two separate operations.

Stepladder Safety

Do not wear loose-fitting clothing when mounting or standing on a stepladder. Pant and shirt cuffs can be secured with rubber bands.

Ladder Precautions

When setting up a ladder to do outside work, make sure the ladder is on a level surface and that it is not placed in front of a door that might be swung open. If you must place a ladder in front of a door, lock the door first so it cannot be opened.

Picking Up a Ladder at Its Balance Point

If you mark your ladder with a stripe of paint at its balance point, you will be able to pick it up and carry it easily with one hand, without a moment of forethought.

Raising an Outside Ladder

When you want to erect an extension ladder, lay it on the ground with its legs against the wall. Lift the other end and keep

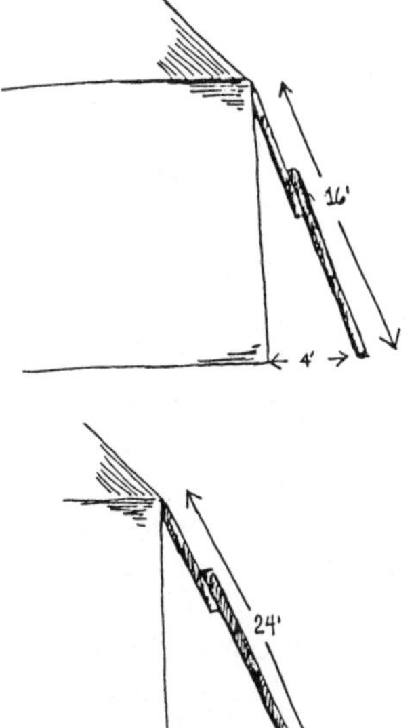

raising it as you walk toward the house. When it is parallel to the wall, pull the rope to extend the ladder. Pull the bottom of the ladder out so that it is about six feet away from the wall if it is a 24-foot ladder, and nine feet away if it is a 36-foot ladder.

Skid-free Ladders

Slipping ladders cause accidents. Whether you use a ladder indoors or outdoors, if it is a

ladder designed to lean against a wall, you can make it skid-free by permanently attaching rubber cut from old tires, old inner tubes, or other nonskid products to the bottom.

Positioning Ladders

Ladders can be dangerous if they are not positioned properly. If the bottom of a ladder is placed too close to a wall, it could fall backwards. To avoid this, place the bottom of the ladder a distance from the wall equal to one-quarter of the ladder's extended length.

Ladder Safety

Keep pieces of an old inner tube tied to your ladder. They come in handy when the ladder has to be placed on a smooth surface.

Alternatively, old asphalt shingles will work as well. The rough

surface of the shingles will keep the ladder from sliding on smooth surfaces like polished floors, stone, or grass.

Ladder Aid

A ladder can serve you much better if you add a long crossbar to the top—either a one-inch round dowel (see illustration) or a piece of three-quarter-inch pine or plywood four inches wide and long enough to extend two or three inches beyond the width of the window.

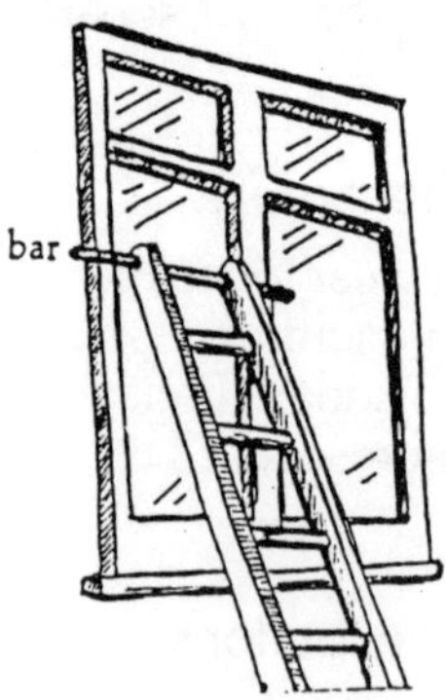

If you are using a round dowel, bore a 1⅛-inch hole through the two sides of the ladder about 1½ inches from the top. You can use a dowel with a wooden or an aluminum ladder. The precut holes in most aluminum ladders will accept a one-inch dowel. With this support and protection, you can use the ladder to get to windows that are often difficult to reach.

Replacing Roofing Shingles

Asphalt roofing shingles are sometimes damaged by strong winds. To replace a torn shingle, raise the shingle that overlaps it, remove the damaged shingle, and hammer down the old nails. Insert a new shingle in the position of the missing one. Drive three zinc-coated roofing nails through the tables of the overlapping shingle and the upper section of the new one. Cover the head of each nail with a spot of roofing cement about the size of a quarter.

Replacing House Shingles

Sometimes it is necessary to remove a damaged shingle. To accomplish this without damaging adjoining shingles, insert a prybar under the lower edge of the damaged piece and raise it just enough to insert the blade of a small metal-cutting saw. Cut through all the nails that hold the lower edge. Then, do the same with the lower edge of the next higher shingle. The shingle can then be slipped out and a new one inserted. Drive in new nails at least one inch from where the old ones were.

Protecting Outside Faucets

Water that remains in an outside faucet may freeze during the winter and crack the supply pipe or faucet. To avoid this, trace the supply pipe of the outside faucet and find the cutoff valve. Usually it will be two to three feet behind the faucet in the basement. Close the cutoff valve and open the outside faucet. This will drain the faucet and protect it and the pipe

all winter. If you use outdoor spigots throughout the winter, have your plumber install a frost-free valve. As with conventional outdoor valves, frost-free valves are opened and closed outside, but the water-stopping mechanism is located inside the building, where it is not subject to intense cold.

Sized-to-Order Gutters

After long usage, roof gutters eventually corrode and start to leak. Though patching postpones the inevitable, the time comes when gutters must be replaced. It is possible to purchase standard-size gutter sections in building supply centers and piece them together by yourself. A better idea is to contract with a company which installs continuous, seemless gutters (see under "Gutters" in the Yellow Pages). Such contractors fashion one-piece gutters to size on your premises. In addition to eliminating leaks, seemless gutters are easier to patch so that rain water drains properly into downspouts.

Strengthening a Leader Elbow

The aluminum elbow or nozzle at the bottom of a drainpipe leader often gets loose and falls off. The elbow helps divert water away from the foundation of the house. An easy way to keep it from falling off is to drill a hole through both elbow and leader and to insert an aluminum screw just slightly smaller in diameter than the hole drilled. Another solution is to drill a hole through the leader and elbow and to force in a long aluminum nail or a wood dowel.

Dry Wells

If your downspouts are not tied into a sewer system and you have sufficient land, you might be able to provide a do-it-yourself remedy by digging a dry well. Secure a used 55-gallon drum (an oil company might have some for sale at $10 to $15), open the drain plugs, punch additional one-inch holes in the side of the drum, and cut off the top of the drum. Next, dig a hole in the ground sufficiently deep so that, when the drum is placed in the hole, its top will lie 18 inches below the soil line. Fill the barrel with stones at least two inches in diameter. Connect the bottom of the downspout with the drum using four-inch plastic drainage pipe. The drainage pipe should be placed in an 18-inch trench and inserted into the top of the drum. Cover the barrel with plastic before backfilling with soil to prevent earth from clogging the dry well.

Foundation Cracks

Large cracks in the foundation of a house are a sign of improperly laid footings and should be at-

tended to. Call in a competent building contractor or consultant to look over the foundation as soon as you notice such cracks.

Fighting Wood Rot

Wood directly exposed to the earth will rot in a few years. You can delay or prevent the deterioration by using one of the wood-preserving chemicals on the market. Ask your local hardware or paint dealer for recommendations.

Old Engine Oil as a Wood Preservative

The old engine oil from your automobile or other power equipment makes a worthy wood preservative for posts or planks that will come into contact with the ground. Coat lightly several times over several hours to allow the oil to sink in. Coating the surface is not sufficient. Make sure that the coating extends *above* the soil line.

Screening Damp Sand

A length of chain placed on the sifting screen before pouring on the sand will break up damp or lumpy sand and push it through the screen as you move the chain around.

Patching Exterior Walls

If outside walls are covered with stucco, brick, or other masonry, check in early fall for cracks or open joints that will allow moisture to enter. In very cold weather the water in the cracks freezes and expands, causing the cracks to open further. Small cracks can be filled with caulking compound; large ones should be filled with vinyl-concrete patching cement. Defective mortar joints in brick or cement block walls should be filled with freshly mixed mortar cement. Before filling the cracks, scrape out about one-half inch to one inch of the old mortar.

Stucco is a plaster that contains Portland cement instead of gypsum, which makes it waterproof when cured and therefore impervious to rot and fungus. To repair cracks in stucco, widen the crack, remove all loose material, and inject a stucco repair compound, such as DAP Fast 'n Final Exterior Spackling, which is available in hardware stores.

Homemade Cement Mix

You can make your own cement mix that will be as good as any premix product on the market by adding pure (Portland) cement to an equal amount of lime. Mix the cement and lime and keep it handy in a dry spot. When you have cement repair work to do, add three shovels of sand to one of the cement-lime mixture. Mix well, then add water until a consistency similar to that of mustard or mayonnaise has been achieved. The cement mixture is good for filling cracks in walls, openings around pipes, and recementing loose stone or brick. It creates a strong bond with the old cement, especially when the crack is one-quarter inch or more deep.

Curing Concrete

Newly poured concrete must be cured, which means that it should be kept moist for four to five days. The thinner the cement slab that has been poured, the more the curing that is required. The periodic sprinkling of water on the concrete will prevent the moisture in the mixture from evaporating and, consequently, prevent shrinkage and cracking.

Reinforcing Concrete

To reinforce cement, throw in any kind of scrap iron, including nails and chain links, that is free of scaling, rust, oil, grease, and dirt. This reinforcement will help prevent the concrete from cracking and will add strength to the slab by tying it together as one unit.

Sonna Tubes

Cement pilings often replace footings under porches, decks, and sheds to prevent sagging and protect the integrity of the structure. For do-it-yourself projects, such piles are easily erected using wax-coated cardboard cylinders, known as Sonna tubes, available in several widths and lengths from building supply centers.

A hole is dug in the ground using a hand auger (power-driven hand-held augers can be rented for big jobs), and the Sonna tube is inserted to the proper depth. Where frost heave is a consideration, cement columns should be 30 to 42 inches deep; where it is not, 24 inches is sufficient. Place a reinforcing rod in the hole and fill with cement. For a minimum number of holes, premixed concrete requiring only water is a convenience. When erecting cement pilings, be certain that they all rise to the same relative height. Test with a level by connecting the holes with builder's twine.

Low-Cost Patios

The price of concrete contributes significantly to the high cost of building a patio. To reduce the cost, use two-inch-thick slates for the foundation and flat stones for the surface. If you want a continuous surface, cement the stones at the edges. For a really level surface, you'll need to reset and recement the stones every several years. By using the slates rather than concrete for the foundation, you'll save nearly 90 percent of the cost of a concrete base.

Galvanized Nails

When using nails on a roof or patio or anywhere that is exposed to the elements, use galvanized nails that are especially coated to resist rusting.

Holes in Driveways

Blacktop driveways develop holes as a result of weathering and the oil drippings from cars. Before patching, the oil should be removed with trisodium phosphate (TSP), which can be purchased at a hardware store. It should be mixed with water according to directions on the package. Remove the TSP by flushing the driveway with water.

Patch holes and cracks with a mix of sand or fine gravel and cold liquid asphalt, also available at hardware stores. Very fine cracks can be filled with liquid asphalt poured from a small can. Allow 24 hours without traffic for asphalt to harden.

Larger holes in driveways can be patched by cleaning out the hole and filling the bottom with clean, good-sized (¾-inch) stones. Cover with stone-and-tar mix or cement, depending on the surface. Premixed cement and sand can be purchased for such patching jobs.

Resurfacing Blacktop Driveways

Blacktop driveways that have been patched and freed of oil and grease can be resurfaced with cold, liquid asphalt or a special black vinyl latex paint. Both are heavy liquids that usually come in five gallon cans. Pour out a gallon at a time on the driveway and smooth it with an old push-broom. The vinyl paint is slightly thinner than the liquid asphalt and is unaffected by oil, which dissolves asphalt, but it must be renewed each year.

Overhead Garage Door Track

If your overhead garage door is not functioning properly, use a level to determine whether the vertical tracks are perfectly vertical. Also measure the distance between the tracks at three points (top, center, and bottom) to see if the distance is the same at all points. If not, make adjustments in the mounting brackets, which have slotted mounting holes.

Wobbly Overhead Garage Doors

If your overhead garage door fails to open properly, it might be because the mounting screws and bolts that hold the vertical track to the door and door frame, or the screws holding the door sections, have begun to loosen. The door will tend to wobble as a result.

Garage-door Hinge Pins

A few drops of lightweight oil should, from time to time, be squirted into each hinge pin that holds together the sections of an overhead garage door.

13
Painting

Introduction

Painting is one of those skills that can be performed at many levels. Often, it is the passage of time that is the ultimate test of the quality of the work. A well-done paint job will last many years; a careless job will show its character in weeks or months.

Regardless of the task, proper preparation is the first step in painting. And for simple reason: the surface to be covered must be put in condition to receive the substance to be applied. If the undercoating is unstable, the covering material will not adhere. Minimally, all surfaces that are to be covered with paint, varnish, shellac, or stain should be clean. If the existing covering is not flaking, washing with soap and water will be sufficient. (In fact, in many cases, a simple washing will reveal that a paint job is not required at all.) If the surface to be painted is flaking, it should be scraped or sanded. If it is pocked or marred, it should be filled.

The choice of materials is crucial. Good paints are expensive. While their price is in part inflated by their reputation, quality brand names also contain superior materials, which increase the durability of the product. Unless you seek nothing more than to temporarily cover something with paint—with longevity and durability not a factor—"supermarket" paints, which often sell at half the cost of quality paints, should be shunned in favor of brand names.

The final factor in a successful paint job is proper application.

Paints should be applied in moderate temperatures (never less than 50 degrees Fahrenheit) and moderate humidities, allowing sufficient time to dry after work is completed in advance of anticipated precipitation. Make sure to have clean, soft, properly sized brushes and rollers for the task at hand. A four-inch brush is impossible to use in corners or crevices, while a one-inch brush on a large wall will turn a few hours of work into a lifetime pursuit. Paint applicators come in various price ranges, with animal-hair brushes more expensive than synthetic ones. But, a properly cleaned brush (use soap and water for latex paints; turpentine or another distillate for oil-based paints) manipulated with smooth even strokes will last through many paint jobs.

GENERAL PAINTING GUIDELINES

Best Time to Paint

The ideal time of year to paint the exterior of a house is late spring or early fall, when the weather is warm but not hot and when there are fewer insects. Allow three to five days for paint to dry between coats. Two coats are recommended when repainting.

When Not to Paint

Do not start a paint job during or soon after a rain, when the wood is still wet. Also, do not paint when the temperature is below 50 degrees Fahrenheit.

When to Repaint

If you're thinking of repainting a house more than once every four years, that's probably too often. The outer coat will wear at the rate of about one-thousandth of an inch yearly. When a house is painted too often, the outer coat becomes so thick that it peels and cracks. Be sure the house needs a new coat of paint before doing the job. Very often you can give the exterior of the house a clean, fresh look by simply washing it down with water and a good cleansing agent. Ask your hardware dealer to recommend one.

The Price of Paint

Bargain prices in house paint cannot be found very often. Better paints cost more because their ingredients cost more, and when you use good paint, you will not need to repaint as often.

Outdoor Ladders

Place an old sock over the ends of each of the legs of a ladder that will be pressing against the house as you work. You will thus avoid marring the paint or bricks.

Coating a New House

How many coats of paint does the exterior of a new house need? Two would be the usual answer. But it's the third coat that adds years of wear to the wood of a new house.

Starting an Outdoor Paint Job

To increase paint durability, prepare exterior surfaces prior to painting by cleaning them with a solution consisting of one quart bleach, one cup laundry detergent, and three quarts of warm water. Apply to surfaces and allow the solution to sit for about 15 minutes, then rinse thoroughly with plain water and allow to dry. Do not use this solution on aluminum siding or raw wood.

Paint on Clean Surfaces

Always start with a clean surface. Wash off all dirt, grease, and oil. Scrape off or sand off loose paint and rust. If the surface is glossy, be sure to sand off the gloss.

A sandpapered surface offers a better grip for paint and retards the cracking and blistering of the paint. Sandpaper also removes dirt and grease and permits the paint to go on more easily. A product called Liquid Sandpaper, which can be easily applied, is available in paint stores. After sanding, be sure to wipe off any residue before painting.

Sanding With Pumice

Before starting to sandpaper, sprinkle some fine pumice on the painted surface. This will keep the paint from clogging the sandpaper. Because the pumice is abrasive, you'll do the job that much faster, and the sandpaper will last longer.

PAINT, BRUSHES, ROLLERS, ETC.

Glossy Paint

High-gloss and semi-gloss paint is better than flat paint for surfaces that are regularly covered with moisture, such as moldings and trim in bathrooms and kitchens.

Solvent-thinned Oil-based Paints

Solvent-thinned oil-based paints (also called alkyd-based paints) are preferred by many professionals because they are more durable, especially on kitchen and bathroom surfaces, where a glossy covering is required to keep moisture from penetrating the painted surface. Paintbrushes and rollers used to apply oil-based paints must be cleaned with solvents such as turpentine, gasoline, or paint thinner.

Water-thinned Latex Paints

Latex paints are used widely because they are easier to apply, build up a thicker film with just one coat, dry more quickly, and do not have an objectionable odor. Latex paints can be thinned by adding water, and brushes and rollers are easily cleaned with soap and water.

The Paint-skin Bypass

The skin that develops over the surface of paint not used in a while is often a great nuisance and time-consuming to remove. A simple way of tackling the problem is to close the lid tightly on cans you do not plan to use shortly and then to store the cans in an upside-down position. When the can is opened the next time the paint is to be used, you will find that whatever skin has formed is on the bottom, not the top.

Screening Paint

If film has formed on the surface of paint, or if paint looks lumpy, remove the hardened film with a piece of wood or a wide

blade. Then stretch a nylon stocking or nylon screening across the opening of the can and strain the paint into a clean can. Metal screening can be used as well.

Wax Paper Keeps Paint Soft

After you have finished painting for the day, it is a good idea to cover the paint can with wax

paper and then press the lid into it. This will keep the air out. When you are ready to use the paint once again, simply discard the wax paper.

Bucket-holder for Painting Equipment

Laying a paintbrush across the top of a can of paint is a dangerous practice, especially when painting on a ladder or scaffold. The brush may get knocked off and land in the paint or fall to the floor.

To avoid trouble, place the can of paint in a large bucket. Attach an S-hook to the rim of the bucket and hang the brush so that, when not in use, it is positioned between the can and the bucket. Any dripping from the brush will land in the bottom of the bucket, and the floor will never get messed up. You may have to drill a larger hole in the top of the paintbrush handle in order to accommodate the hook.

You can also use the bucket as a convenient place to keep a

paint scraper, a putty knife, or a rag. You can either lay these articles in the bucket or hang them from additional S-hooks. The bucket or pail can hang from a hook attached to a ladder.

Selecting Paintbrushes

Buy the best paintbrushes you can afford for painting a house. Better brushes hold more paint, lay the paint down more evenly, and last longer.

Keeping Brushes Soft

A paint brush used with an oil-based paint can be kept soft between coats of paint without being thoroughly cleaned by pouring about two inches of paint thinner into a tall coffee can with a plastic lid. Cut an X in the center of the lid. Exercise the brush a bit in the thinner, then push the handle through the X in the plastic lid. Adjust the handle so that the bristles are covered by thinner but do not touch the bottom of the can. When ready to paint again, just wipe the bristles with a rag and start painting.

Storing Brushes

It's not necessary to clean a paintbrush used with an oil-based paint if it is to be used the next day. Sprinkle a few drops of turpentine or linseed oil on the brush and wrap it tightly in a plastic bag or plastic wrap. Store the brush flat.

Suspending a Paintbrush in Paint

Avoid cleaning a brush that will be used very soon again by drilling a hole in the brush handle and suspending the bristles in the

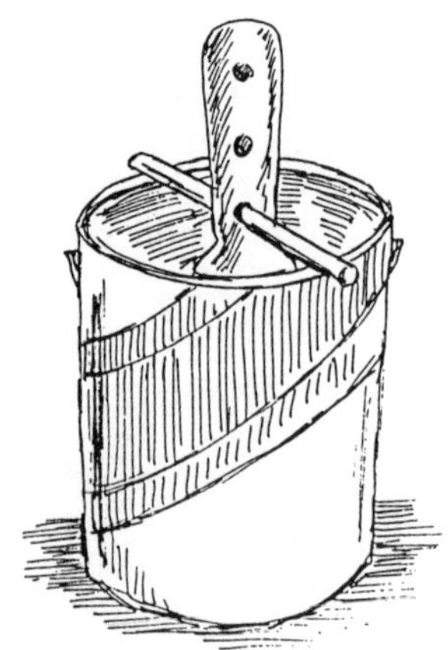

paint. Insert a long thin dowel (or curtain rod) through the hole. The hole in the brush handle should be made in two or three spots so that the rod can be inserted at the right spot to keep the bristles of the brush from touching the bottom of the can.

Wire for Suspending a Brush

Another way to prevent a paintbrush from drying out between uses is to attach a thin wire to the paintbrush. The wire should extend about six inches. Immerse the brush in the paint can to the point where it almost touches the bottom. Seal the can with its cover tightly, with the wire on the outside, and the wire will be held in place. The paintbrush will be in perfect condition to proceed with the paint job.

Brushes With Varnish

When refinishing furniture or doing a job requiring repeated coats of varnish or paint remover, you can avoid the bother of having to clean the brush between coats by wrapping it in aluminum foil, placing it in a plastic bag, and storing it in the freezer.

Selecting Paint Rollers

Using a paint roller can speed up the painting process, but you must select the proper roller. To paint smooth surfaces (such as most indoor walls), use the shortest, least bulky nap available. For slightly textured surfaces, a medium length nap is best. To cover rough, heavily textured surfaces, use a roller with a long nap. Long nap rollers are also best suited for irregular surfaces like wood shingles and chain-link fences.

Storing a Paint Roller

If you are undertaking a paint job that will last for several days, an easy way to keep the paint roller in good, usable condition is to store the entire roller and the tray with paint in it, in an airtight plastic bag. Before putting the assembly in a plastic bag, roll the roller in the paint that is in the tray so as to moisten the nap. This will keep the roller soft and fresh for the next time you use it, whether it's a day or a month later. This type of storage will save you the trouble of cleaning rollers and the expense of buying new ones.

Sponge Brushes

If you have small areas in the house that require touching up, there is no need to bother with a paintbrush. Use the edge of an ordinary kitchen sponge as you brush.

Shake the can of paint well. Remove the cover, and dip the end of the sponge lightly into the paint left on the inside of the can cover. Paint with even strokes. When you are finished, cut off the edge of the sponge and use the rest of the sponge for any purpose you desire.

Pad Applicators

Pad applicators paint as smoothly as brushes and are easy to use. But remember, use pad applicators only with latex paints.

PAINTING HINTS AND TIPS

Color Durability

White paint is the most durable of all colors. The lighter the color of the paint, the slower it will fade.

For Brighter Rooms

When you redecorate, paint walls in light pastel colors and ceilings in white or off-white. Use a flat or semi-gloss paint on walls and ceilings to help diffuse the light and make the room appear brighter.

Testing Paint Colors

To see how a particular color will look in a room, buy small cans of various colors you are considering and brush a four-to-six-inch swab of each color on one of the walls and the ceiling of the room. After the paint has dried, take note of which color is most satisfactory at different times of day.

Spray-painting

When applying spray paint, best results will be achieved if the can is held eight or nine inches away from the surface to be painted and moved back and forth in a straight horizontal line rather than in an arc.

Electric Paint Mixer

Mixing paint properly is a time-consuming job. With an electric drill and a special paint mixer attachment that is inserted like a drill bit, you can save time and get a more thorough mix. The paint-bit-mixer is available in most hardware stores. Dip it in the can of paint before starting the drill motor, and do not remove it from the paint can until the twirling motion stops. This will avoid paint spatter.

Save Drill Bits

Do not discard worn-out drill bits with wide blades. Use them in your drill press or hand drill to stir small cans of paint.

Containers for Mixing Paint

Quart and half-gallon milk containers are extremely useful for small quantities of paint and stain, and it is wise to keep some on hand for future use. Cut away the top of the container, leaving anywhere from one to five inches of the bottom section. If you are going to work with a larger amount of stain or paint, you should cut the container to a height of four or five inches. Select a container that will accommodate the full width of the brush you are planning to use.

Stir Paint Thoroughly

Before applying paint, make sure you have stirred thoroughly, working it up from the bottom of the can. The paint must be blended properly before it is used.

When using a spray can, shake well until you hear the mixing ball moving freely.

Reducing Paint Odors

If the odor of paint is more than you can bear, add vanilla extract to the paint. Add two teaspoons of extract to each quart.

Eliminating Paint Odors

Believe it or not, an onion cut in half and placed in a large open pan of cold water will absorb the odor of fresh paint in a matter of hours. Use a large onion for best results.

Painting Platform

Painting ceilings and the tops of walls can be exhausting. Save wear-and-tear by making a platform to stand on. Use two *sturdy* kitchen chairs of the same size, and lay a strong board at least 12 inches wide across the two seats. The longer and wider the board, the better. You will have more mobility, and the platform will be more secure.

Avoid Paint-can Drip

Each time you press a paintbrush against the rim of a can to clean off excess paint, the groove around the rim of the can catches some of the paint. Unless you are extremely careful, in time the paint will run down the side of the can. Avoid this by punching several holes in the bottom of the

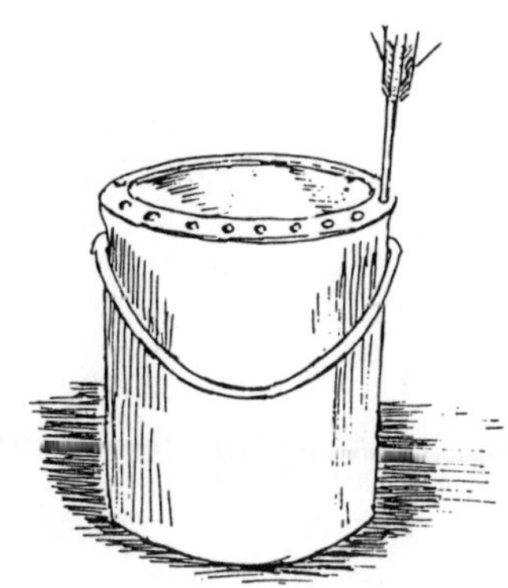

groove into which the lid fits. The excess paint will flow back into the can, and the resealing of the lid will not be affected because the lid seals against the sides rather than the bottom of the groove.

Painting Procedure

When painting a room, start at the upper right-hand corner and work down. Try to finish each day's work at a corner or near a window so as to prevent overlaps when you resume painting. Paint one wall at a time.

Avoid Roller Spattering

You can avoid spattering of paint when working with a roller if you roll the paint on with a slow, steady motion. Too much pressure on the roller causes spattering.

Drippy Rollers

To avoid or at least minimize dripping and running paint, when working with a roller always make the first stroke in an upward direction.

Working a Roller

When working with a roller, you will get even coverage if you add paint to the roller as soon as the roller starts to become dry.

A Handy Dropcloth

Use a dropcloth whenever you paint. An old shower curtain that has become discolored or whose eyelets are torn need not be discarded. Lay it away as is, and save it for "painting day." A shower curtain is not only heavier than the plastic dropcloths available today at paint stores but also more durable.

Protective Measures

If you do not have a dropcloth handy when painting, the plastic bags from the cleaners or ordinary plastic trash bags can be cut open and spread out over all the furniture and the floors. Walk on the plastic carefully so as not to tear it.

Leftover Paint

Small amounts of paint left over when a job is finished should not be stored in a large can. If poured into a smaller can, the surface area will be reduced and, consequently, less paint skin will form.

Protecting Ceiling Fixtures

Large plastic dry-cleaner bags are ideal for protecting hanging lamps and chandeliers from dropping plaster and spattering paint. The most effective way of protecting ceiling fixtures is to

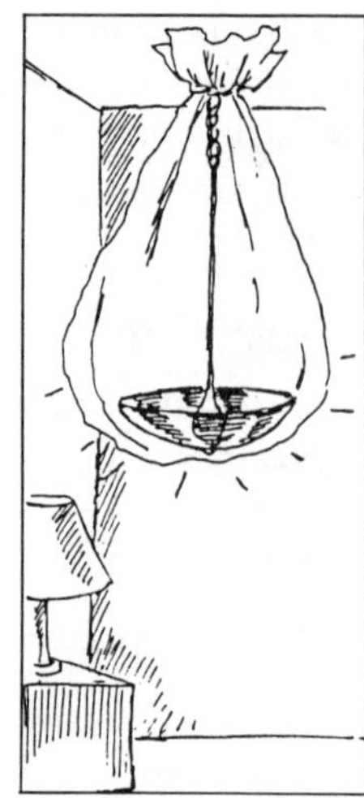

release the cover plate that is screwed into the ceiling and let it slide down the chain. Pull the plastic sack up over the entire unit and tie a cord around it as high up on the chain as you can.

Touch-up Paint

It is wise to save leftover paint. You never know when you may wish you had just a little bit of paint to touch up a marred surface. For such touch-up jobs, instead of a brush use the kind of applicators doctors use to swab throats. You can make your own by twirling some cotton around the tip of a toothpick or a wooden dowel.

Stripping Furniture

Stripping old finishes from furniture is relatively easy and inexpensive when you use common household lye. Dilute the lye first by adding about six ounces to one and one-half quarts of water. Any container is fine except aluminum, which will be corroded by the lye. After stirring the mixture slowly, apply it to the furniture with a brush or sponge; allow it to set, then rinse. Wear gloves and long sleeves during the process, as lye will burn the skin. If any lye does spatter on you, wash the area immediately and thoroughly with plenty of water.

Paint Stripping

When removing the finish from old furniture with jellied paint stripper, remember to wear rubber gloves so as to avoid the possibility of burning your hands. Do not use plastic gloves because some plastics are easily dissolved by paint stripper.

When stripping paint, always work in a well-ventilated area, since the fumes can be quite toxic. Above all, do not smoke while working; most paint strippers are highly flammable.

Removing Paint Sludge

After paint stripper has been applied to a surface, allow it to stand for a while. Then, dust the surface lightly with sawdust, woodshavings, or excelsior. Next, use a dry rag to remove the stripper. The sawdust and woodshavings increase the friction on the normally slippery surface and make removal of the sludge much easier.

Emergency Staining

If you want to stain small areas of unfinished wood but have no stain on hand, use liquid shoe polish. When dry, the area can be coated with any paste wax.

Staining Without Brushes

Save the effort, nuisance, and cost of handling messy brushes by using a cloth rag or a sponge to apply stain (or varnish). Dip the cloth or sponge in the stain and apply it to the wood, rubbing it in well until the stain is evenly distributed. With varnish or shellac use a light stroke, moving only with the grain.

Tea as a Stain

Strong brewed tea makes a good, low-cost stain for pine, giving an antique-like finish. When the stain is dry, apply two coats of fresh white shellac.

Different Types of Wood Stain

Water-based wood stain penetrates the wood and actually dyes its fibers. *Oil-based* wood stain contains oil-soluble dyes; it requires about 24 hours to dry fully. *Varnish* stain (stain that contains varnish) does not penetrate wood as well as plain oil- or water-based stains.

Turpentine as Varnish Solvent

Use turpentine or a special varnish remover to remove varnish from unwanted areas and to clean brushes used to apply it.

Shellac/Varnish Test

To determine whether a wood surface is covered with varnish or shellac, apply a small amount of rubbing alcohol to an inconspicuous spot. If after a few minutes the finish becomes soft, it is shellac. Varnish will not react with alcohol.

Alcohol as Shellac Solvent

Denatured alcohol is the ideal solvent to thin and prepare shellac. It is good for cleaning and refinishing shellacked surfaces and for cleaning brushes used with shellac.

Restoring Shellacked Floors

Shellacked floors, like all others, wear out most quickly along the paths of greatest traffic. Such paths can be somewhat restored by rubbing them with a rag soaked in alcohol. Make sweeping strokes with the rag so that dissolved shellac is brought from the less worn adjacent sides into the path. You can also brush on new shellac that has been diluted with an equal amount of alcohol (one cup of shellac to one cup of alcohol).

Shellacking Baseboards

If you want to prevent dust from sticking to baseboards, apply a coat of shellac to the surface. Not only will the task of cleaning the corners be easier, but paint will not chip off as easily.

Knots That Bleed

Knots in lumber such as pine, hemlock, or fir often contain resin that bleeds through white or light-colored paints. Stains appear in the form of brownish rings. If this happens, cover the brown spots with four-pound cut white shellac. When the shellac has dried, sand the surface lightly with fine sandpaper, then wipe clean and paint. White pigmented shellac primer can also be used.

Shellac Before Painting

If you want good, even coverage when painting walls, coat them first with shellac to assure even absorption of the paint. Use fresh shellac, since it dries very quickly and you will be able to paint the walls the same day they have been shellacked. Even better results will be assured and you will prevent peeling if the old paint is removed before the shellac is applied.

Painting Cellar Walls

When painting cellar walls, bear in mind that there is an advantage to using light colors. They may soil more quickly, but they do reflect more light and will keep the area bright and cheerful.

Painting Brass

A brass surface must be carefully prepared if paint is to adhere to it. First, wash the brass with a household cleaner that does not contain soap. Then, wipe the surface with denatured alcohol and proceed with the painting.

Cabinet and Closet Painting

when painting a closet or cabinet, avoid getting paint all

over your person by painting the interior top, bottom, and sides before painting the area near the door.

Painting Cabinet Knobs

Knobs of cabinets can be spray-painted easily and quickly without getting any paint on your fingers. First, remove the knob and its screw from the cabinet. Then turn the screw into the knob only partway. Next, place the knob on a bottle with a narrow neck. The neck of the bottle will serve as a support while you are painting, and the bottle can be turned as required without getting paint on your fingers. The knob can be left on the bottle until completely dry.

Painting a Floor

Save a backache! Instead of a paintbrush use a new pushbroom with soft bristles to paint a floor. Put the paint in a shallow pan large enough to accommodate the broom.

Painting Flowerpots

Painting an empty flowerpot is a simple procedure if you place the pot upside down on a can tall enough to raise the pot above the surface on which you are doing the job. Protect the surface with old newspapers to catch dripping paint.

Painting Metal Surfaces

It is not always easy to apply paint to the metal surfaces of wastepaper baskets and garbage cans. To make painting easier and to make sure the paint adheres, clean the surface thoroughly first, then spray with shellac. When the shellac is dry, apply the paint.

Painting Nails

When paint is applied to untreated nails, rust will bleed through in time. Before repainting, apply a coat of pigmented shellac-based sealer. This will seal the area and prevent bleeding.

Painting Plywood Edges

If you are going to paint plywood and you want the edges to look presentable, fill in the end grain with a wood filler or a latex spackling compound. Smooth on with a flexible putty knife and sand when dry. If the wood is to be stained, the edges can be covered with strips of wood veneer, available in many shades from lumber yards and hardware stores.

Painting Stairs

A clever way of painting stairs is to paint every other stair so that you can walk up and down on the unpainted steps. When the painted stairs are dry, paint the unpainted ones and you'll still be able to use the stairs while the paint is drying.

Painting Stripes

Paint stripes of any width and length can be made perfectly with

masking tape and a can of spray paint. First, clean the surface of dirt, dust, oil, and grease. Place masking tape strips in parallel lines spaced as desired. Measure with a ruler so the lines will be straight. Protect the surrounding wall by taping newspaper over it. Spray the area between the tape strips, holding the spray can about 12 inches from the surface. Lift the tape before the paint is entirely dry to avoid ragged edges caused by chipping of hardened paint.

Painting a Window Screen

Clean the screen itself well before beginning to paint. Use a paint roller or a clean rag to apply the paint. After painting, place the screen on a flat surface for drying. This will prevent the paint from dripping.

CLEANUP

Paint Remover

Trisodium phosphate, commonly called TSP, is a paint remover. Paint stores sell it under trade names such as Oakite, Soilax, and Spic 'n Span. A solution can be made up by mixing one pound of TSP with one gallon of hot water. Apply with a brush to the area where the paint is to be removed, and after one-half hour paint will begin to loosen. Scrape off with a putty knife and rinse off with clean water. Wipe with a wet sponge and dry the area with a cloth.

Ready-made paint removers are available under the trade names Red Devil, Dap, Savogram, and No-flame.

Cleaning Paintbrushes

Use turpentine or mineral spirits to clean brushes that have been used with oil-based or alkyd-based paints. Brushes to apply lacquer should be cleaned with lacquer thinner. And those used to apply shellac can be cleaned with alcohol. Brushes used for varnish are easily cleaned with paint thinner or turpentine.

Cleaning Paintbrushes

To clean a brush used with water-thinned acrylic or latex paint, simply wash thoroughly with warm sudsy water after getting rid of as much paint as possible by brushing the excess paint on newspaper or a piece of wood.

Use a comb or a brush to keep bristles separated.

On Hanging Paintbrushes

After being thoroughly cleaned, paintbrushes should be hung up to dry with hairs facing down.

Cleaning Paint Rollers

It is most important to remember that if you want to reuse paint rollers, they should be washed *immediately* after completing each job. First, remove as much of the excess paint as possible by rolling it back and forth over a stack of old newspapers. Remove the top sheets as they become saturated, and keep rolling until most of the paint is gone. Then, if the roller was used with latex paint, wash it in a tub of sudsy water. Work out all remaining paint with your fingers. If the roller was used with oil-based paint, clean it with a solvent or paint thinner.

Removing Excess Water

Because paint rollers are designed to hold fluids, it is often difficult to get all the rinse water

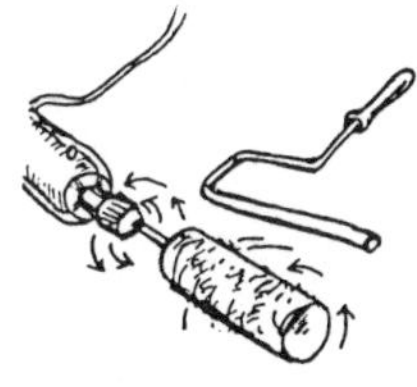

out of them after they have been cleaned.

Whirling the roller with an electric drill is one good way to get rid of the excess water quickly. To prepare the drill buy a length of one-quarter-inch threaded steel rod at a hardware store. Cut the rod with a hacksaw so that the piece is two and one-half inches longer than the roller. Put the rod through the roller and add a washer and butterfly nut at each end of the roller. Tighten the nut and select a location where spattering water will not create a problem. Put one end of the rod in the chuck of your drill; close the chuck and turn on the drill.

Storing Spray Paints

After using a can of spray paint, turn it upside down and hold the spray button down until air alone emerges. Then, wipe off the nozzle opening with a cloth. This will help prevent the hole from clogging up, and the spray should work easily the next time you use it.

An alternative is to keep handy a small jar containing about an inch of turpentine or lacquer thinner. After using a can of spray paint, remove the nozzle and keep it immersed in the liquid. Keep the jar covered. The paint will not clog the nozzle opening.

Linseed Oil as Thinner

Linseed oil is an excellent wood preservative. Use it rather than turpentine to thin outdoor paint. Turpentine tends to evaporate and does not help the wood.

Linseed oil restores some of the wood's original vitality.

Turpentine Substitute

Paint thinner and benzene serve the same function as turpentine, and they are much cheaper.

Acetone as Lacquer Solvent

Acetone is the solvent for lacquer. Use it to remove old lacquer before refinishing an article. Use also as a thinner for lacquer. The main ingredient in nail polish remover is acetone.

Hard-to-open Windows

For windows that have been painted and cannot be opened because paint has hardened, a special tool is available at hardware and paint stores. Sometimes called a window zipper or zip tool, it has fine, sharp teeth to cut through paint film. Of course, you should first try a two- or three-inch-wide plastering spatula, which will usually loosen a window that has been painted shut.

Spattered Concrete Floors

A strong solution of lye and water should do the job of removing paint from concrete. Rinse well afterwards with a large amount of clean water.

Paint on Brickwork

To remove spattered paint from brickwork, use another brick as a scrub brush. For concrete, use a broken piece of concrete. The dust created by the scrubbing will camouflage the faint traces of spatter that remain.

Removing Paint From Tiles

Paint that has been spattered on tiles can be removed with a little turpentine on a clean cloth. To make the job easier, first remove as much as you can with a razor blade.

14
Cleaning & Stain Removal

Introduction

Though rarely listed with food, shelter, clothing, and medical expenses as a primary household budget item, laundry and household cleaning bills can contribute several hundred dollars to the yearly family outlay. By familiarizing oneself with basic cleaning techniques, it is possible to shave significant sums off the family budget. As important, many stains are best removed as soon as they occur. It thus behooves every household to keep a selection of cleaning solutions at hand to deal with unforeseen "catastrophes." Many a dinner party has lost its shine for want of a timely spot remover.

CLEANING PREPARATIONS AND TECHNIQUES

All-purpose Cleanser

Sprinkle baking soda on a damp sponge or make a paste by adding water to one tablespoon of baking soda. Use as a cleanser. Being only mildly abrasive, baking soda will not scratch surfaces.

Or, dissolve two tablespoons of baking soda in water and pour into a squeeze bottle. Keep the solution handy to clean soiled windows, chrome, and enamel surfaces.

Vinegar and Its Many Uses

Vinegar has long been hailed as an effective cleaning agent and deodorizer. Because it contains about 5% acid (acetic), it dissolves many greasy spots. Vinegar cleanses the white stains left on furniture by beverage glasses and cleans glassware without leaving a residue.

Keep on hand a solution of one quart of water to which one-quarter cup of white vinegar has been added. After mixing thoroughly, add a tablespoon of baking soda and a tablespoon of salt. Keep the solution in a spray bottle, and use as needed as a stain remover, glass and tile cleaner, and deodorizer.

Lumpy Detergents

When buying detergents for your washer, always shake the box to make sure the powder is not lumpy. Lumpy detergent will dissolve more slowly and thereby reduce the efficiency of the washer.

Homemade Window Cleaning Solution

Windex and similar commercial products are effective, but you can save money by making your own window cleaning solution. Simply fill a bucket with warm water and add to it one-half cup of white vinegar, one-half cup of ammonia, and two tablespoons of cornstarch. Divide into two or three parts. Use only as much as needed and save the remainder for future use.

Soapless Detergents

Spic 'n Span and Oakite, among other brands, are soapless detergents. These commercial products are effective in removing wax from floors and grease from walls, woodwork, bathtubs, and kitchen appliances.

First Aid for Spills and Stains

When a liquid spills, to avoid permanent staining, immediately blot the spill with a cloth or paper towel until most of the liquid has been absorbed. Don't rub the stained area. If the stain has not been caused by a greasy substance, flood the area with cool tap water. Do not use hot water. Then, proceed with a treatment appropriate for this type of stain.

Stain Absorbers

When stains are still moist, they can often be blotted up with one of three common absorbents: talcum powder, cornstarch, and cornmeal.

Stretch the stained article on a clean cloth and spread one of the absorbents over the stained area. Move the absorbent around with the fingertips until it becomes gummy. Brush off. Repeat the procedure as necessary.

Salt as an Absorbent

To remove a sticky spill, pour on salt, allow to dry, then scoop up.

Old Stains, New Stains

It is much easier to remove new stains than those that have had time to set. Many old stains, such as those caused by ink and paint, are almost impossible to remove. So, be wise and act quickly.

Testing for Colorfastness

Before using any stain remover, including water, test it on an inside hem or pocket to be sure that it will not harm the fabric or dye.

Make a test by soaking a hidden area of the garment in a diluted solution of the stain remover for 20 minutes, then let dry. Compare to the rest of the garment. If no change has occurred, wash as usual.

Dry Spotter and Wet Spotter

The word *spotting* refers to stain removal. *Dry Spotter* is used to remove stains that do not dissolve in water. *Wet Spotter* is effective in eliminating water-soluble stains.

To prepare Dry Spotter, mix one part coconut oil (or mineral oil) and eight parts dry-cleaning solvent. This solution is used to remove adhesive tape marks and many other kinds of stains. Oil lubricates the fabric and reduces the possibility of damaging it as it is rubbed. Dry Spotter keeps well if stored in a tightly capped container.

Many stains that are soluble in water can be removed from fabrics with Wet Spotter, a preparation consisting of one part glycerin to one part liquid dishwashing detergent and eight parts water. This mixture can be kept in a squeeze bottle. Shake well before applying.

Removing Stains With an Enzyme Product

Enzymes are proteinlike substances formed in plant and animal cells that act as organic catalysts which speed up specific chemical reactions.

Some popular laundry detergents contain enzymes that help dissolve stains caused by blood and other body fluids, egg and egg-containing products, milk, cream, chocolate, and gravy.

These products may be stored as purchased, but they become active if stored after they have been made into a solution.

Simple Detergents to Remove Stains

The simplest form of detergent is ordinary dishwashing liquid. Mixed with cool water, it makes an effective stain remover for fabrics that are not affected adversely by water. Cool water must be used, for hot or even warm water is known to cause stains to set and thus become difficult to remove.

TSP (Trisodium Phosphate)

TSP is the prime ingredient in many strong, general-purpose floor and wall cleaners. Among the products containing TSP are Soilax, Spic 'n Span, and Wilmore.

Two tablespoons of TSP plus two tablespoons of baking soda in a gallon of water will take care of most floor and wall cleaning jobs.

Chlorine Bleach as a Stain Remover

Chlorine bleach is used to remove stains such as catsup, chocolate, and syrup. Check the label of the bleach to be sure that it contains chlorine.

Chlorine bleach damages some fibers, dyes, and finishes. It may be used to whiten cottons, linens, and synthetics but should never be used on silk, wool, leather, or rayon with a wash-and-wear finish. Check the care label of the fabric for cautions regarding the use of bleach, and read the label on the bleach container. Test the fabric in an inconspicuous place before using bleach on the stain. Do not use chlorine bleach on fabric with a fire-retardant finish unless the care label states otherwise.

Popular Bleaching Substances

The most popular bleaches are chlorine, lemon juice, ammonia, hydrogen peroxide, and vinegar. Synthetic bleaches, such as Clorox, are widely used. All forms can be made weaker by diluting them with water.

Ammonia Caveats

- Do not use ammonia on aluminum pans.
- Ammonia should never be mixed with chlorine bleach or other household chemicals. A dangerous reaction may ensue.

Removing Stains With Ammonia

Ammonia will restore many articles soiled by smoke. It can be used for cleaning glassware, mirrors, enamel-coated items, formica, straw items, and wicker furniture.

Use plain household ammonia. Do not use ammonia with added color or fragrances.

Ammonia changes the color of some dyes. To restore the color, rinse the color-changed area thoroughly with water and apply a few drops of white vinegar. Rinse well with water again.

For use on wool and silk, dilute ammonia with an equal amount of water.

Glycerin Solvents

Pure glycerin, available in pharmacies, is usually used in combination with other solvents. Used alone, it will often soften stubborn stains and thus hasten their removal.

Sodium Perborate

This odorless, crystalline white compound, used chiefly as a bleaching agent, is effective in removing yellow perspiration stains that do not clear up when vinegar or ammonia is applied to them.

Magic Wand

Magic Wand is a commercial product in stick form that can remove from washable fabrics a variety of stains, such as those caused by ballpoint ink, chocolate, blood, wine, grass, and perspiration.

Goo Gone

An all-purpose easy-to-apply stain-and-grime remover called Goo Gone was introduced recently by the Magic American Corporation. It works on most surfaces and fabrics. If not available in your local shopping center, write to the company. See the Appendix for the address.

Carbona

Carbona is a popular, effective spot remover that cleans grease spots, oil, tar, wax, chewing gum, and adhesive tape. Before using, test the Carbona on a hidden part of the fabric. Do not use on rubberized fabrics or styrene plastics.

Borax

Borax is a commercial product that cuts grease and acts as an antiseptic to retard the growth of molds and the spread of bacteria. A white crystalline salt with an alkaline taste, it is used in the manufacture of glass, soaps, and antiseptics.

Benzene and Benzine

Benzene is a good spot remover for gum and fat stains. Benzine, which is chemically different from Benzene, is likewise a good solvent for greasy stains. Both are highly flammable materials.

Grease and Oil Solvents

Carbona and K2r are two popular oil solvents that will usually remove stains containing oil or some other greasy substance. Popular detergents, such as Fab, Shout, and Spray 'n Wash, contain these solvents and are effective spot removers.

Alcohol as a Solvent

Pure alcohol (not rubbing alcohol) can be used as a solvent on stained garments that may not be cleaned with water. The liquid content of the alcohol evaporates quickly, and the fabric is not damaged. Always test an inconspicuous part of the garment first, since alcohol can make most dyed fabrics bleed. For use on acetate, dilute alcohol with two parts water to one part alcohol. If alcohol is not available, substitute vinegar.

Acetone as a Cleaning Agent

Acetone is an ideal thinner for many types of epoxy and fiberglass resins. It dissolves grease, wax, and dirt. To remove label adhesives that cling to a bottle or jar after a label has been removed, mix four parts water to one part acetone and immerse the container in a shallow pan until the residue has softened.

Acetone should not be used on acetate.

Removing Stains by Spooning

The bowl of a smooth stainless steel teaspoon is an effective tool for loosening stains.

Place the stain directly on a working surface without any absorbent material underneath. Add the stain remover.

Move the bowl of the spoon back and forth about one-quarter inch in each direction. Short strokes are the most effective. Do not press down with the spoon. This may damage the fabric.

Do not use this procedure on delicate fabrics.

Sponging Procedure

When directions call for sponging, place the stained area, stained side down, over a pad of absorbent material. Dampen another piece of absorbent material with the stain remover. Sponge the stain lightly, working from the center to the edge. You are less likely to form rings if you keep working out from the center.

Nonoily Stain-removal Solution

Simple stains on washable fabrics can often be treated successfully by using a solution of equal parts ammonia, dishwashing liquid detergent, and water. Dab the solution liberally, let stand for a few minutes, then wash out with clean water.

Removing Stains from Water-sensitive Fabrics

Some fabrics show water stains easily. When using a solvent on such fabrics, choose a water-free solvent such as Carbona, Renuzit, or Energine. Apply with a sponge and, starting from the epicenter of the stain, scrub in an ever-widening circular motion.

REMOVING SPECIFIC STAINS

Adhesive Tape Stains

Marks made by adhesive tape can be removed by applying Dry Spotter to the stain. Using an absorbent pad, keep the area moist with Dry Spotter until the stain has been removed. Then, sponge the material with water.

If the above procedure is not effective, apply Wet Spotter and a few drops of ammonia, again using a pad of absorbent material. Keep the area moist until the stain has disappeared, then sponge with water (see earlier hint on sponging technique).

Alcoholic Beverage Stains

Liquor or wine stains on garments, upholstery, and rugs often can be treated successfully with club soda. After dousing with soda, cover the area with toweling and press down to absorb the liquid.

Alternatively, immediately soak liquor and wine stains with cold water to which a small amount of glycerin has been added. If the stain persists, pour vinegar onto the stain.

If these methods fail, try scrubbing the area with a strong detergent.

Asphalt Stains

Should asphalt come into contact with clothing, apply dry-cleaning solvent and blot with a moistened pad of absorbent material. Apply Dry Spotter, again blotting with a moistened pad. Continue alternate soakings in the two solutions until all stain has been removed. Flush with dry-cleaning solvent and allow to dry.

Battery Stains

If acid from a batter comes in contact with a garment, immediately pour household ammonia over the affected area. After a minute or two rinse liberally with cold water.

Beverage Stains

Many beverage stains can be removed by the following method:

Soak washable fabrics for 15 minutes in a solution of one quart warm water, one-half teaspoon liquid dishwashing detergent, and one tablespoon vinegar. Rinse with water. Stubborn stains can be treated with a laundry detergent containing an enzyme product.

Nonwashable fabrics should be treated by applying Wet Spotter with a few drops of vinegar and blotting with a moist pad of absorbent material until the stain has been removed.

Beer Stains

Beer stains can be removed by blotting the area and then applying cool water mixed with rubbing alcohol or vinegar. If necessary, rinse again with water and dab some hydrogen peroxide on the fabric. Before doing so, however, test for colorfastness.

Treating with a one-to-one solution of chlorine bleach and water may be necessary to remove traces of stain from garments. Always test for colorfastness first.

Blood Stains

- To remove a blood stain from washable material, soak in cold water and, when the stain has lightened considerably, wash it out with warm water and a detergent. If the stain persists, apply a few drops of Dry Spotter.
- For blood stains on nonwashable fabric, sponge the area with lukewarm water, then add a few drops of hydrogen peroxide solution to the sponge and rub until the stain disappears. If this doesn't work, apply Wet Spotter. Hydrogen peroxide is safe for all fibers, but dyed fabrics should be tested for colorfastness before using.
- Blood stains can also be removed by covering the area with a paste made of meat tenderizer and water. After about one-half hour, sponge with lukewarm water.
- Blood stains that are old and have set may be removed from cottons and linens by soaking in a warm solution of trisodium phosphate (TSP).

Butter Stains

If soapy water to which a small amount of glycerin has been added doesn't work, use an oil solvent such as Carbona. Follow the same procedure for removing margarine stains.

Calamine Lotion Stains

Stains caused by calamine lotion may be removed by applying Dry Spotter to the stain. Using an absorbent pad, keep the area moist with Dry Spotter until the stain has been removed. Then, sponge the material with water.

If the above procedure is not effective, apply Wet Spotter and a few drops of ammonia, again using a pad of absorbent material. Keep the area moist until the stain has been removed. Then, sponge the material with water.

Candy Stains

Rub the area with hot water. When dry, rub with a cleaning fluid or a soapy detergent to remove the balance of the stain.

Candle Wax Stains

After scraping off the wax, place the fabric between two pieces of paper toweling and press with a warm iron.

Carbon Stains

Garments soiled by carbon paper, carbon typewriting ribbon, or correction fluid can be cleaned by applying Dry Spotter to the stain and blotting it with a pad of absorbent material until the stain disappears. Flush with dry-cleaning solvent.

If the above procedure is not effective, apply amyl acetate (banana oil) to the stain and blot with a pad of absorbent material. Allow to stand for 15 minutes, then flush with dry cleaning solvent.

If traces of stain remain on the fabric, treat with a one-to-one solution of chlorine bleach and water. Before doing so, test for colorfastness.

Charcoal Stains

Stains caused by charcoal can be effectively removed by rubbing the area with liquid soap to which a few drops of ammonia have been added. Rinse with cool water.

Catsup Stains

To remove catsup stains, saturate the soiled area with cold water and rub with a cloth soaked in a laundry detergent. If this doesn't work, apply Dry Spotter. Using an absorbent pad, keep the area moist with Dry Spotter until the stain has disappeared. Then, sponge with water.

If the above procedure is not effective, apply a few drops of liquid detergent and a few drops of ammonia, again using a pad of absorbent material. Keep the area moist until stain has been removed. Then, sponge the material with water. Stubborn stains can be treated with a detergent containing an enzyme product.

Treating for two minutes with a one-to-one solution of chlorine bleach and water may be necessary to remove lingering stains caused by catsup and steak or chili sauce. Before using, test for colorfastness. Flush with water after using.

Chewing Gum Stains

- Apply a cube of ice to the area until the gum has hardened, then scrape off with a dull-edged knife.

  After scraping off as much as possible, saturate the stained fabric with cleaning fluid.
- Gum stuck on a carpet (or in one's hair) can be softened with peanut butter and then removed.

Chocolate Stains

Chocolate (or cocoa) stains may require special treatment in addition to the procedures outlined below. Begin by applying Dry Spotter to the stain. Using an absorbent pad, keep the area moist with Dry Spotter until the stain has been removed. Then, sponge with water.

If the above procedure is not effective, apply a few drops of liquid handwashing detergent and a few drops of ammonia, again using a pad of absorbent material. Keep the area moist until the stain has been removed. Then, sponge with water. Stubborn stains can be treated with a detergent containing an enzyme product.

Treating for two minutes with

a one-to-one solution of chlorine bleach and water may be necessary to remove lingering stains caused by chocolate. Test for colorfastness before using. Flush with water after using.

If the above remedies fail, try bleaching chocolate stains with hydrogen peroxide. Keep the area moist with peroxide and a drop or two of ammonia for up to 15 minutes. Rinse with water.

Coffee Stains

Coffee stains usually will dissolve if boiling water is poured over the area. If a stain persists, sprinkle glycerin over the area and allow to soak.

If cream and sugar have not been added to the coffee, pour a liberal amount of club soda on the stain and rub with a cloth.

Cooking Oil Stains

For heavy stains caused by all types of cooking oil, apply dry-cleaning solvent and blot with a moistened pad of absorbent material. Apply Dry Spotter, again blotting with a moistened pad. Continue alternate soakings in the two solutions until all of the stain has been removed. Flush with dry-cleaning solvent and allow to dry.

Crayon Stains

To remove crayon marks caused by a wax or grease crayon, first scrape off as much as possible, then launder in the usual manner with a cup of baking soda added.

If this is not effective, apply Dry Spotter to the stain. Using an absorbent pad, keep the area moist with Dry Spotter until the stain has been removed. Then, sponge with water.

If neither of the procedures is effective, apply Wet Spotter and a few drops of ammonia, again using a pad of absorbent material. Keep the area moist until the stain has been removed. Then, sponge with water.

Crayon on Carpets and Walls

- Wax crayon on carpets can be removed by covering the soiled area with paper towel and ironing the towel with a warm iron. The wax will melt and be absorbed by the towel.
- Crayon marks on a painted wall can be erased by dabbing fingernail polish remover on a clean cloth and rubbing the area.

Cream and Milk Stains

To remove cream and milk stains, launder washable fabrics in warm water to which suds or a detergent has been added. Nonwashable fabrics should be sponged with warm water and the stained area rubbed with dry-cleaning fluid after the water has dried.

Cheese Stains

Stubborn stains caused by cheeses can be treated by applying Dry Spotter to the area. Using an absorbent pad, keep the area moist with Dry Spotter until the stain has been removed. Then, sponge with water.

If the above procedure is not effective, apply a few drops of liquid handwashing detergent and a few drops of ammonia, again using a pad of absorbent material. Keep the area moist until the stain has disappeared, then sponge with water. Stubborn cheese stains can be treated with a detergent containing an enzyme product.

Treating for two minutes with a one-to-one solution of chlorine bleach and water may be necessary to remove lingering stains caused by cheese. Always test for colorfastness first. Flush with water after treatment.

Deodorant Stains

Stains caused by deodorants can usually be removed by sponging with white vinegar. If this doesn't work, saturate the area with rubbing alcohol.

Red and Yellow Dye Stains

Red fabric stains can be caused by dye in food coloring, hair coloring products, fabric coloring agents, ink, mercurochrome, or water-color paint. *Yellow* stains may result from using products which contain a derivative of picric acid.

To remove such stains, washable fabrics should be soaked for 30 minutes in a solution of one quart warm water, one-half teaspoon liquid dishwashing detergent, and one tablespoon ammonia. Rinse with water to remove all ammonia. Soak in a solution of one quart warm water and one tablespoon vinegar for one hour. Rinse and allow to dry. If this procedure is not effective, moisten the stain with alcohol and blot with an absorbent pad. Flush with water.

Nonwashable fabrics should be treated by applying Wet Spotter with a few drops of ammonia and blotting with a moist pad of absorbent material until the stain has been removed.

Treating for two minutes with a one-to-one solution of chlorine bleach and water may be necessary to remove lingering stains caused by red dye. Always test for colorfastness first. Flush with water after treatment.

Other Dye Stains

Most dyes are meant to be permanent and are difficult to remove. For dye stains *except* those caused by red and yellow dyes, try the following method, which works well for stains caused by fabric dye, food coloring, bluing, gentian violet, ink, hair dye, shoe dye, and watercolor paint.

Soak washable fabrics for 30 minutes in a solution of one quart warm water, one-half teaspoon liquid dishwashing detergent, and one tablespoon vinegar. Rinse with water. Moisten the stain with alcohol and blot with an absorbent pad, then flush with alcohol. Soak for an additional 30 minutes in a solution of one quart warm water, one-half teaspoon liquid dishwashing detergent, and one tablespoon ammonia. Rinse with water.

Nonwashable fabrics should be treated by applying Wet Spotter with a few drops of vinegar and blotting with a moist pad of absorbent material. Flush with water. Wet Spotter with a few drops of ammonia may be applied to stubborn stains. If traces of stain remain, treat for two minutes with a one-to-one solution of chlorine bleach and water. Test for colorfastness first. Flush with water after treatment.

Egg White Stains

Washable fabrics soiled by egg white should be soaked for 20 minutes in a solution of one quart warm water, one-half teaspoon liquid detergent, and one tablespoon ammonia. Then, rinse with water. Stubborn stains can be treated with a laundry detergent containing an enzyme product.

Nonwashable fabrics should be treated by applying Wet Spotter with a few drops of ammonia and blotting with a moist pad of absorbent material until the stain has been removed.

Egg Yolk Stains on Fabrics

Using the back of a knife, scrape off as much of the egg as possible, then sponge the fabric with *cold* water. Washable materials can then be laundered in the usual way. Nonwashable materials should be sponged with drycleaning fluid after the fabric has dried.

Follow this procedure for removing mayonnaise stains as well.

Egg Stain on Porcelain

Egg stains on porcelain dishes should be washed off immediately with cold water. Washing with hot water will make stain removal more difficult.

Eye Makeup Stains

Fabric soiled by eyebrow pencil, eyeliner, eye shadow, mascara, or any similar type of eye makeup may be cleaned by applying Dry Spotter to the stain until the stain has been removed. Then, sponge the material with water.

If the above procedure is not effective, apply Wet Spotter and a few drops of ammonia, again using a pad of absorbent material. Keep the area moist until the stain is gone, then sponge with water.

To removal the final traces of stain caused by eye makeup, use a solution of one teaspoon chlorine bleach to one teaspoon water. Apply with a dropper for no longer than two minutes. Flush with water, apply one teaspoon of vinegar to the stain, and flush with water again.

Face Makeup Stains

Face powder, rouge, or makeup of the liquid or pancake variety may cause stains on collars. These are best removed by applying Dry Spotter to the stain. Using an absorbent pad, keep the area moist with Dry Spotter until the stain has been removed. Then, sponge with water.

If the above procedure is not effective, apply Wet Spotter and a few drops of ammonia, again using a pad of absorbent material. Keep the area moist until the stain has been removed, then sponge with water.

Felt-tip Marker Stains

Clothing stains caused by felt-tip magic marker ink can be removed by applying Dry Spotter to the stain. Using an absorbent pad, keep the area moist with Dry Spotter. When the stain has disappeared, sponge with water.

If the above procedure is not effective, apply Wet Spotter and a few drops of ammonia, again using a pad of absorbent material. Keep the area moist, and when the stain has disappeared, sponge with water.

To remove the final traces of stain caused by felt-tip marker ink, use a solution of one teaspoon chlorine bleach to one teaspoon water. Apply with a dropper for no longer than two minutes. Flush with water, apply one teaspoon of vinegar to the stain, and flush with water again.

Hairspray for Felt-tip Marker Stains

To remove felt-tip marker stains from fabrics, spray with hairspray. After the spray has dried, brush off with a sponge moistened with a solution of vinegar and water (three tablespoons of water to each tablespoon of vinegar). If this fails to do the job, rub with a cloth dipped in bleach. Wash thoroughly with clean water. Test for colorfastness before using.

Fruit and Vegetable Stains

The juice from various types of fruits and vegetables may cause stains on fabrics. Commercial solvents such as Spray 'n Wash or Shout are often effective in removing fresh fruit and vegetable juice stains. If the stain has set, soak washables for 15 minutes in a solution of one quart warm water, one-half teaspoon liquid dishwashing detergent, and one tablespoon vinegar. Rinse with water. Stubborn stains can be treated with a laundry detergent containing an enzyme product.

Nonwashable fabrics should be treated by applying Wet Spotter with a few drops of vinegar and blotting with a moist pad of absorbent material until the stain has been removed.

Treating for two minutes with a one-to-one solution of chlorine bleach and water may be necessary to remove lingering stains caused by vegetables. Test for colorfastness first. Flush with water after treatment.

Removing Glue or Lacquer

To remove glue or lacquer stains use amyl acetate (banana oil). Ask for "chemically pure amyl acetate" when ordering it in your drug store.

If you cannot obtain amyl acetate, you may substitute fingernail polish remover. Do not use the oily-type nail polish remover.

Amyl acetate is a strong solvent for plastics. Do not allow it to come in contact with plastics or furniture finishes.

Glue Stains

For ordinary white glue stains, soak the soiled area in warm water, then sponge off with vinegar.

For stains caused by mucilage, airplane glue, plastic glue, liquid solder, and plastic cement, apply Dry Spotter to the stain and blot with a pad of absorbent material until the stain has been removed. Flush with dry-cleaning solvent.

If the above procedure is not effective, apply amyl acetate (banana oil) to the stain and blot with a pad of absorbent material. Allow to stand for 15 minutes, then flush with dry-cleaning solvent.

Grass Stains

For mild grass stains soak the soiled area in warm water to which pepsin (available in pharmacies) has been added. If the stain persists after a half-hour of soaking, sponge the area with rubbing alcohol.

Gravy Stains

After soaking the fabric in cool water, gravy stains may be treated with an oil solvent such as Carbona spot remover.

Grease and Oil Stains

Cornstarch or baby talcum powder should be applied immediately to all greasy stains. The area becomes gummy as the stain is soaked up, and the gum can then be scraped off. After scraping, proceed with an in-depth treatment, as follows:

Most types of grease used in cooking (e.g., lard, margarine) and lubricating oils, salves, and ointments used in the home may be removed by applying Dry Spotter to the stain. Using an absorbent pad, keep the area moist with Dry Spotter until the stain has disappeared, then sponge with water.

If the above procedure is not effective, apply Wet Spotter and a few drops of ammonia, again using a pad of absorbent material. Keep the area moist until the stain has been removed, then sponge with water.

Grease Stains on Polyester

Grease stains on polyester garments can be rubbed with talcum powder. Use your fingertips. Allow the powder to stand for 24 hours, then brush off. Repeat the procedure if necessary.

Attacking Grease With Salt

Salt will absorb oil and grease. If you apply salt immediately to grease or oil on a nonabsorbent surface, it should prevent damage. Allow time for the salt to absorb the grease and oil before wiping off with a damp cloth.

Grease Stains on Wallpaper

Place a paste made of cornstarch and water on the grease

spot and leave it there until dry. Then, brush off the paste and the stain should disappear. If this does not work, try again with a paste of fuller's earth and carbon tetrachloride. Both can be purchased at paint and hardware stores.

Removing Grease Stains From Suede

Fresh grease stains can be removed from a suede garment or suede shoes by rubbing with a sponge or cloth dipped in vinegar or club soda.

Greasy Glass

There are several ways to remove grease from glass. A bit of vinegar added to some water is effective. Jars and bottles that are soiled by grease can be cleaned by adding a spoonful of ammonia to a glass of tap water.

Hair Coloring Stains

Hair coloring stains that have hardened on a fabric should first be softened with an application of glycerin and then dabbed with vinegar and rinsed.

India Ink Stains

India ink stains are most effectively dealt with by applying Dry Spotter to the stain. Using an absorbent pad, keep the area moist with Dry Spotter. When the stain has disappeared, sponge with water.

If the above procedure is not effective, apply Wet Spotter and a few drops of ammonia, again using a pad of absorbent material. Keep the area moist until the stain has been removed, then sponge with water.

Herb Stains

A solvent in which glycerin is an ingredient should first be applied. If the stain persists, apply a mixture of half water and half alcohol to which a few drops of vinegar have been added.

Hairspray Stains

The sticky residue left by hairspray on fabric surfaces can be removed by applying Dry Spotter to the stain. Using an absorbent pad, keep the area moist with Dry Spotter until the stain has disappeared. Then, sponge with water.

If the above procedure is not effective, apply Wet Spotter and a few drops of ammonia, again using a pad of absorbent material. Keep the area moist until the stain has been removed. Then, sponge with water.

Stains created by hairsprays can also be removed with an alcohol application. Test the fabric first, especially if it is colored.

Ink Stains—Ballpoint

Ballpoint ink stains are difficult to remove, and you might have to engage the services of a cleaning professional. But, before doing so, you might try the following:

- Ballpoint inks consist of a variety of ingredients. Acetone is a solvent that will lift some ballpoint ink stains. If acetone doesn't work, try applying a cloth moistened with lukewarm glycerin. Be persistent if the stain doesn't come out initially. If this doesn't work, try using Wet Spotter. If necessary, treat for two minutes with a one-to-one solution of chlorine bleach and water to remove last traces of the stain. Test for colorfastness.

- To get rid of some ballpoint ink stains, saturate the soiled area with alcohol, then scrub. Follow this procedure by sponging the stain with a dry-cleaning solvent and then washing it out with a household detergent.

Hand Lotion Stains

Hand lotion can cause troublesome staining when brought into contact with sheer or delicate fabrics. To remove, apply Dry Spotter to the stain. Using an absorbent pad, keep the area moist with Dry Spotter. When the stain has disappeared, sponge with water.

If the above procedure is not effective, apply Wet Spotter and a few drops of ammonia, again using a pad of absorbent material. Keep the area moist until the stain has been removed, then sponge with water.

Insecticide Stains

A special problem during the summer months, insecticide stains on clothing can be treated by applying Dry Spotter. Using an absorbent pad, keep the area moist with Dry Spotter until the stain has been removed. Then, sponge the material with water.

If the above procedure is not effective, apply Wet Spotter and a few drops of ammonia, again using a pad of absorbent material. Keep the area moist until the stain has been removed, then sponge with water.

Iodine Stains

Dry iodine stains are difficult to remove. If the stain is still damp, it can be removed by rubbing with soap and water or ammonia.

Removing Lacquer Stains

Stains resulting from contact with lacquer and varnish (including fingernail polish or nail hardener) can be treated by applying Dry Spotter to the stain and blotting with a pad of absorbent material until the stain has been removed. Flush with dry-cleaning solvent.

If the above procedure is not effective, apply amyl acetate to the stain and blot with a pad of absorbent material. Allow to stand for 15 minutes, then flush with dry-cleaning solvent.

Lipstick Stains

Pour liquid detergent directly on a lipstick stain and blot with paper toweling. Repeat several times if necessary. If this doesn't work, use a dry-cleaning solvent or vaseline and then scrub the area with a detergent. If the stain persists, apply hydrogen peroxide.

Jam and Jelly Stains

Children's clothing is often soiled by sticky jams, jellies, fruit preserves, and fruit juices. Remove stains from washables by soaking for 15 minutes in a solution of one quart warm water, one-half teaspoon liquid dishwashing detergent, and one tablespoon vinegar. Rinse with water. Stubborn stains can be treated with a laundry detergent containing an enzyme product.

Nonwashable fabrics should be treated by applying Wet Spotter with a few drops of vinegar added and blotting with a moist pad of absorbent material until the stain has been removed.

Treatment for two minutes with a one-to-one solution of chlorine bleach and water may be necessary to remove lingering stains. Always test first for colorfastness. Flush with water after treatment.

Meat Juice Stains

Saturate the soiled area with water to which pepsin has been added. The stain should disappear in about 30 minutes.

Meat Soup Stains

Greasy stains caused by soups containing meat can be treated in the following manner. Washable fabrics should be soaked for 20 minutes in a solution of one quart warm water, one-half teaspoon liquid dishwashing detergent, and one tablespoon ammonia. Then, rinse with water. Stubborn stains can be treated with a laundry detergent containing an enzyme product.

Nonwashable fabrics should be treated by applying Wet Spotter with a few drops of ammonia and blotting with a moist pad of absorbent material until the stain has been removed.

Mercurochrome Stains

Mix equal amounts of water and rubbing alcohol and apply to the stained area. If the stain persists, rub with glycerin, then wash out with liquid detergent.

Mucus or Vomit Stains

A washable fabric soiled by mucus or vomit can be cleaned by soaking the fabric for 20 minutes in a solution of one quart warm water, one-half teaspoon liquid detergent, and one tablespoon ammonia. Then, rinse with water. Stubborn stains can be treated with a laundry detergent containing an enzyme product. Uric acid stains can also be removed by this method.

Nonwashable fabrics should be treated by applying Wet Spotter with a few drops of ammonia, then blotting with a moist pad of absorbent material until the stain has been removed.

Mud Stains

Ground-in dirt in children's playclothes is a perennial problem. Soak washables for 15 minutes in a solution of one quart warm water, one-half teaspoon liquid detergent, and one tablespoon vinegar. Rinse with water.

Stubborn stains can be treated with a laundry detergent containing an enzyme product.

Nonwashable fabrics should be treated by applying Wet Spotter with a few drops of vinegar, then blotting with a moist pad of absorbent material until the stain has been removed.

To remove lingering stains caused by mud and dirt, treat for two minutes with a one-to-one solution of chlorine bleach and water. Test first for colorfastness. Flush with water after treatment.

Mustard Stains

Fresh mustard stains can be washed out with a household detergent or liquid soap. If the stain is not completely removed, wash again with a mixture of water and glycerin or water and rubbing alcohol.

Dried mustard stains should be treated by placing the stained area on a smooth surface and carefully scraping off the excess mustard. Then, flush with dry-cleaning solvent and allow to dry. Follow this by sponging the fabric with water, applying Wet Spotter and vinegar, then flushing again with water.

If this does not remove the stain, apply hydrogen peroxide and a drop of vinegar, and allow to stand for 15 minutes. Flush with water and allow to dry.

Nail Polish Stains

Nail polish remover is specifically made to remove nail polish and will usually remove nail polish stains. If you have acetone on hand, it will do the job. If a stain persists, try using peroxide or alcohol with a few drops of ammonia added.

Nose Drop Stains

Fabric stains caused by nose drops can be removed by applying Dry Spotter to the stain. Using an absorbent pad, keep the area moist with Dry Spotter until the stain has been removed, then sponge with water.

If the above procedure is not effective, apply Wet Spotter and a few drops of ammonia, again using a pad of absorbent material. Keep the area moist. When the stain has disappeared, sponge with water.

Mildew Odor

To get rid of odor caused by mildew stains mix two tablespoons of Borax in a bowl of water. Let soak for a few minutes. Rinse the article, squeeze out the water, and hang up to dry.

Mildew Stains

- Chlorine bleach is effective in removing mildew stains and in preventing mildew spores from multiplying. But first try washing with soap and water.
- Mildewed fabrics can be treated with denatured alcohol and water mixed in equal parts. Allow to dry in fresh air if possible. The musty odor should disappear.
- Mildew stains on garments can be washed out with liquid detergent. If the mildew per-

sists, sponge the area with lemon juice and salt.

Oil-based Paint Stains

Use turpentine to remove fresh paint stains caused by oil-based paints. If turpentine is not available, paint thinner or regular gasoline can be used.

Oil Stains on Garage Floor

To instantly remove oil or grease spots from a garage floor, simply pour on some gasoline and rub. If you don't have gasoline on hand, douse the area with turpentine or paint thinner. After ten minutes sprinkle sand or dry cement or baking soda over the area, and five or six hours later sweep up and the condition will be greatly improved. Repeat if necessary.

Paint Stains

Water-based paint that has dried on fabric should be scraped off gently and the fabric then washed in hot water with detergent.

Oil-based paint stains should be removed by soaking the fabric in turpentine or gasoline. Commercial paint remover fluids are available in paint and hardware stores.

Perspiration Stains on Clothing

To remove a perspiration stain from a washable fabric, soak it for 30 minutes in a solution of one quart warm water, one-half teaspoon liquid dishwashing detergent, and one tablespoon ammonia. Rinse with water to remove all the ammonia. Soak again in a solution of one quart warm water and one tablespoon vinegar for one hour. Rinse and allow to dry.

If this procedure is not effective, moisten the stain with alcohol and blot with an absorbent pad. Flush with water.

Nonwashable fabrics should be treated by applying Wet Spotter with a few drops of ammonia and blotting with a moist pad of absorbent material until the stain has been removed. Remaining traces of stain may be treated with alcohol, as above.

Bleaching with chlorine may be necessary to remove lingering stains caused by perspiration. If so, follow the procedure outlined in the section on eye makeup stains.

Some people have discovered that perspiration stains will disappear from cotton clothing if soaked in salt water for several hours and then washed out in the usual manner.

Putty Stains

Fresh stains caused by putty can be cleaned up with ammonia or turpentine.

Rubber Cement

Rubber cement can be removed by applying rubber cement thinner or dry-cleaning solvent and blotting the stain with a moistened pad of absorbent material. Apply Dry Spotter, again blotting with a moistened pad. Continue alternate soakings in the two solutions until all stain has been removed. Flush with dry-cleaning solvent and allow to dry.

Rust Stains

Rust stains can be removed from fabrics by moistening the soiled area with water and then squeezing lemon juice directly upon it. Then hold the fabric over the steam of a boiling pot of water. Rinse with water and repeat the procedure if necessary.

Alternatively, scrub the soiled area with lemon juice to which some salt has been added. If necessary, mix three tablespoons of oxalic acid in a pint of water, saturate the stained area, and scrub with a clean cloth or sponge.

A commercial product named Whisk-Away is effective in removing rust stains from porcelain sinks and kitchen appliances.

Soup and Sauce Stains

For fabric soiled by gravy, mayonnaise, soup, or salad dressing, apply Dry Spotter to the stain. Using an absorbent pad, keep the area moist with Dry Spotter until the stain has been removed, then sponge with water.

If the above procedure is not effective, apply a few drops of liquid dishwashing detergent and a few drops of ammonia, again using a pad of absorbent material. Keep the area moist until the stain has been removed, then sponge with water. Stubborn stains can be treated with a detergent containing an enzyme product.

Starch Stains

In washable fabrics, stains caused by too much starch should be soaked for 20 minutes in a solution of one quart warm water, one-half teaspoon liquid dishwashing detergent, and one tablespoon ammonia. Then, rinse with water. Stubborn stains can be treated with a laundry detergent containing an enzyme product.

Nonwashable fabrics should be treated by applying Wet Spotter with a few drops of ammonia, and blotting with a moist pad of absorbent material until the stain has been removed.

Sugar Stains

To remove sugar stains it is wise to keep handy a small bottle consisting of eight tablespoons of liquid dishwashing detergent to which one spoonful of glycerin has been added. Rub the area with a clean cloth.

Syrup Stains

Corn or maple syrup, molasses, cough syrup, and caramelized sugar can be the cause of bothersome stains. Soak washables for 15 minutes in a solution of one quart warm water, one-half teaspoon liquid dishwashing detergent, and one tablespoon vinegar. Rinse with water. Stubborn stains can be treated with a laundry detergent containing an enzyme product.

Nonwashable fabrics should be treated by applying Wet Spotter with a few drops of vinegar and blotting with a moist pad of absorbent material until the stain has been removed.

Treating for two minutes with a one-to-one solution of chlorine bleach and water may be necessary to remove lingering stains caused by caramelized sugar. Test first for colorfastness. Flush with water after treatment.

Tar Stains

- Tar stains sometimes can be softened by applying Vaseline. Then, a product containing carbon tetrachloride, such as Renuzit, should be applied to the softened tar with a sponge and rubbed until the stain disappears.
- Tar stains on clothing may appear hopeless but will usually yield to an application of Dry Spotter. Using an absorbent pad, keep the area moist with Dry Spotter until the stain has been removed. Then, sponge with water.
- If the above procedure is not effective, apply Wet Spotter and a few drops of ammonia, again using a pad of absorbent material. Keep the area moist until the stain has been removed, then sponge with water.

Tea Stains

For removing tea stains, follow the same procedure as for coffee stains (page 190).

Tobacco Stains

Tobacco stains can be removed by soaking washables for 15 minutes in a solution of one quart warm water, one-half teaspoon liquid dishwashing detergent, and one tablespoon vinegar. Rinse with water. Stubborn stains can be treated with a laundry detergent containing an enzyme product.

Nonwashable fabrics should be treated by applying Wet Spotter with a few drops of vinegar, then blotting with a moist pad of absorbent material until the stains have been removed.

If stains persist, treat for two minutes with a one-to-one solution of chlorine bleach and water. Test first for colorfastness. Flush with water after treatment.

Toiletry Stains

Remove stains caused by toothpaste, shaving cream, suntan lotion, and home permanent solutions by soaking washables for 15 minutes in a solution of one quart warm water, one-half teaspoon liquid detergent, and one tablespoon vinegar. Rinse with water. Stubborn stains can be treated with a laundry detergent containing an enzyme product.

Nonwashable fabrics should be treated by applying Wet Spotter with a few drops of vinegar and blotting with a moist pad of absorbent material until the stain has been removed.

Treating for two minutes with a one-to-one solution of chlorine bleach and water may be necessary to remove lingering stains caused by suntan lotion. Test for colorfastness before applying. Flush with water after treatment.

More Toiletry Stains

Washable fabrics that have been stained by bath oil, after-shave lotion, mouthwash, or eyedrops should be soaked for 20 minutes in a solution of one quart warm water, one-half teaspoon liquid dishwashing detergent, and one tablespoon ammonia. Then, rinse with water. Stubborn stains can be treated with a laundry detergent containing an enzyme product.

Nonwashable fabrics should be treated by applying Wet Spotter with a few drops of ammonia, then blotting with a moist pad of absorbent material until the stain has been removed.

Urine on Rugs

Dried urine is difficult to remove, but try sponging the soiled area with vinegar or pure bleach. Test first for colorfastness.

It is best to act quickly to remove urine. After blotting up as much as possible, saturate the area with cool water, then apply a dishwashing detergent solution. Rinse again with water.

Urine-stained Clothing

Warm, soapy water to which a small amount of ammonia has been added will take out most urine stains. Rub well, then wash the garment in a washing machine or rinse well by hand.

Vinegar and Lemon Juice Stains

To remove stains caused by acids in such foods as vinegar and lemon juice use a solution of one part ammonia to eight parts water. After application, rinse, blot, and dry.

Water Stains

To remove water stains, dip a soft cotton cloth in spirits of camphor and rub well. Or, if you prefer, prepare a solution of one part ammonia, one part turpentine, and one part linseed oil. Stir thoroughly, then apply to the stained area. This solution is also recommended for wood surfaces.

To remove water stains from stainless steel or chrome trim in the kitchen or bath, try using club soda. Rubbing alcohol also helps to remove water stains from stainless steel.

Wax and Polish Stains

To remove fabric stains caused by floor wax, furniture polish, or shoe polish, apply Dry Spotter. Using an absorbent pad, keep the area moist with Dry Spotter, and when the stain has disappeared, sponge with water.

If the above procedure is not effective, apply Wet Spotter and a few drops of ammonia, again using a pad of absorbent material. Keep the area moist until the stain has disappeared, then sponge with water.

To remove the final traces of stain caused by wax and polish, use a solution of one teaspoon chlorine bleach to one teaspoon water. Apply with a dropper for no longer than two minutes. Flush with water, apply one teaspoon of vinegar to the stain, and flush with water again.

Wine Stains

Blot wine stains immediately with an absorbent cloth or paper napkin. If possible, place absorbent material under the stained area. Apply tap water to the area and continue blotting. If the stain persists, stretch the fabric over a bowl, apply salt, and pour hot water over it.

Alternatively, apply cold water as soon as possible and then sponge with glycerin and a detergent or with a solution of equal parts water and vinegar. Rinse with warm water. To remove any discoloration that remains apply a few drops of ammonia.

Hardened Wax

Hardened wax on a fabric can be scraped off with a dull-edged knife without damaging the material. If the stain remains after pouring hot water over the remaining wax, rub the area with acetone or a dry-cleaning solvent, then rinse off with water. Apply more solvent if the stain persists.

15
Clothing Care

Introduction

It is said that "clothing makes the man." It is equally true that clothing can *break* the man . . . and the woman. With the high cost of clothing, it is important to get maximum mileage out of our purchases, and nothing is more vital in this regard than proper cleaning. Our instincts, for example, tell us that the hotter the water, the cleaner the clothes. But, modern cleaning agents, formulated to maintain colors and pamper fine fabrics, often work as well or better with cold water.

In deciding on cleaning strategy, it is vital to consider the type of fabric being laundered. Much of the guesswork is removed by the care labels found in so many garments. A garment label requiring dry cleaning should not be ignored. Nor should a warning not to clean with dark colors. Though the proper cleaning agent exists for almost every source of grime, some of these substances are highly potent. It is thus wise practice to always test a substance on a nonvisible corner of the garment before committing it to a visible part of the garment.

The drying phase is crucial to any cleaning operation. Not all garments are suited to high-heat drying. In cases, the garment will shrink; in other cases, the elastic in the garment will lose its stretch. If you are not certain that an item of clothing can withstand a dryer, allow it to air-dry, or subject it to just enough machine drying to fluff it after most of the moisture has evaporated. Certain garments, such as fine wool sweaters, are best done by hand. Spread such garments—wet, without distorting the garment shape—on a towel so that they retain their original shape.

KEEPING YOUR CLOTHES CLEAN AND FRESH

Read the Label

Before trying to remove a stain from a garment, read the label. The law requires that clothing must have attached to it a permanent label giving instructions for its proper care and cleaning.

When Dry Cleaning Is a Must

A fabric in its pure state may be washable, but one with a multicolored print design or with trim in contrasting color should be sent to a dry cleaner. If washed at home with soap and water, the dyes may run. Naturally, it is imperative that clothes labeled "Dry Clean Only" be treated in just that manner.

Professional Dry Cleaning

If a label states "Professionally Dry Clean Only," do not try to wash or attempt to remove stains at home unless you own the proper chemicals or cleaning agents. Incidentally, the term "French Dry Cleaning" has no practical meaning today.

Hand Wash Only

Garments bearing labels that state "Hand Wash Only" should not be dry cleaned. They should be laundered in water no hotter than lukewarm, using a suitable cleaning agent, such as dishwashing liquid.

Help the Dry Cleaner

Your garment will be returned to you with the stain cleanly removed if you tell the dry cleaner what caused the stain. He is not always able to determine the cause by simply looking at the garment. Always show the dry cleaner exactly where the stains are located. Competent establishments will mark the spot with a sticker.

Dry Cleaning Vinyls

Some vinyl articles are resistant to dry-cleaning solvents, while many others are likely to be damaged by solvents. Dry-cleaning solvents may remove the plasticizers from garments and cause them to stiffen.

If removal of an oil or grease stain is attempted, the procedure should consist of very lightly sponging the surface of the vinyl with a cloth barely dampened with dry-cleaning solvent. Do not make more than a few strokes. Repeated rubbing will remove the plasticizer and may change the appearance of the vinyl surface.

Stain-removal procedures using water and liquid detergent with vinegar or ammonia are usually safe for vinyl. Test a hidden hem before trying to remove the stain. A blotting action is the safest method for treating stains on vinyl.

Washable Clothing

Any garment carrying a label indicating that it is washable can either be laundered by machine or dry cleaned. Normal machine washing is safe.

Color Test for Bleach

Before using bleach on colored fabric, test the effect by mixing one tablespoon of bleach with one-quarter cup of water. Dab the solution on a hidden seam, hemline, or cuff. Wait one minute, then blot dry with a paper towel. If there is no change in color, the fabric can be safely washed with the bleach.

Prevent Running

To prevent colored fabrics from running, first soak the garments in cold water to which vinegar has been added. Then, wash in the usual manner.

Colored Trimmings

Colored garments or garments with colored trimmings such as collars, cuffs, or monograms should not be washed with all-white clothes unless the label on the garment indicates that it is colorfast.

Premix Detergent

Some detergent packages require that the detergent be premixed with water before clothing is added to the washing machine. This insures a more uniform distribution of the cleaning agent than is the case when the detergent is simply scattered over the clothing before water is added. Fill the drum one-third with water, add detergent, swish around with your hand, then place the clothing in the drum and allow it to fill with water.

Water Temperature

In running a washing machine, use hot water for white cottons and diapers and warm water for permanent press, bright colors, and delicate fabrics. Use cold water for colors that fade or bleed.

Mixing White Fabrics in Washing Machine

All-white nylon or polyester garments may be safely washed with white cotton fabrics provided that the former can stand the high water temperature used for cottons.

Presoaking

Soiled clothing will come out cleaner if it is presoaked before being put in the washing machine. The simple procedure involves rinsing off the heavy soil then pouring on the soiled area a product such as Wisk, Fab, or Tide and allowing the clothing to stand for about 15 to 30 minutes. Rinse off, then place in the washing machine. Avoid presoaking for an extended period, because this may cause the dye to run, even on a colorfast garment.

Heat on Garments

Garments containing the warning "Dry Away From Heat" should never be placed in a clothes dryer, even at a low temperature setting.

Ring-Around-the-Collar

The detergent industry has made millions with products they claim can successfully remove "ring-around-the-collar" and other yellow oil stains from light fabrics. A recent study by the Department of Textiles and Apparel at Cornell University, however, shows that unless the culprit dirt is removed soon after it has been deposited, no laundry product is likely to clean the garment. In just one week, the study found, the oil can react with the cellulose fibers in the cloth, changing its color as if it had been dyed.

Preventing Collar Stains

To prevent a ring from forming around the collar of your shirt or dress, dab Witch Hazel or another astringent around your neck. Another method is to apply talcum powder to the back of the neck to absorb the oil. This will reduce, if not completely eliminate the ring problem.

Oil Stains on Clothing

Cotton and polyester shirts and blouses whose collars and cuffs may have absorbed oil stains caused by skin secretions from the neck or wrist should first be soaked with a detergent that identifies itself as an "enzyme presoak."

Stained Handkerchiefs

Badly stained dishcloths and handkerchiefs can be restored to a natural state by first washing them thoroughly with warm suds and then leaving the articles in a solution of three tablespoons of bleach added to a quart of cold or lukewarm water. Allow them to sit in the bleach solution for about five minutes, then rinse well.

Acetate Fabrics

Even though manufacturers offer laundering instructions for acetate garments, it is always wise to have such clothing dry cleaned. Laundering must be done with great care.

Acetate Velvet Pile

Velvets with acetate pile should never be treated with a stain remover that contains water. Even the slightest rubbing can damage the matting.

Loosely Woven Fabrics

Loosely woven fabrics and fabrics woven from low-twist yarns are likely to suffer yarn slippage if brushed or rubbed while wet.

Stains on Silk

Silk fabrics are generally not compatible with water and therefore require dry cleaning. However, some garments can be washed with water. Check the label on the garment.

Washable silk garments can best be cleaned by hand in lukewarm water to which has been added a teaspoon of borax to soften the water. (Never use chlorine bleach on silks.) Dry by rolling in a towel, then hang on a hanger.

STORING AND MAINTAINING YOUR WARDROBE

Giving Clothes Air

Before hanging in a closet or placing in a drawer the clothing you wore during the day, allow it to air out for an hour or two. It is wise to leave bureau drawers and closet doors slightly ajar.

Resting Wearing Apparel

Garments and shoes will last longer and be refreshed and odor-free if not worn for two consecutive days.

Mothproofing a Closet

Clothes closets can be made mothproof by lining the walls with thin pieces of cedar. Try to locate pieces that are one-quarter inch thick. The wood has a strong fragrance that repels moths. Attach with nails or glue to your closet walls.

Preventing Moth Damage

When storing woolen sweaters, coats, and suits for the summer, stack some mothballs or whole cloves into the pockets of the garments. The odor will repel the moths.

Doorless Closets

Where closet door swing space is limited, consider removing the door and instead hanging a full-length bamboo blind over the closet opening. The blind is not only decorative but will keep your clothes from full view while providing adequate ventilation. An accordion door is another option for places where door swing space is limited.

Herbs in Closets

Leaving a sachet of dried herbs in drawers and closets will help keep clothing fresh-smelling.

Damp Closet Cures

Clothing stored in a damp closet is apt to be smelly and subject to mildew. One cure is proper ventilation. Either leave the closet door open for several hours a day, or replace the old door with a louver door.

Another solution is to provide some heat to remove the dampness. One means of doing so is to install a 60-watt closet light. Be careful that the closet bulb does not present a fire hazard (see page 237).

Wrinkled Clothes

Put a terry cloth towel dampened with water in the closet with newly unpacked wrinkled clothes and close the door. In a few hours most of the wrinkles will disappear. Before hanging, give the clothing a thorough shaking.

If you hang your clothes on hangers while the garments still retain your body heat, wrinkles will fall away more quickly.

Wrinkled Wool

Wrinkled wool and wool mixture suits that do not appear badly wrinkled when first unpacked can usually be worn immediately because most of the wrinkles will disappear in about an hour.

Garment Steaming

After wearing tailored clothes, particularly silk and wool, for a whole day, hang them in the bathroom while bathing or showering. The steam will rid the fabric of wrinkles as it deodorizes it.

Wooden Hangers

Some wooden hangers are rough and cause damage to clothes. To keep wooden hangers from snagging clothing, run sandpaper over them lightly, then coat with clear shellac.

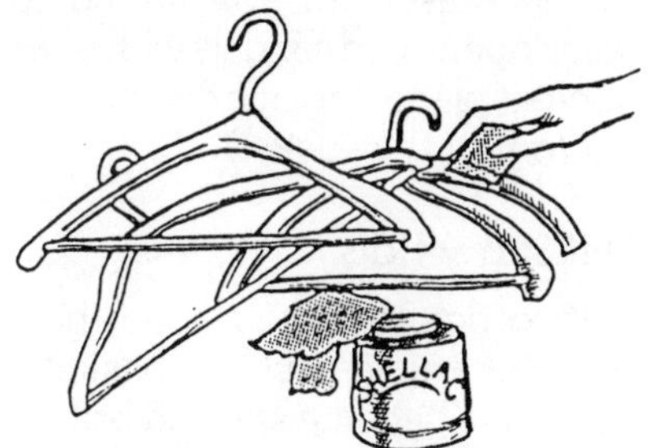

Wire Hangers

Avoid using wire hangers whenever possible. Clothes lose their shape when hung on them regularly. Wooden and heavy-duty plastic hangers are preferred. If you must use wire hangers, place two together for added strength.

Homemade Garment Bags

Make your own garment bag to protect suits and dresses by slitting old pillow cases at the sewn end just enough to pull them over hangers holding the garments.

Buttoning Clothes

To be assured that clothes will hang straight, close the top button on all garments.

Belt Shape

A belt will keep its shape if, when not worn, it is hung in a closet by the buckle.

Shelving Knitwear

Most knits stretch and lose their shape when hung on hangers. Lay sweaters and the like on closet shelves or in dresser drawers.

Freshening Suede Gloves

To freshen suede gloves, put them on your hands and rub with a slice of stale bread. Use thick slices if you can. When the bread appears to be sufficiently soiled, take another slice and repeat the process.

Getting Rid of "Pills"

Safety-razor blades can be used successfully to remove "pills" and fuzz that form on sweaters and other woolen garments. An electric razor blade works well on nylon and polyester fabrics.

Buzz-Off, a battery-operated clothes shaver specifically designed for this purpose, is available in most variety stores.

Storing Lace

To keep lace looking better longer, store lace articles in wax paper. It will help keep the threads from rotting.

Storing Fur

Fur stored in humidified closets will look better and last longer. You can make your own humidifier by placing a bowl of water with a sponge in it in the closet. Add water periodically to replace the water that has evaporated.

Removing Hairs

Removing animal hair or lint from clothing with a whisk broom is almost impossible. One effective method of doing so is to use adhesive tape or a piece of moistened masking tape. Press the sticky side lightly against the surface of the clothing several times and you will succeed in picking up most, if not all, of the lint and hairs.

Reconditioning Nylon, Dacron, and Orlon

To whiten yellowed or grayed nylon, dacron, or orlon, use two tablespoons (one-eighth cup) of bleach to one gallon of lukewarm water. Immerse the fabric in the solution for about 20 minutes. Rinse with clean water. Repeat if necessary.

The Missing Sock

To solve the perennial mystery of the sock that seems to disappear in the washing process, pin each pair together before placing them in the washing machine. You will, of course, want to be careful not to damage delicate fabrics.

Pairing Socks

To reduce the time you spend pairing socks after washing, consider using an indelible marker to code the socks. Mark the same letter or number on the toe of each sock partner. The appearance of the sock will not be harmed and your work load will be decreased. (If you intend to wear open-toed sandals with your socks, place the marks on the *bottom* of the socks.)

Stiff Straw Hats

In order to soften straw hats or other articles, such as baskets, that have become stiff and brittle, wipe with a cloth saturated with glycerin.

Stubborn Zippers

If a zipper does not slide easily, do not rush to have it replaced. First try spraying lightly with graphite or rubbing with a lead pencil. If this does not work, use a lubricant such as WD40. Squirt some on your fingers, then rub it into the zipper. Be careful not to soil the garment when applying the lubricant.

Longer Life for Buttons

After sewing a button onto a garment, dab some clear nail polish on the thread in the center of the button and the repair will last much longer.

Soap as a Pin Cushion

Keep a bar of soap (wrapped in a piece of cloth if you like) in your sewing basket and use it to hold pins and needles. The soap will also serve to lubricate the pins and needles, making them easier to push into fabrics.

Attracting Pins and Needles

To reach those elusive pins and needles in your sewing basket, keep a magnet handy and reach in to attract them.

ALL ABOUT FOOTWEAR

On Buying Shoes

The best time to buy shoes is late afternoon. By that time your feet will have expanded. This is especially true in hot weather. If you buy shoes in the morning, they are likely to pinch your feet by afternoon.

Also, it is good to remember that since one foot is usually larger than the other, it is wise to make sure that the shoes you buy fit the larger foot comfortably.

Protecting New Shoes

Polish new shoes before wearing them for the first time. Also, if you wish to add years of good wear to shoes, polish them frequently. This will keep the leather fresh and soft.

Changing Shoes

Double the life of shoes by changing them daily. Shoes need air circulation to keep them fresh and to allow the perspiration that collects in them to evaporate.

Hardened Shoe Polish

Hardened shoe polish in a metal container can be softened by heating the container in a pot of water.

Opening a Shoe Polish Can

If you are among those who are always looking for a coin (or similar object) to pry open a shoe polish can, try the following: Simply select a washer of the correct thickness. Screw it to the handle end of the polishing brush so that it protrudes about one-quarter inch. Use the washer as a handy can opener.

Shoe Polish Applicator

One of the softest applicators for shoe polish is a powder puff. If you decide to use a puff instead of a brush, make sure it is new and clean.

A Substitute Shoe Polish

In an emergency, floor wax can be used as shoe polish. Since floor wax is neutral in color, it can be used on light- or dark-colored shoes.

The Best Leather Polish

Wax polish is best for leather shoes. Rub hard after applying the polish in order to obtain a sparkling and durable shine. Liquid wax self-shining polishes are generally alcohol-based and tend to dry up leather by smothering the surface pores.

Soiled Shoes

To remove oil stains or other street grime from the heels and soles of shoes wipe them with turpentine or any paint thinner.

Salty Shoes

The salt that is dispensed on the streets to melt ice during the cold winter months can be very damaging to shoes. Use a mixture of water and vinegar to get rid of the salt buildup.

Touching Up Scuffed Shoes

Black acrylic paint or paint used to touch up cars is useful in restoring badly scuffed shoes. A wax crayon of the same color can also do a good job.

Scuffed Shoes

If you have scuffed shoes that do not hold shoe polish when it is applied, try rubbing the scuffed portions with alcohol before applying the polish.

Waterproofing Shoes

To waterproof shoes and boots, rub on saddle soap or spray on a lanolin-based compound such as neat's-foot oil. Products of this type are available in shoemaker shops and some pharmacies.

Restoring Rain-soaked Shoes

Shoes that have become rain-soaked take two days to dry out, and when they do, the leather is left stiff and hard. To restore wet shoes, clean them with saddle soap while they are still damp, and let the soap remain on them while they dry. Remove the dried soap with a slightly damp soft cloth in 48 hours.

If the shoes are very wet, stuff them with paper toweling to preserve the shape.

Slippery Soles

Slippery soles are dangerous. Correct the problem by sandpapering the soles lightly. It is especially important to do this on children's shoes as a slip prevention measure.

Spots on Suede

A good way of removing stains on suede shoes, hats, and handbags is to brush the surfaces gently with an emery board.

Suede Shoes

To keep suede shoes looking good, rub them with a dry sponge (or try a piece of stale bread) after each wearing.

Another method of keeping suede shoes in condition is to first remove all dust and dirt particles, then hold the shoes, one at a time, over a pot of boiling water or some other source of steam. When the nap has been raised, stroke the raised nap with a soft brush and allow the shoes to dry thoroughly before wearing them.

Cleaning Patent Leather

One way to clean patent leather is to saturate a clean rag with vinegar and rub well until all blemishes disappear.

Cleaning Shoebrushes

From time to time shoebrushes must be cleaned. Soak them for one-half hour in warm, sudsy water to which a few drops of turpentine have been added. After soaking, hang up to drip dry.

Patent Leather Shoes

Cold weather often affects patent leather shoes, causing them to crack. You can protect against this by applying a slight film of petroleum jelly to the shoes. Then, polish with a clean cloth.

Shoe Eyelets

Metal eyelets on shoes often become discolored as a result of the pressure exerted on them by the shoelaces. You can prevent this discoloration by coating the eyelets with shellac, which is colorless. To do this, first remove the shoelaces.

Frayed Shoestrings

When the metal or plastic tips come off shoestrings, the material frays quickly. To prevent fraying, dip the ends in hot paraffin, twist, and allow to dry thoroughly. Dipping the shoestring tips in nail polish is also an effective way of preventing the ends from separating.

Sneaker Cleaning

Canvas sneakers can be cleaned in the washing machine, using hot water. Wash together with soft articles of clothing to reduce the knocking as the sneakers spin. Dry in fresh air.

Leather sneakers can be cared for in the same manner as leather shoes.

16
Coping With the Seasons

Introduction

Which is worse, the heat of summer or the cold of winter? In answer to that much-asked question, most people seem to choose winter. And with good reason. Extreme cold, experienced for even very short periods of time, can be painful and even life-threatening. Physical discomfort aside, the health hazards of summer can usually be relieved by getting out of the sun and replenishing depleted liquids.

Be it winter or summer, there is much that can be done to make our homes more comfortable. Where winter temperatures dip regularly into the 40s, all homes should be adequately insulated. Insulation traps air and keeps the warmth inside the house. Storm windows create an additional wind and air barrier between the outside and the inside. In the coldest climates, double-paned windows do an even better job. In emergencies, and where cost is a consideration, cutting sheets of plastic to size and thumb-tacking them to each window will do much to keep a house warm.

With the availability of low-energy models, air conditioners are more affordable than ever before. If the added electric cost is a burden, however, or if you are just one of those who does not like the noise and sensation of air conditioning, do not short-shrift the electric fan. An average-size electric fan consumes as much electricity as a 40-watt bulb and costs 10¢ or less per 24-hour day to operate compared to several dollars for an air conditioner.

As much as by controlling the environment, the effects of heat and cold can be mitigated by the clothing that we wear. It has long been known that dressing in layers in winter, which traps body heat, is the most effective means of combatting cold. Equally important is to realize that the extremities—the head, the hands, the feet—drain the body's heat most rapidly. The head, in particular, functions very much as a chimney expelling heat in short order. Bald people, beware! Thus, if you want to keep warm, wear a hat, gloves, and socks. In summer, try the reverse: wear single-layered cotton clothing (which absorbs perspiration) and take along a hat to shield the sun's rays. And don't neglect Baseball Hall of Famer Satchel Paige's summer advice: "Move slowly and think cool thoughts."

KEEPING WARM IN WINTER

Preparing for Winter

Prepare for winter immediately after Thanksgiving:

- Remove screens and store them flat. If they need repair or painting, this is the time to do it.
- Clean window frames and door frames before fitting storm doors and windows. If caulking is needed around the frames, do it now.
- Insulate any exposed plumbing pipes that are likely to freeze.

Winter Mode for Storm/Screen Combos

Storm/screen combinations typically come with two storm windows and one screen. Both storm windows are kept in the up mode in summer, but many people lower the wrong storm window in winter. To be sure that you have lowered the correct window, check to see that the upper window fits into the upper track, leaving no gap between the top of the window and the track.

Keeping Out Cold

To prevent cold air from coming in through cracks at the top, bottom, and middle portion of

your windows, open the window, place folded cloth or newspaper at those points, and close the window tight. This will make an instant tight seal.

Frost-free Windows

To keep frost from forming on your windows in cold weather, rub the outside with alcohol or salt water and then polish the surface with newspaper.

Use the Sun's Warmth

If you are blessed with a southern exposure, exploit it in the winter to reduce your heating bills. Even in temperatures well below freezing, enough warmth will filter through a picture window on a winter day so that no additional heating will be required. To conserve the day's heat, cover the window at sundown and keep it covered on cloudy days.

Glycerin as an Antifreeze

Glycerin is an antifreeze agent. It is recommended that two tablespoons of glycerin be added to water to be used to wash windows in cold weather. Rubbing alcohol will serve the same purpose. Both leave a film on the glass that will prevent the window from icing up.

Drafty Doors

If too much of a draft is coming in through the bottom of an outside door, correct the situation by attaching a simple device available in practically any hardware store: an aluminum frame with a movable strip of neoprene. The strip drops to the floor when the door is shut and lifts up when opened.

There is also available a less expensive frame in which a strip of plastic or rubber can be moved

up and down manually. Either product will help conserve energy in the summertime and in the wintertime.

Tacking a piece of heavy cloth to the inside bottom of the door and letting it drag on the floor is a do-it-yourself solution to the problem.

Rock Salt Caution

The use of an excessive amount of rock salt to deal with ice in winter is discouraged because it has the potential of seeping down to the root systems of plants and interfering with the chemical balance in the soil. It can also cause the yellowing of tree shrub leaves. Sand is a safer solution to the winter ice problem.

Snow Shovels

To prevent snow from sticking to a shovel, cover the shovel with wax before using. The wax can be applied manually, or it can be sprayed on.

Preventing Locks From Freezing

Before winter sets in, squirt WD40, a nonoily lubricant, into all keyholes exposed to rain and snow. It will prevent them from freezing.

Frozen Padlocks

Ice or snow that accumulates on a padlock can seep into the lock and cause freezing and subsequent rusting. It is, therefore,

a good idea to protect the lock by placing a piece of tape over the keyhole and a piece of leather or plastic over the entire lock.

Frozen Locks

If you can't get your key into a keyhole or turn a lock that seems to be frozen, squirt very hot water into it or over it and the difficulty will usually be solved.

An alternative is to heat the key with a match, insert it into the keyhole, and turn gently. Repeat if necessary. Take care not to burn your fingers.

Homemade Storm Windows

To make your own storm window, measure the size of the window. Cut an oversized piece of heavyweight clear plastic large enough so that the plastic can be doubled over around the outer moldings of the window. Tack or staple through the bunching around the window's edge. This makeshift storm window will provide a relatively airtight seal that will keep the house warmer and reduce heating bills.

Hot-water Bags

To temporarily mend a rubber hot-water bag that has sprung a leak, dry it off thoroughly and apply a piece of adhesive tape over the leaky spot. For permanent repair, apply an inner-tube patch. Kits of inner-tube patching materials can be purchased at automotive supply stores or bicycle shops.

Cold-weather Attire

The best way to keep warm in cold weather is to dress in layers, one garment over another. The warmth generated by the body is trapped in the air between the layers.

Gloves for Winter Wear

The best gloves for winter wear are mittens. If your gloves have fingers, you will keep warmer in cold weather if you allow the glove fingers to hang limp while you curl up your own fingers, forming a fist inside the glove. In extreme cold, a pair of light wool gloves placed inside a pair of mittens will provide exceptional warmth.

Wear a Hat

If you're cold in the winter, make sure to wear a hat. The head functions as both a thermostat and a chimney. The best way to conserve body heat, therefore, is to cover the head. Woolen ski caps are most effective. Conversely, if you feel overheated after winter outdoor exercise, remove your hat.

Chapped Hands

There are times when it is necessary to work outdoors in cold weather without gloves. At such times, hands should be protected from chapping. Castor oil rubbed into the hands before going outdoors and when coming back inside will offer that protection.

Keeping Your Feet Warm

Use two pairs of socks to keep warmer. The air barrier between them serves as effective insulation. Placing baggies over your socks will keep your feet warmer, but it will also deprive the feet of air circulation.

Exercise for Warmth

In winter, the body sometimes becomes chilled and no amount of clothing will relieve it. One remedy is to exercise—run in place, do sit-ups, walk up and down the stairs—until the body heats up. An alternative for the leisure-seeking is to sit in a hot tub.

Rugs Add Warmth

Most people know about the virtues of insulating a house to keep cozy-warm in winter. Many, however, overlook the fact that carpets and rugs add immeasurably to the warmth of a house. Even if you prefer bare flooring, covering the floor with a rug in winter is a good comfort and energy-conservation strategy.

Thicker Is Warmer, So Are Layers

The thicker a blanket, the warmer it will be. Test the nap of a wool blanket by giving it a squeeze then releasing it; the nap should spring back.

On exceptionally cold nights, cover yourself with a second blanket. The same "layers increase warmth" principle that applies to clothing also applies to bedding.

Electric Blankets

Make an electric blanket for a king-size bed by sewing together two twin-size electric blankets. Not only will this cost about 20 percent less than a king-size electric blanket, but it will also offer dual control of heat.

Cardboard as Fireplace Kindling

Small slivers of wood and small-diameter branches are commonly used to generate sufficient heat to allow larger pieces of fireplace wood to ignite. In place of these, try pieces of cardboard cut from corrugated boxes. Cut or tear the cardboard into roughly two- or three-inch squares, and place them on top of the paper and beneath the heavier wood. In addition to the substantial heat-generating capacity of the cardboard, the corrugations improve the flow of air critical to combustion.

Adjust the Damper

When starting a fire, the fireplace damper should be opened maximally to provide the new fire with proper draft. Once the fire has settled into its burning routine, however, the damper should be adjusted according to the nature of the fire. Leave the damper open if you want a large hot fire. If you want a smaller fire that will burn more slowly, close the damper a notch or two, monitoring for smoke. Never close the damper completely or the room will fill with smoke.

Starting a Fire

Many a fireplace fire fails to start because those who build it overpack it with wood and paper. To start a fire most efficiently, space two pieces of four-inch diameter wood one foot apart. Next, crumple a single, large sheet of newspaper (using too much paper will impede the development of the fire) and place it between the two floor logs. Cover the newspaper with five to ten pieces of cardboard (see previous hint) and then, with progressively larger diameter wood, build a log cabin. Make sure that the second tier wood is no more than two inches in diameter.

When choosing wood to start a fire, avoid round wood or wood with bark on it. Bare, split, rough-textured wood provides superior burning surface. Crucial in starting a fire is providing sufficient draft for the fire to ignite. Any material—paper, cardboard, wood—if too heavily packed, works against this.

Fireplace Aroma

To add a sweet smell to the house when using the fireplace, from time to time throw apple, lemon, or orange rinds onto the burning logs—or do the same with dried aromatic herbs.

The Best Wood for Logs

Do not use logs cut from soft wood such as pine, fire, and cedar. These burn quickly and send off many sparks. They also coat the chimney with creosote, which is flammable. Hardwoods are denser and generate more heat, so try to purchase oak, walnut, and fruitwood logs. They are sometimes more costly but are well worth the higher price. Regardless of the wood used, make sure it is well dried before burning.

Storing Fireplace Logs

Never store fireplace logs in your house. If you do, you might find that insects that have made their homes in the logs will eventually find their way into furniture and carpeting. Bring into the house only as much wood as will be used within one day's time.

Homemade Logs

Ecology and money-minded individuals who use a fireplace will be interested in learning that

"logs" can be made out of old newspapers and magazines. You can buy a portable logger, or you can roll your own.

Reducing Fireplace Soot

The amount of soot that accumulates in a fireplace will be greatly reduced if salt is sprinkled on the burning logs from time to time.

Cleaning a Fireplace Flue

If a fireplace that has always worked well suddenly begins to smoke, or if the logs burn sluggishly, you probably have an obstruction in the flue preventing the smoke from escaping through the chimney in a normal manner. Birds may have decided to make a nest in the flue, or possibly you burned old newspapers or gift wrappings and the ashes have clung to the walls of the chimney flue. Usually, the most effective solution is to tie a long rope to a sack that has been weighted with a few heavy rocks. Lower the sack down the flue, and raise it and lower it several times. This should dislodge the obstruction.

Fireplace Cleaning

To clean a brick fireplace that doesn't have glaring stains, scrub it down with Beatsall (available in hardware stores) and hot water. Use two tablespoons per gallon. After using the Beatsall-water solution, rinse with clear water. When undertaking this job, wear rubber gloves and use an old terry towel or something similar for scrubbing.

Chimney Downdraft Cure

If a chimney is subject to downdrafts, the fireplace will not function properly and the house will be filled with smoke. Downdrafts occur when outside air is sucked into the chimney, and this can happen if the chimney is not at least two feet higher than any other part of the house roof, or if there are other obstructions nearby, such as trees that are taller than the house. This can be rectified by adding two or more layers of brick to the chimney, by capping it to make a smaller opening, or by doing both. You can test whether capping will solve the problem by cutting a hole smaller than the chimney opening in a piece of metal and securing it temporarily to the top of the chimney. If this smaller opening solves the problem, make a permanent opening of that size with brick or stone. If that doesn't work, extend the height of the chimney.

KEEPING COOL IN SUMMER

Cold Water for Hot Days

Fill a plastic gallon jug (such as a milk container) with water, then freeze. When frozen, move it from the freezer to the refrigerator. As the ice melts in the container, you'll have a good supply of cold drinking water that can be poured off as needed.

As the water in the jug is used up, replace it with fresh water until the ice is completely melted. This generally takes three or four days. Keep another jug in the freezer while the first one is defrosting.

Draw Window Shades in Hot Weather

A great deal of heat is absorbed through window glass. So, keep electric bills down by keeping the window shades drawn while the air conditioner is running.

Air Conditioning

It is best to turn on an air conditioner before a room gets hot. The unit uses up much more energy to cool off a very hot room than to maintain the temperature of a cool one.

Mounting an Air Conditioner

When mounting a window air conditioner, make sure the portion hanging out of the window tilts downward so that the moisture being removed from the room does not return to the room.

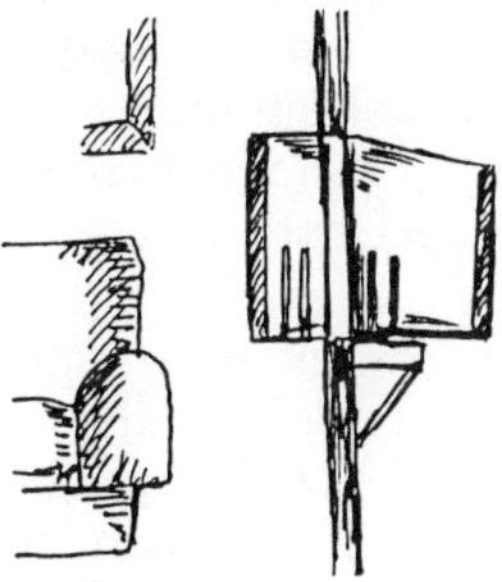

Air Conditioning Speeds

During extremely hot weather, set air conditioner thermostats high. In this way, more energy is saved than if the unit is set at a lower speed and constantly goes on and off.

Air Conditioner Protection

Try to protect your window air conditioner from the rays of the sun by covering it with some type of shading. When the hot sun hits the condenser that projects from the window, the unit has to work that much harder and as a result is more costly to run.

Air Conditioner Vent

The best way to run an air conditioner is to keep the vent closed at all times, except when the unit is being used as an exhaust to eliminate room odors.

Air Filters

Air conditioners contain air filters that must be washed periodically to remove accumulated grime and dust. A clogged filter puts extra strain on the air conditioner motor and increases the energy cost and reduces performance.

Foam air conditioner filters can be washed easily in the kitchen sink. Use dishwashing liquid with the water. Filters can also be cleaned well outdoors by shooting a stream of water at them with a garden hose. Allow to dry thoroughly before returning them to the air conditioner units.

Don't Shortsell the Electric Fan

The proliferation of air conditioning notwithstanding, the electric fan is still the most cost-effective and often the most convenient means of keeping cool in summer. Because, as the saying goes, what is most oppressive in summer is not the heat but the humidity, a fan—at low setting, blowing on you when you sleep and evaporating perspiration—often provides as much relief as an air conditioner, and for literally pennies per day. Also, fans are usually less noisy.

Exhaust Fans

An exhaust-style fan that fits into the window is an effective means of reducing room temperature. An exhaust fan placed in an attic will cool the house significantly. Such fans often operate automatically on thermostats.

Cross-ventilation

An open window will do nothing to relieve summer heat unless there is an outlet for the hot air. Always keep windows at opposite ends of the room open in hot weather to provide cross-ventilation. If only one window can be opened, make sure that it is opened top and bottom.

WAYS TO SAVE ENERGY THE YEAR ROUND

Home Energy-saver

The best way to make a home more energy-efficient is to fix broken or cracked windows and seal window frames if they are not tight, especially in places where slivers of light shine through.

Caulk to Save Energy

To help conserve fuel during the heating season and electricity during air conditioning season, check the outside of your house regularly and seal up cracks, particularly around windows. Use a caulking gun with a good grade of caulking compound. Latex caulking compounds are the least expensive, and they bond well to most surfaces.

Conserving Room Energy

Even if your home is adequately insulated, caulked and weatherstripped, you save additional energy as follows:

- Make sure radiator covers do not restrict the flow of heat. At least 75% of the surface of a radiator cover should be a grille to allow for free heat flow.
- Cover the floors with rugs or carpets. They offer much more insulation than tile, linoleum, wood or slate. The thicker the carpet, the greater the insulation value. Wool and acrylic fibers provide the best insulation.
- Position your furniture far enough away from radiators and vents to permit free circulation of heated or cooled air.
- Much radiator heat warms up the wall rather than the room.

Aluminum foil placed behind radiators will help reflect heat back into the room.

Insulation "R" Factor

When buying insulation for your house, don't just look for a low price. Consider the "R" factor, which is a measure of resistance to heat. The higher the "R" value, the more efficient the insulation.

Storm Windows

Storm windows can keep electric bills down in the summer as well as in the winter. If your house is air conditioned, keep the lower glass of the storm window in the same position in summer as in winter. The cool air will not be dissipated as quickly.

17
Plumbing & Heating Electric & Lighting

Introduction

Of all the do-it-yourself tasks that can be performed in the home, plumbing and heating offer the fewest options. The skills and knowledge necessary to solder pipes, open systems under pressure, and reset tolerances are not quickly acquired. Nonetheless, there are tasks which the homeowner can safely handle, and mastering them can save considerable service expense. These include changing washers in leaky faucets, resetting sink stoppers that do not seat correctly, and relieving clogged sink drains and toilets. Before performing any plumbing or heating repairs, however, it is essential to acquire the appropriate tools. Using pliers to remove a drain plug when a wrench is needed, or a flat screwdriver in place of a Phillips, can turn a routine task into a nightmare.

Simple electric and lighting work can be safely attempted by those otherwise daunted by technical tasks. Appliances should be disconnected from the electrical source and the electrical system itself turned off (by closing a circuit breaker or removing a fuse) while repair work is underway. Frayed wires and faulty plugs on appliances are easily replaced; dimmers can be installed to create a whole range of lighting effects; lamp sockets can be replaced; and outdated or unpleasing permanent fixtures can be replaced with new ones. Though the work is often unfamiliar, the task may require no more than replacing the old with the new. The first rule when doing any electrical work on a live system is to isolate the circuit on which you will be working and disable it. This is easily accomplished by activating the switch or receptacle on which you will work and flipping breaker switches until it is deactivated.

PLUMBING AND HEATING BASICS

Identify the Main Cut-off Valve

As a homeowner, you will find it helpful if an identifying tag is placed on the main water cut-off valve. Each family member should be shown the location of the cut-off valve and be told how to use it. This knowledge will spare water damage should a break develop in the water line.

Hard-water Test

If you are not sure whether the water in your house is hard or soft, test it by adding one teaspoon of powdered laundry detergent to one-half gallon of warm water. If, after shaking the mixture, suds do not appear, or if they appear but then disappear quickly, the water is hard. Since hard water produces a mineral coating on plumbing pipes, consult with a plumber to determine if the problem is sufficiently serious to require a water softener.

Unclogging Drains

- While commercial drain uncloggers such as Drano and Plumber's Helper do an effective job, you can keep kitchen and bathroom drains in good working order by pouring one-half to one full gallon of boiling hot sudsy water into them every week or two. This will help soften accumulated grease and allow it to be flushed through the system.
- If a drain is only slightly clogged, drop five heaping tablespoons of baking soda into the drain and pour boiling hot water over it very slowly.

Preventing Clogged Drains

Never pour grease or cooking oil down the drain. It will harden and cause clogging. Instead, collect grease in an empty tin can, allow it to harden, then discard.

Also, do not pour tea leaves or coffee grounds into a drain. They will cling to the grease in the drain and are difficult to dislodge.

Removing a Stopper

If a sink is clogged and it is necessary to remove the stopper in order to use a snake or a plunger, the linkage of the stopper, which is beneath the sink, must be removed. Loosen the thumbscrew that holds the upper and lower rods together. Pull the upper rod out through the top of the sink. This will free the lower rod and enable you to pull out the horizontal rod that goes into the bottom of the stopper. Take out the stopper and use the plunger or snake.

Using a Plunger

If your sink gets clogged often, use a rubber plunger. Fit it tightly over the drain hole and force the plunger handle up and down

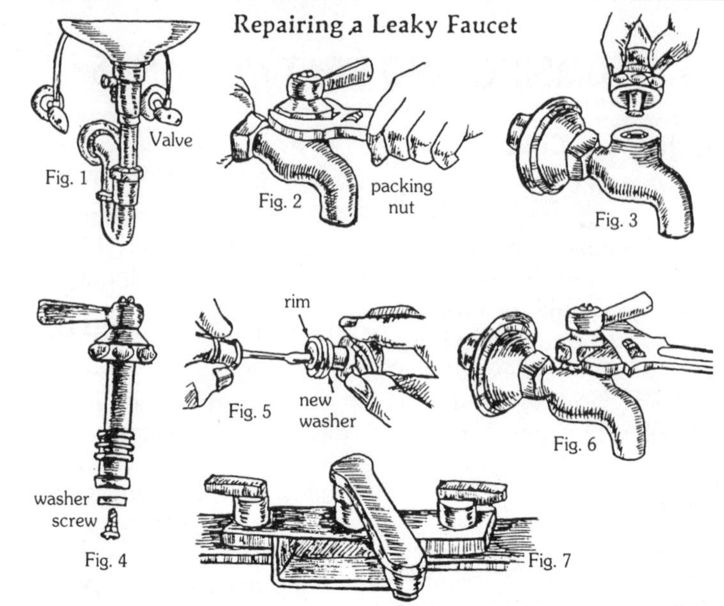

REPAIRING A LEAKY FAUCET

Dripping faucets should be fixed immediately. One drip per second, over a period of one year, amounts to 700 gallons of water.

You should be able to replace a worn-out washer, which is usually the cause of a dripping faucet. The following procedure can be followed in most situations:

1. Turn off the water at the shut-off valve nearest to the faucet that is to be repaired. Then, open the faucet until the water stops flowing (fig. 1).
2. Loosen the packing nut with a wrench (fig. 2). Most nuts loosen by turning counterclockwise. Pull out the valve unit (fig. 3).
3. Remove the screw holding the old washer at the bottom of the valve unit (fig. 4).
4. Put in a new washer that fits snugly, then replace the screw (fig. 5).
5. Put the valve unit back in the faucet, with the handle in the same position as when it was removed.
6. Tighten the packing nut (fig. 6).
7. Turn on the water at the shut-off valve.

quickly several times. This may loosen the clogged materials. When using a plunger, better results are achieved if an old towel or piece of cloth is stuffed into the overflow opening, thus creating better suction.

Nighttime Relief From Dripping Faucets

If a dripping faucet keeps you awake during the night, as a temporary measure insert a straw or dowel into the faucet opening and secure it. the water will run down noiselessly, and you can replace the defective washer in the morning.

Another way of handling the problem is to tie an old sock or hand towel around the spout, allowing the bottom to touch the bowl or the sink.

To Speed Up Slow-flowing Faucets

If the water from a faucet flows out slowly, the aerator might be clogged. The aerator is screwed onto the end of the faucet and

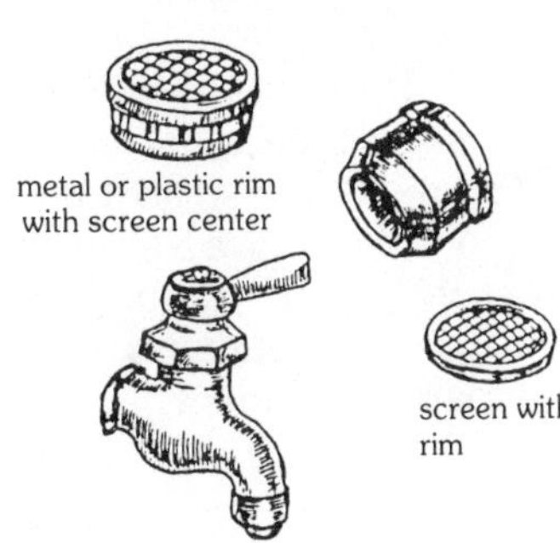

consists of two or more round screens. These screens force air between the water droplets, insuring a uniform flow. When the fine openings of the screen are clogged, the water flows evenly and in reduced quantities.

To correct the problem, remove the aerator and clean away the trapped particles. Be sure to remember the order in which you removed the round screens so you can replace them exactly as they were. This task can often be performed with the hand alone.

Leaky Pipes

A small hole in a copper or iron pipe can be repaired temporarily with a pipe clamp and a piece of rubber sheeting from an inner tube.

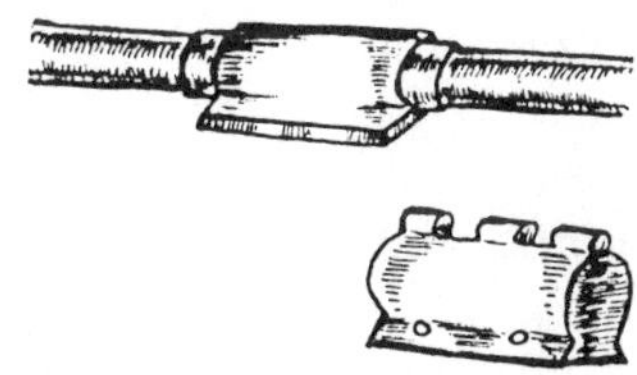

Wrap the rubber sheeting tightly around the pipe, then secure a clamp on either side of the hole.

Antifreeze Dripping

If you will be away from home and are concerned that the water pipes in a marginally heated area of the house might freeze, try allowing one or two faucets to drip a bit. This will keep the water flowing through the pipes.

Pipe Condensation

Cold water pipes often sweat during warm weather, and the wetness can leave stains on the floor and cause mildew. Insulation is the simplest way to control condensation. An alternative to conventional pipe insulation is to buy some quarter-inch sponge rubber self-sticking weatherstripping, which comes packaged in coils and is relatively inexpensive. Remove the protective paper from the adhesive and apply the stripping in a tightly wound spiral until the pipe is covered. Be sure the pipe is dry before applying the insulation or weatherstripping.

Basement Water Stains

If you discover water stains or rust around the base of your furnace, washer, or dryer, check for leaks. Place a piece of cardboard over the stain to see if it persists.

Repairing Air Ducts

If your heating system has a loose joint in one of the ducts through which warm air is escaping, repair it with duct tape, which is especially made for the purpose. Available in many hardware stores, duct tape is a heat-resistant cloth material with a plastic coating and a powerful adhesive. Remove dust and dirt from the duct with detergent and water. Strip protective paper from the adhesive and press the tape against the loose joint.

Hot Furnaces

If your basement is too hot, check the furnace. Browned areas near the warm-air ducts or scorched areas above the heater are conveying a message: it is time to call in an expert to check over the heating unit.

Wind Teflon Tape Clockwise

When connecting plumbing fixtures, teflon tape is commonly wound around pipe threads to seal the spacing and ensure a tight, leak-proof connection. When winding teflon tape around threading, be sure to wind the tape in the opposite direction the threaded pipe will turn. If this is not done, the tape will unravel as the connection is tightened.

Black Smoke

Black smoke coming out of a chimney is an indication that it's time to call the serviceman.

Furnace Checkup

You will save money and conserve energy by calling in a serviceman to clean the furnace and replace the filters every summer. This should be done by experienced personnel only. It might be worthwhile to sign a service contract with your oil supplier. Annual furnace cleanup is part of the standard agreement.

ELECTRIC AND LIGHTING BASICS

Loose Power Cords

See to it that every power cord in your home fits snugly into its outlet. A receptacle that does not hold a plug firmly is a fire hazard and must be replaced.

Sparking Electrical Receptacles

If an electrical receptacle sparks when a plug is inserted, withdraw the plug by gripping it with a work glove or a thick dry towel while standing on a dry surface.

Unplugging a Plug

Never pull a plug out of a socket by the wire. Pull it out by the plug itself.

Electrical Hazards

It is hazardous to hold electrical appliances with wet hands. Avoid touching sink faucets or pipes in the kitchen or bathroom when plugging in an electrical appliance.

Cleaning Electrical Appliances

Never immerse an appliance in water, and always unplug the appliance before cleaning to avoid electrical shocks.

Plugging in Appliance Cords

To avoid sparks, when using an appliance that has a cord with plugs at both ends, always insert the cord that fits into the appliance first. Then plug the other end into the wall receptacle.

Overloading an Outlet

Overloading outlets with multiple plugs may lead to fires. Keep to a minimum the number of plugs in each outlet.

Long Extension Cord Inefficiency

An extension cord that is too long causes a drop in current, and this will affect the efficiency of the appliance. Keep extension cords short if possible, and avoid joining several to each other.

Extension Cords

Electric extension cords—unless designed specifically for the purpose—should not be used outdoors on rainy or damp days.

Fastening Electrical Wires

When winding wires around the screw of an electrical plug or

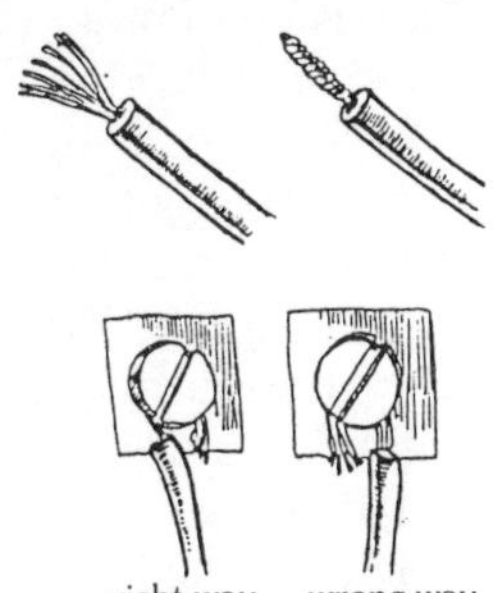

outlet, always twist the strands tightly together and wrap around each screw in a clockwise direction. Then, tighten with a screwdriver. Winding the wires in a counterclockwise direction will cause them to unravel and lose contact with the screw as the screw is tightened.

Protecting Extension Cords

When using hedgetrimmers, snowblowers, and other appliances that require long extension cords, play it safe and wrap three feet or more of garden hose over the cord near the appliance. Simply slit the hose, spread it with a screwdriver, and push in the electric wire.

Wall Switches

Small appliances that do not have their own on-off switches can be operated using plug-in wall switches. An advantage to this is that you don't have to pull out or push in the plug to turn the appliance off or on, and no installation is required.

Dimmer Controls

Add flexibility to your home lighting by using dimmer controls on fixtures in bedrooms, bathrooms, halls, and living rooms. Gradations of light, from full bright to very dim, are possible simply by turning a knob. A low level of lighting is helpful in the care of small children, sick persons, and others who need assistance during the night.

You can make dramatic changes in the mood of a room by softening lights with a dimmer switch. Lights can be lowered when listening to music or enjoying a fire on the hearth.

Dimmer controlled lamps give greater flexibility than three-way lamps that use three-way sockets and require three-way bulbs.

Be sure to close the power source before installing any dimming device.

Selecting Lampshades

Light, transparent lampshades reflect more light than those of darker colors. The more light, the better you'll see, and the cozier the room will look.

Floor Lamps

In choosing a floor lamp, keep in mind exactly where in the home it is to be placed. Choose lamps sized and constructed for proper placement without interfering with household traffic. Small floor lamps—standard, swing-arm, or bridge-type—may be 43 to 47 inches from the floor to the bottom of the shade. Large lamps—standard or swing-arm—measure 45 to 49 inches from the floor to the bottom of the shade.

Soldering Wires

Before soldering electrical wires, twist them together in a firm mechanical joint. To solder properly apply flux, or use solder in wire form with a flux core and heat the wire joint with the tip

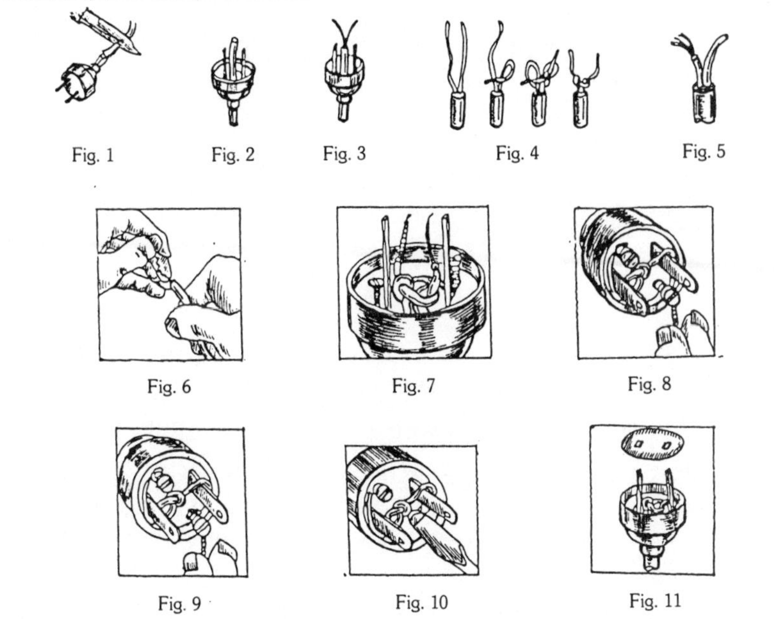

Fig. 1 Fig. 2 Fig. 3 Fig. 4 Fig. 5

Fig. 6 Fig. 7 Fig. 8

Fig. 9 Fig. 10 Fig. 11

REPLACING ELECTRIC PLUGS

If a lamp or appliance does not work, the problem may be a defective plug. A prong may be loose or broken, or the cord may be damaged in some manner. To play safe, buy a new two-prong plug and wire it. This is how to do it:

1. Cut the cord off the old plug, making sure to remove any damaged part (fig. 1).
2. Slip the new plug onto the cord (fig. 2).
3. Split and separate the cord (fig. 3).
4. Tie an underwriter's knot (fig. 4), which prevents the wire from slipping through the plug hole.
5. Remove one-half inch of the insulation from the end of the wires (fig. 5).
6. Twist small wires together, clockwise (fig. 6).
7. Pull knot down firmly in the plug (fig. 7).
8. Pull one wire around each terminal to the screw (fig. 8).
9. Wrap the wire around the screw, clockwise (fig. 9).
10. Tighten the screw. Insulation should come to the screw but not under it (fig. 10).
11. Place insulation cover back over the plug (fig. 11).

LIGHTING MAINTENANCE

Home lighting equipment needs regular care and cleaning. Dirt and dust on bulbs, tubes, diffusion bowls, lampshades, and fixtures can cause a substantial loss in light output. Clean all lighting equipment at least four times a year. Bowl-type portable lamps should be cleaned monthly.

Here are some suggestions for taking care of lamps and electrical parts:

1. Wash glass and plastic diffusers and shields in a detergent solution. Rinse in clear warm water, then dry.
2. Wipe bulbs and tubes with a damp, soapy cloth. Dry well.
3. Dust wood and metal lamp bases with a soft cloth and apply a thin coat of wax. Glass, pottery, marble, chrome, and onyx bases can be washed with a damp, soapy cloth, dried, and waxed.
4. Lampshades may be cleaned with the soft brush attachment of a vacuum cleaner, or they may be dry cleaned. Silk or rayon shades that are handsewn to the frame, with no glued trimmings, may be washed in mild, lukewarm suds and rinsed in clear water. Dry shades quickly to prevent rusting of frames.
5. Wipe parchment shades with a dry cloth.
6. Remove plastic wrappings from lampshades before using. Wrappings create glare and may warp the frame and wrinkle the shade fabric. Some are fire hazards.
7. Replace all darkened bulbs. A darkened bulb can reduce light output 25 to 30 percent, but it uses almost the same amount of current as a new bulb operating at correct wattage. Darkened bulbs may be used in closets or hallways where less light is needed.
8. Replace fluorescent tubes that flicker and any tubes that have darkened ends. A long delay in starting indicates that a new starter is probably needed. If a humming sound develops in a fluorescent fixture, the ballast may need to be remounted or replaced.

of the soldering iron. In a few seconds the wires will be hot enough to melt the solder. Remove the soldering iron and touch the solder to the wires until the melted metal covers the joint. When the solder is fully melted, it will have turned to a shiny silver finish.

An easier way to solder electrical wires is to apply steel solder. The bond is not as strong, but if wrapped well in tape, the bond will hold.

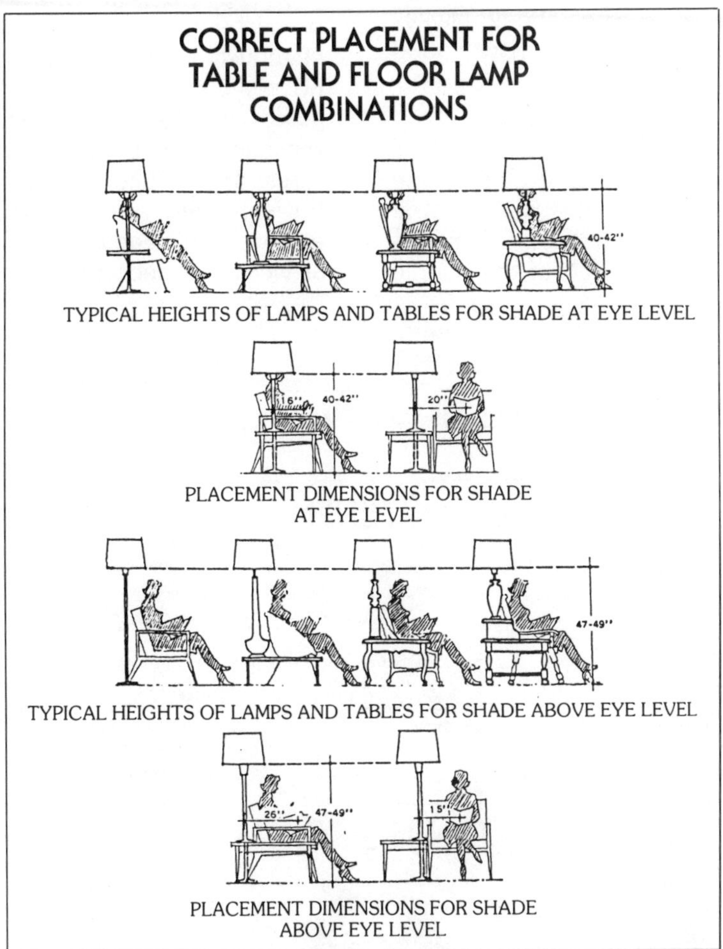

CORRECT PLACEMENT FOR TABLE AND FLOOR LAMP COMBINATIONS

TYPICAL HEIGHTS OF LAMPS AND TABLES FOR SHADE AT EYE LEVEL

PLACEMENT DIMENSIONS FOR SHADE AT EYE LEVEL

TYPICAL HEIGHTS OF LAMPS AND TABLES FOR SHADE ABOVE EYE LEVEL

PLACEMENT DIMENSIONS FOR SHADE ABOVE EYE LEVEL

Reading Lamps

For reading, a floor lamp with a fixed or swing-arm is correctly placed when the light comes from behind the shoulder of the reader, near the rear of the chair, either at the right or the left, but never from directly behind the chair.

High-intensity Lamps

The small high-intensity lamps now on the market are not designed for study, reading, or general work. They can, however, provide a concentrated area of high-level light for special tasks, such as sewing, crafts, or fine-detail work. They should always be used in combination with good general lighting.

Piano Lamp

To read music and play the piano, center the shade of a swing-arm floor lamp 22 inches to the right or left of the middle of the keyboard and 13 inches in front of the lower edge of the music rack.

Types of Lighting Fixtures

The fixtures illustrated below for kitchen, dining room, and bedroom have design features that permit them to function more effectively in certain areas of the house. Use the diagrams as a guide when you are thinking of replacing your current lighting fixtures. When choosing new fixtures, remember to consider the electrical efficiency of the fixture as well as its decorative effect.

TYPES OF LIGHTING FIXTURES

KITCHEN

Closed globe unit. Minimum diameter of bowl is 14 inches. White glass gives good diffusion of light.

Shielded fixture. Three or four sockets, 14 to 17-inch diameter. Shallow-wide bowl is desirable.

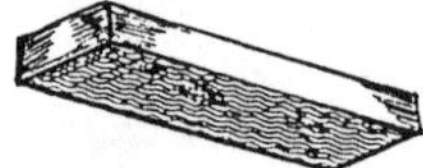

Fluorescent fixture with diffusing shield. Two or four tubes as needed in a 48-inch unit. For a large kitchen, two 2-tube fixtures can be placed end to end.

DINING ROOM

Lantern-style pulldown. Unit has a three-way socket, takes a 50/100/150-watt bulb and a diffusing globe.

Ventilated ceiling fixture. Bent glass diffuser, 14-inch minimum diameter. Interior reflecting surfaces should be white or polished.

Pulldown fixture. Ventilated unit has three-way single socket or three sockets and white glass diffuser.

BEDROOM

Surface-mounted ceiling fixtures. Twelve- or 14-inch width. Surface-mounted, with plain or textured glass or plastic diffuser.

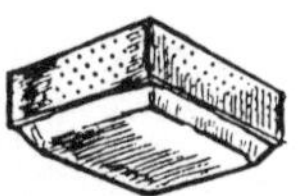

Ventilated ceiling fixture. One or two sockets, diffusing shade to extend below trim to give side lighting. Unit is surface-mounted on ceiling.

BATHROOM

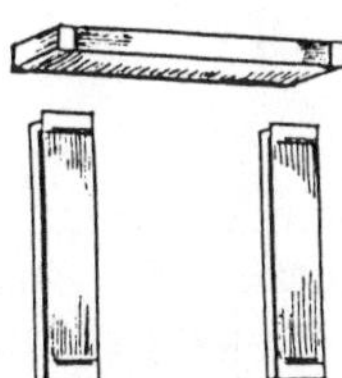

Side and overhead fluorescent fixtures. Pair of 24-inch long fixtures are spaced 30 or more inches apart of mirror sides. Use fixture above mirror if no ceiling light in room.

Vapor-proof ceiling fixture. A good type for a shower stall. Use a 60-watt bulb. Make sure that the switch is located outside of the shower.

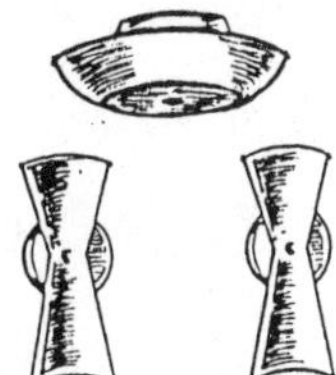

Side and overhead incandescent units. One- or two-socket fixtures or minor sides are centered 60 inches above floor. Note overhead fixture. Bulbs are well shielded to reduce glare.

UTILITY ROOM

Surface-mounted ceiling fixture. Minimum diameter of 12 inches is desirable. Unit may have one or two sockets.

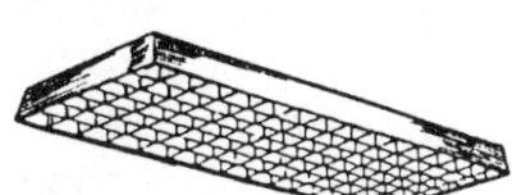

Shielded fluorescent fixture. Two- or four-tube fixture can be centered in ceiling or mounted over work area.

Reflector and reflector bowl bulb unit. Twelve- or 14-inch minimum diameter. Use to reduce glare and to spread light.

HALLWAY

Hanging bowl fixure. Eight-inch diameter. A good choice for lighting a high-ceilinged hall or stairway.

Closed globe fixture. Unit is mounted on ceiling. Choose a white glass globe for diffusion of light.

Wall bracket fixture. May be used to supplement general lighting. Can be mounted on wall near a mirror.

Types of Diffusers

Undershade diffusers are offered by manufacturers for use in study and reading lamps. One is a highly reflective, inverted metal cone. Other diffusers are bowl-shaped, prismatic reflectors. Shields prevent glare.

Combination Outlet

If you have only one ceiling light fixture in your garage or cellar but need a power outlet, there are two adaptors which can provide

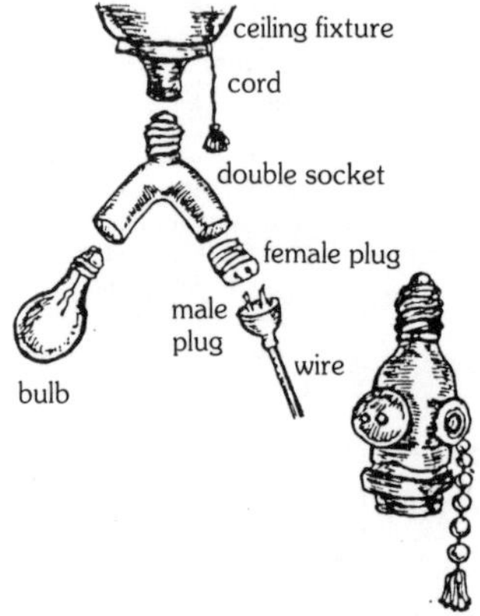

it for you. One is a Y-shaped double socket and the other is a pull-chain current tap with two convenient outlets. Both will provide light and power at one time.

Replacing a Lamp Socket

When a lamp socket switch fails, the entire socket must be replaced. To do so, first remove the plug from the wall outlet. Pull the upper part of the socket from its core, and loosen the wires from the terminal screws. Loosen the setscrew. Remove the old

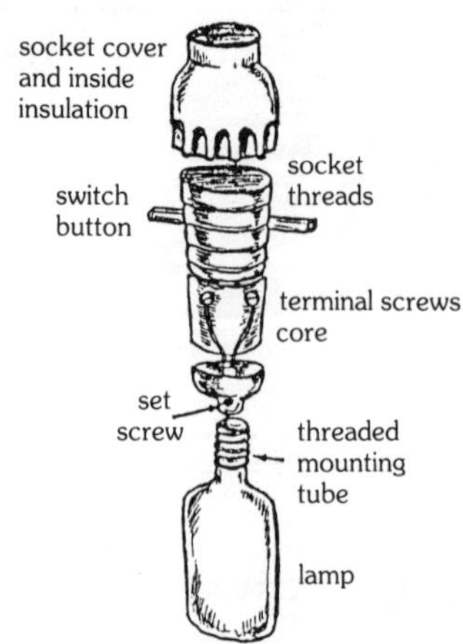

base from the wires, slip the new base over the wires, then screw it onto the mounting tube. Attach the wires to the new terminal screw, and press the new upper socket part firmly onto the base. Tighten the setscrew against the base.

Propane Lamps

When the electric power fails and remains off for a considerable length of time, one of the best and safest emergency lights is the propane lamp which is available widely at hardware outlets. It provides a brilliant light, and its fuel (propane) can be stored safely in its sealed steel cylinders without deteriorating. Although gasoline lanterns also provide brilliant light, gasoline deteriorates with age and is difficult to store safely.

Long-lived Bulbs

If you use electric bulbs in hard-to-reach areas of the home, consider using long-life bulbs. These are available only in hardware stores that cater to industrial clients. Manufacturers claim that they last up to 2,500 hours.

Fluorescent Lighting

Fluorescent lights produce up to four times as much light per watt as do conventional bulbs, and they last as much as twenty times longer.

Fluorescent bulbs that screw into standard (incandescent) sockets are available.

Fluorescent White

There are three types of fluorescent white: daylight, cool white, and warm white. Daylight is used primarily for display lighting, especially for store windows. Cool white blends well with natural light and is used in schools, factories, and offices. Warm white is the most efficient, but highlights orange, yellow, and yellow-green at the expense of other colors, which makes its light warmer and more pleasant, and thus the choice of most homeowners.

Fluorescent Lamp Life

Don't turn fluorescent lights on and off frequently, as this shortens their life. Fluorescents work best in temperatures not below 50 degrees Fahrenheit. When replacing the starter, be sure to purchase the right kind. Check the number on the old starter against the number on the replacement. Flickering bulbs are often the result of defective starters.

Dark Tubes

A fluorescent tube that darkens need not necessarily be replaced. Reversing the tube sometimes will brighten it at the dark end.

Halogen Lighting

Halogen light bulbs, introduced relatively recently, give off a whiter, brighter illumination while using the same wattage as incandescent light bulbs.

While the halogen lights are considerably more expensive than traditional kinds, they are capable of maintaining the same intensity of light for up to 3,000 hours.

Halogen Light Bulb Caution

Halogen light bulbs are silicone-coated to allow them to tolerate very intense heat. For this reason, when handling halogen lights, hold the bulb with a tissue or other soft material. Do not hold the bulb with bare hands, as the oils in your fingers may weaken the silicone coating, and the high temperature of the light may cause the bulb to burst.

Protect Closet Bulbs

Bare light bulbs are often installed horizontally in closets to provide lighting. In tightly packed closets, they frequently constitute a fire hazard. If an article of clothing should fall on the bulb from a shelf, it is likely to ignite. Closet bulbs should be situated so that no object can fall on them. If this is not possible, the bulb should be shielded with a device manufactured for the purpose.

Lightning Protection Indoors

If you are at home during a lightning storm, avoid touching plumbing and heating lines. Although TV antenna systems are designed to absorb and ground electricity, it is best to turn off all television sets while a storm is in progress. Sudden surges of electric current can damage televisions.

Radio and TV Interference

Your radio or TV set is not necessarily in need of repair if, at times, the sound is muffled or the pictured distorted. Interference may be due to an airplane passing overhead or to adverse weather conditions. But there are times when the cause of the problem is right in your own house. If the radio or TV is plugged into an outlet that is on the same line as a fluorescent light fixture, you might experience bad reception. The next time you have bad reception, observe what happens when you turn off the fluorescent fixture. If the fluorescent fixture proves to have been the cause of the problem, try plugging the radio or TV into different outlets until you find one that gives trouble-free reception.

Television Lighting

Watching television in a darkened room is tiring to the eyes because of the contrast between the bright screen and dark surroundings. To avoid eyestrain, make sure there is some light in the viewing area. Portable lamps placed behind or at the sides of the set will prevent reflections on the TV screen.

Electrical Hazards

It is hazardous to hold electrical appliances with wet hands. Avoid touching sink faucets or pipes in the kitchen or bathroom when plugging in an electrical appliance.

Identifying Fuses and Circuit Breakers

To determine which fuse or circuit breaker controls a particular outlet, plug a radio into the outlet in question and turn it up to a high volume. Then, unscrew or close the various fuses or breakers in succession. When the radio has stopped playing, you will know that you have just cut off the fuse that controls the outlet into which the radio is plugged. Mark the fuse accordingly.

Trouble on the Line

When a fuse blows or a circuit breaker trips, the cause could be an overloaded circuit (too many appliances being used at the same time) or a faulty unit plugged into the line. If the appliances on the ciruit were all in use for at least a few moments before the fuse blew or circuit breaker tripped, the cause most likely is an overloaded circuit. Simply reduce the number of items operating on that fuse or circuit breaker. If the fuse blows or circuit breaker trips immediately upon plugging in a unit or turning on a switch, the cause is probably the unit.

New Circuit With External Tubing

Frequently, in existing homes it is desirable to add an electrical circuit. Though adding a circuit breaker box and making the required electrical connections are within the ability of many do-it-yourselfers, situating the wiring inside existing walls presents a problem. One solution is to position new wiring on the outside of existing walls. Decorative tubing through which the new wiring can be run is available in a variety of colors. The new receptacle and switch boxes are positioned on the outside of the wall.

Plugging in Appliance Cords

To avoid sparks, when using an appliance that has a cord with plugs at both ends, always insert the cord that fits into the appliance first. Then plug the other end into the wall receptacle.

Cleaning Electrical Appliances

Never immerse an appliance in water, and always unplug the appliance before cleaning to avoid electrical shocks.

Overloading an Outlet

Overloading outlets with multiple plugs may lead to fires. Keep to a minimum the number of plugs in each outlet.

18
In the Workshop

Introduction

Outfitting the home workshop is not unlike purchasing a wardrobe. Clothing and footwear of every description and for every occasion are available for purchase, but it would be foolish to buy a bathing suit if you never swim, a ski outfit if you live in Florida and intend to stay there, a wedding gown if you are already married (and intend to stay that way), or a tuxedo if you never attend formal affairs. So, too, with the workshop. Hardware stores and tool catalogues offer a bewildering assortment of products for every possible use. Some are offered in sets costing hundred or thousands of dollars. They provide a tempting allure for those fascinated with tools.

The best way to outfit a home workshop, however, is according to need. Wrench and socket sets are indispensable tools, and every handyman will want to have them. But, they come in both metric and American measurements; and unless the machines you work on contain both types of fasteners, you will not need both. Read catalogues and browse in hardware stores so that you are aware of what is available. But purchase tools only as the need arises. In time, your workshop will be custom-stocked to suit your interests and needs.

An inviolable rule when it comes to tools is to purchase quality. Good tools can last a lifetime, and many hand tools carry lifetime guarantees. If you are serious about your home repair work and projects, purchase only established brands. Although many nonbrand-name products carry manufacturer warrantees, the manufacturer might very well be out of business by the time the claim is made. This is not to say that it is always necessary to buy top-of-the-line tools. The Craftsman line, sold at Sears stores, for example, is used by many professionals, carries a lifetime guarantee, and is significantly less expensive than tools sold in professional outlets that are only marginally superior.

Power Tool Precautions

When working with power tools, particularly electric drills and saws, do not wear loose clothing that can get caught in the tools. If your hair is long, put it up in a bun or wear a cap.

Lubricating Power Tools Regularly

Make sure to lubricate each power tool regularly, unless the manual instructs otherwise. Keep track of the dates when each tool was last lubricated. Record dates on a sheet tacked to the wall of the workshop, or place a piece of masking tape directly on each tool and write the date on it.

Wrapping Tools

When tools are not to be used for a long period, you can preserve them and protect them from rust by wrapping them in oil-soaked rags. The oily rags may be a safety hazard, so store the wrapped tools in a metal box. Wrapping tools also protects cutting edges from coming into contact with other tools that might chip or dull the sharp edges.

Rust Prevention

Tools rust when they come in contact with moisture from the air. To prevent tools from rusting, store them in a tool box with mothballs or moth crystals. Or, try to obtain little cloth bags of granules used to absorb moisture. Many hardware stores carry this product. When the granules are saturated with moisture, they change color. When put in the oven for a few minutes, they will dry out and can be used again.

An alternative is to place a few pieces of carpenter's blue chalk in the toolbox. The chalk will absorb moisture, and it too can be reused after being warmed in the oven to evaporate the moisture.

Ammonia and Rust

A drop or two of ammonia applied to a rusted bolt will usually eat into the rust and loosen it. To remove rust, put ammonia on the rusty spots and let it soak in for several minutes. Then, wipe off the rust with a soft cloth. It's not a good idea to use sandpaper or steel wool for removing rust from scissors or other objects.

A Handy Ruler

If you have to measure small objects and don't have a ruler, open your wallet and you will find a handy gauge. Every bill in your wallet from one dollar to one hundred dollars measures exactly 6⅛″ x 2⅝″ and will serve you well when you need an approximate measure of things.

Reading a Ruler

When taking measurements, especially for cabinet work, it's important to be accurate. If you place a ruler or tape measure against the object to be measured and try to read it while looking at it from any angle other than a right angle, you will get a wrong reading. The proper way to take a reading is to lay the measuring tool flat and position yourself so you are looking directly over the spot where the end of the object being measured touches the ruler or tape.

Measuring With a Tape

When you want to measure a large article and are working alone, try the following. Place one end of a steel or cloth measuring tape at one end of the distance to be measured. Secure it with Scotch tape or masking tape. This will leave you free to move and stretch the measuring tape as far as necessary without dislodging the other end from its set position.

At the end of a steel tape there is usually a "grabber." Since the grabber most often has play in it, be sure to draw the tape tight before taking your reading.

Using Old Gloves for Storage

Don't throw away old gloves. If they are still in reasonably good condition, nail them on the side of the work table and use the glove fingers to hold nailpunches, small screwdrivers, and other tools that are reached for regularly.

Drawing a Long Straight Line

When you need to draw a long straight line, select the two end points and drive nails into the surface. Tie a length of string (builder's twine is preferred) to both nails and rub chalk on the string. Use blue chalk if the surface is white. Make sure the string is taut. Hold the string in the middle, between the thumb and middle finger, pull out one or two inches, and snap the string against the surface by releasing it. A straight chalk line will thus be laid down on the surface.

Drawing a Straight Line on a Wall

To draw a straight horizontal line on a wall, you need not mark two points. Select the height at which you want the line drawn, and position your level firmly at that point. When the bubble in the glass indicator is in the center, draw the line. You can be certain it is straight.

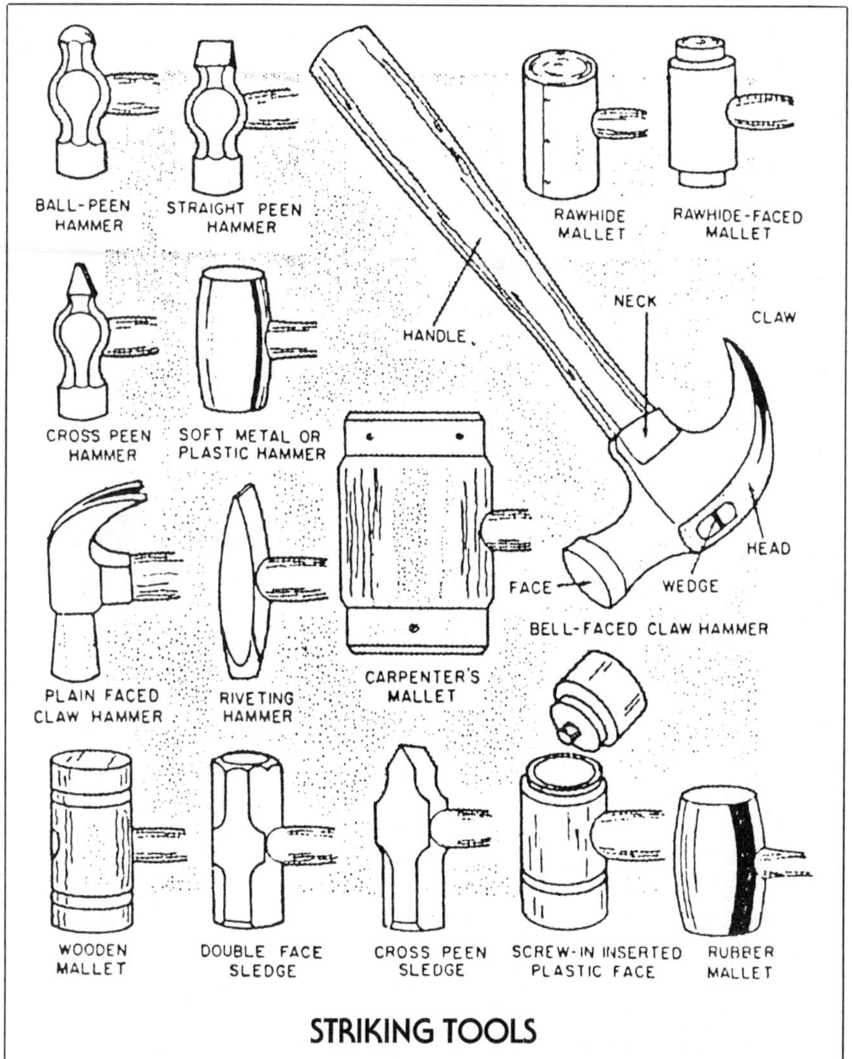

STRIKING TOOLS

Hammers, mallets, and sledges are used to apply a striking force. The tool you select will depend upon the intended application. The carpenter's hammer is designed for one purpose while the machinist's hammer has other primary functions.

Hammers for Beginners

If you can afford to buy only one hammer, you will find the clawed style, which is suitable for driving in and pulling out nails, to be most useful.

Buy a hammer of average weight, between twelve and sixteen ounces. A sixteen-ounce hammer is most commonly used. For more hitting power, hold the hammer near the end of the handle. When starting the nail, hold it firmly and tap it gently into the wood until it takes hold—then drive it in.

Hammer Safety

A hammer handle should always be tight in the head. If it is loose, the head may fly off and cause an injury.

Hammers for Hardened Nails

The face of the ordinary claw hammer (also called a nail hammer) is tempered for soft steel nails. When used on hardened steel, such as a cold chisel, or even on the hardened nails used in concrete work, the face of a claw hammer may chip, and fragments of steel may fly into the worker's eyes. Use a ball hammer or hand-drilling hammer.

Hammering a Chisel

Hammering on a cold chisel or star drill can produce an uncomfortable stinging sensation. If wearing gloves or wrapping a sponge around the chisel doesn't offer enough protection, make a

protective handle for the chisel out of a small hollow rubber ball. Cut a hole in the ball the same diameter as the chisel handle, and force the handle through the ball. By squeezing the ball, you'll be able to grip the tool tightly and hammer without the unpleasant sting.

PURCHASING NAILS

Different types of nails are referred to by different names. Become familiar with them:

Common nails have heavy flat heads and are used for general

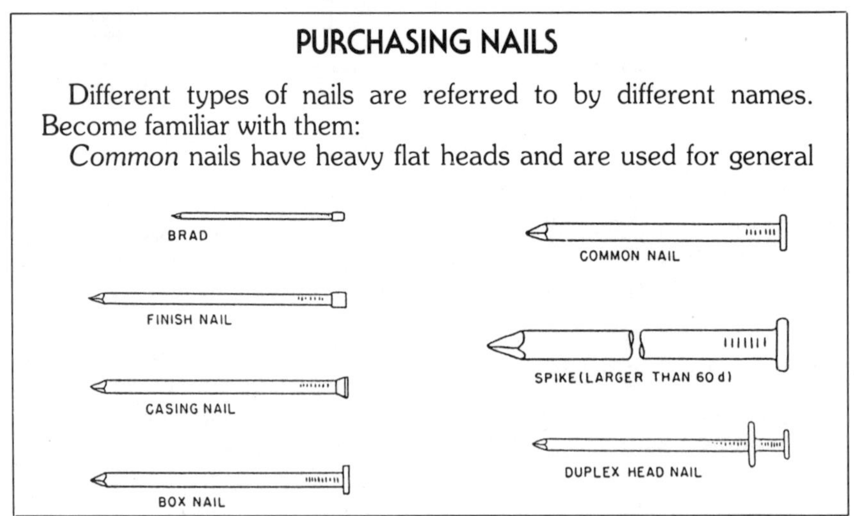

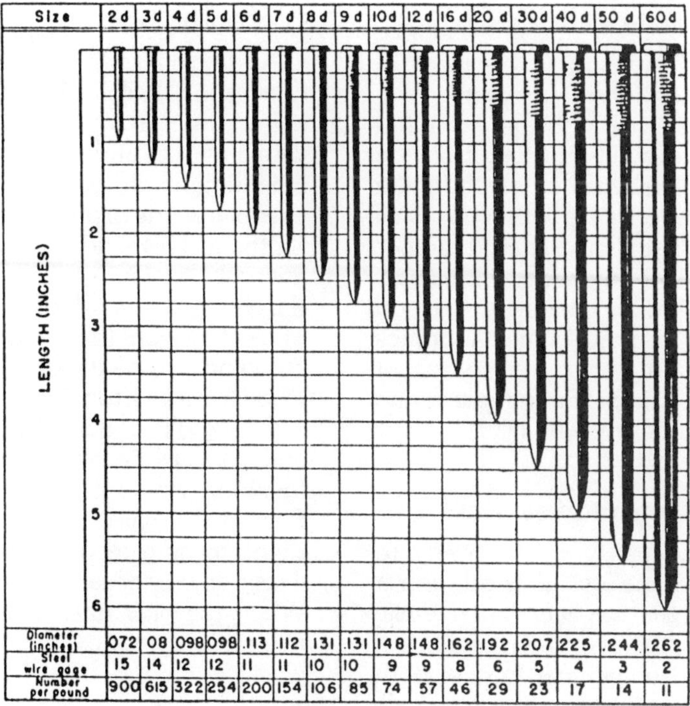

Size	2d	3d	4d	5d	6d	7d	8d	9d	10d	12d	16d	20d	30d	40d	50d	60d
Diameter (inches)	.072	.08	.098	.098	.113	.112	.131	.131	.148	.148	.162	.192	.207	.225	.244	.262
Steel wire gage	15	14	12	12	11	11	10	10	9	9	8	6	5	4	3	2
Number per pound	900	615	322	254	200	154	106	85	74	57	46	29	23	17	14	11

Common Nail Sizes.

work. *Box* nails are relatively thin and have flat heads. They were first used for nailing together boxes built of wood that was thin and therefore split easily. *Finish* and *casing* nails have small heads that can be set beneath the wood surface. They are used for furniture, cabinets, and for trim work. *Brads* are small finishing nails and are used to nail thin stock such as molding.

Use a *nail set* to drive a casing, finishing, or brad nail beneath the surface of the wood.

The term *penny,* abbreviated d, was once applied to nails to indicate the cost per hundred, but now it is used as a measure of length.

Nail Removal Technique

There is an easy way to remove a nail from a piece of wood, as long as the head is somewhat above the surface. Grasp the head of the nail with the claw hammer, slide a block of wood under the head of the hammer, and push the hammer back against the block. If the nail is long, use a thicker piece of wood. The nail will come out with little effort, without marring the wood, and may even be straight enough to be reused.

Stubborn Nails

If you want to save a piece of wood for future use but a protruding nail cannot be extracted with a claw hammer, cut off the head of the nail as close to the wood as possible with a hacksaw or cutting pliers. Then, hammer the nail into the wood with a nail-set and cover the hole with wood filler. If the point of the nail comes out at the other end, extract it with a pair of cutting pliers and fill the opening with filler.

Removing Headless Nails

If the nail you are trying to remove has lost its head, grip it with a pair of pliers. Then, while holding the pliers with one hand, use a claw hammer to raise both the pliers and the headless nail.

Temporary Nailing

Temporary wooden structures that have been nailed together can be more easily dismantled when duplex head nails are used. These nails have two heads, one at the very end and the other about an inch below (see illustration). When driven into wood, the nail stops at the lower head, leaving the upper head protruding so it can be removed with a claw hammer.

Nailing Hardwood

If you are having trouble getting nails to penetrate hardwood, dip them in oil or apply soap to them to facilitate entry.

Concealing Nails

Aside from the normal way of concealing nails (driving them below the surface of the wood with a nail-set and then filling the indentation with wood filler), an effective way is to prepare a cover for them. This is done by pushing a wood chisel into the surface of the wood to a depth of about 1/16 or 1/8 of an inch, then pushing the chisel on a plane parallel with the wood to make a tongue about one inch long. The tongue will curl up, and you will be able to drive a finishing nail into the space. Recess the nail with a nail set, then smear glue over the area. Press down and apply a weight. When the glue has bonded the two surfaces, sand off the excess glue.

Corrugated Fasteners

Corrugated fasteners are more effective than nails in holding together small pieces of wood. The divergent type in which the center corrugations diverge from each other are especially effective because they lock the two pieces together. Corrugated fasteners are also useful in holding together glued mitered pieces, such as the corners of picture frames.

Use Screwdrivers Properly

A screwdriver is the most frequently abused of all handtools. It is designed for one function only—to drive and remove screws. A screwdriver should not be used as a pry bar, a scraper, a chisel, or a punch.

Screwdrivers Must Fit

Each household should have two types of screwdrivers: the straight blade and the Phillips, which has the X-shaped tip. No matter which type you are using,

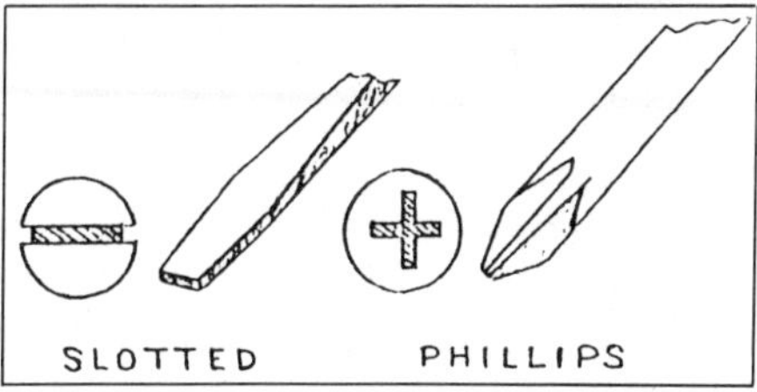

make sure it fits snugly into the screw slot and is neither too wide nor too narrow. Otherwise, you could damage the wood or ruin the screw slot.

Fixing Screwdrivers

Damaged flat-blade screwdrivers can be made usable by filing the tip and restoring it to its original square edge. If you have an electric grinder, the job can be accomplished very quickly, but placing the screwdriver in a vise and squaring it with a metal file is almost as effective.

Purchasing Screws

When purchasing screws, specify the length and diameter desired. Numbers 1 to 16 indicate the diameter. If the screw shank is a #16, it is the largest; if it is #1, it is the smallest.

Hiding Screw Heads

Screw heads can be concealed by the use of round wooden plugs. For a medium-sized screw, drill a half-inch hole one-quarter inch deep. Drill a second hole in the middle of the first one with a bit slightly narrower than the thickness of the screw shank. Turn the screw into the second hole until its head is flush with the bottom of the half-inch hole.

Make a plug by cutting off a quarter-inch slice of a half-inch wooden rod or dowel. Place a little glue on the underside of the plug and slip it into the hole. The plug may be sanded flush with the surface, or you may allow it to protrude for decorative effect.

Enlarged Screw Holes

Hinges and handles become ineffective and difficult to use when a screw hole has become enlarged. To correct the situation, first make sure that the wood surrounding the hinge or handle is not split. If it is, remove the hinge or handle, fill the split with wood filler and let it dry. Then, make a tapered woodplug (or use wooden match sticks) and force it into the opening. Make a pilot hole with your drill or with an awl, then insert the screw.

Screws in Hardwood

Driving screws into hardwood can be difficult, and a little soap on the threads usually makes the job easier. Save pieces of bar soap that are too small for use in the bath or shower (and that would normally be discarded) and use them for this purpose.

Before inserting the screw, make a pilot hole with a drill bit that is slightly smaller than the diameter of the screw at its widest point.

Use Lag Bolts

For heavy-duty screw applications, consider using lag bolts instead of screws. Lag bolts are threaded screws with hex- or square-sided heads. They come in a variety of sizes and can be driven with ratchet tools, which spare considerable labor.

Dowels for Screws

If you want to join two pieces of wood without leaving telltale signs, drill a hole through both pieces, drop in white glue, and hammer in a dowel to fit the hole snugly. Then, sand off the end of the dowel and the point of entry will be almost invisible.

PLIERS—WHICH IS WHICH?

Pliers are made in many styles and sizes and are used to perform many different operations. Pliers are used for cutting purposes as well as holding and gripping small articles when it is inconvenient to use the hands.

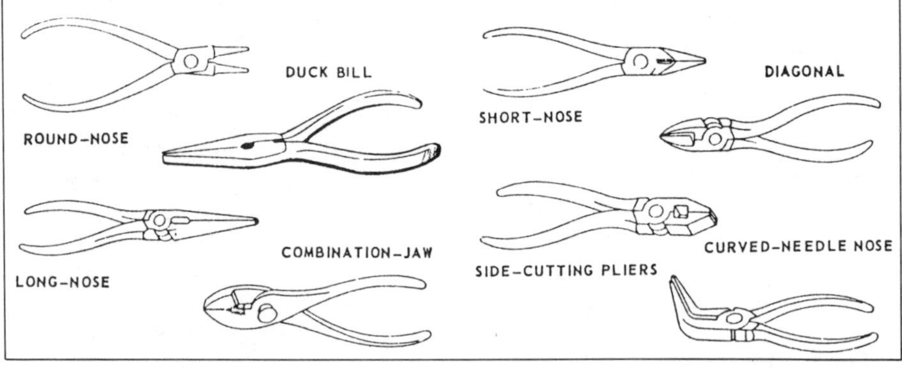

Rubber Grips for Pliers

For a more comfortable and more secure grip, place a continuous piece of rubber tubing over both handles of a pair of pliers.

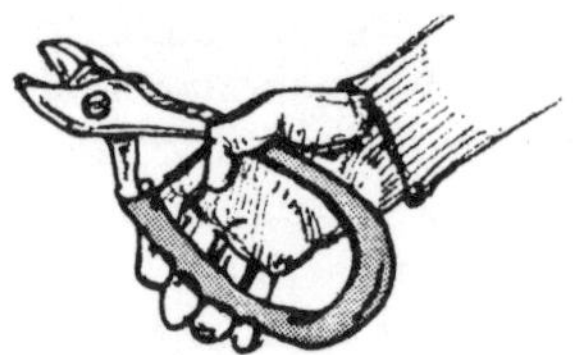

The rounded part of the tubing will keep the pliers open when you relax your grip. The heavy rubber tubing will serve as a safety device by insulating the handles and preventing an electrical shock when you perform electrical work.

The Handiest Wrench

A handy all-purpose wrench

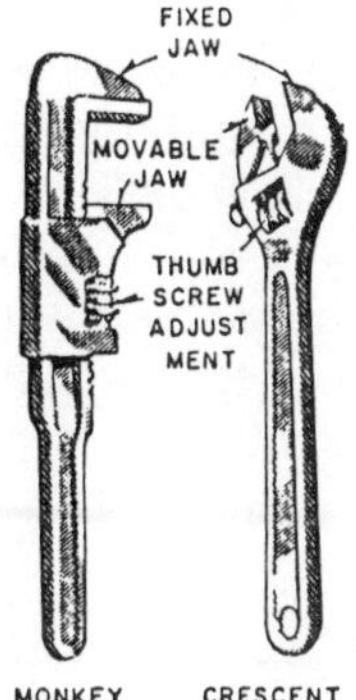

that is generally included in every toolbox is the adjustable open-end wrench. Adjustable wrenches are available in varying sizes ranging from four to 24 inches in length. The size of the wrench selected for a particular job is dependent upon the size of nut or bolt head to which the wrench is to be applied. As the jaw opening increases the length of the wrench increases.

THE VERSATILE SOCKET WRENCH

The socket wrench is one of the most versatile wrenches in the toolbox. Basically, it consists of a handle and a socket type wrench which can be attached to the handle.

A complete socket wrench set consists of several types of handles along with bar extensions, adapters, and a variety of sockets. See the illustration.

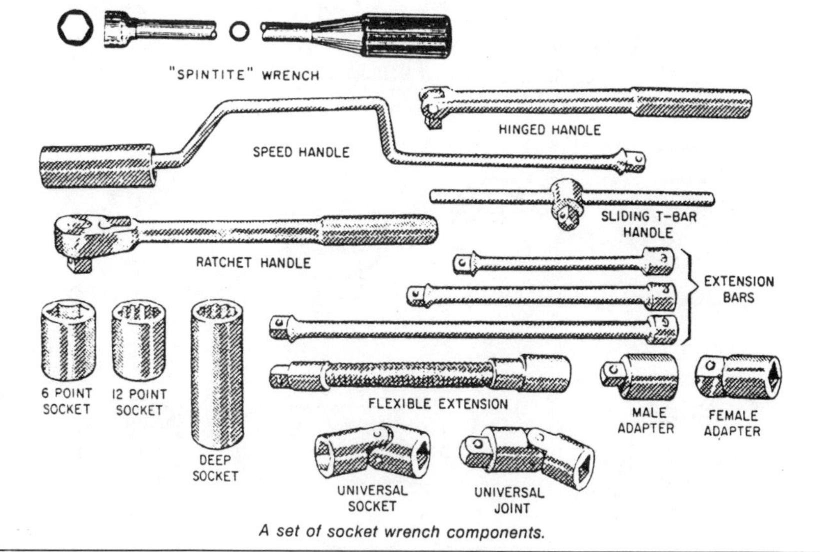

A set of socket wrench components.

Safety Rules for Wrenches

There are a few basic rules that you should keep in mind when using wrenches:

- Always use a wrench that fits the nut properly.
- Keep wrenches clean and free from oil. Otherwise they may

slip, resulting in possible serious injury to you or damage to the work.

- Do not increase the leverage of a wrench by placing a pipe over the handle. Increased leverage may damage the wrench or the work.
- Determine which way a nut should be turned before trying to loosen it. Most nuts are turned counterclockwise for removal. This may seem obvious, but even experienced people have been observed straining at the wrench in the tightening direction when they wanted to loosen it.

AVOID NUT CONFUSION

There are many types of nuts, and each has a special use: *Square* and *hexagonal* nuts are standard, but they are supplemented by special nuts. One of these is the *jam* nut, used above a standard hex nut to lock it in position.

Castellated nuts are slotted so that a safety wire or cotter key may be pushed through the slots and into a matching hole in the bolt. This provides a positive method of preventing the nut from working loose.

Wing nuts are used where the desired degree of tightness can be obtained by the fingers. *Cap* nuts are used where appearance is an important consideration. *Thumb* nuts are knurled, so they can be turned by hand for easy assembly and disassembly.

SQUARE

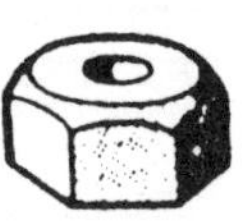
HEXAGONAL

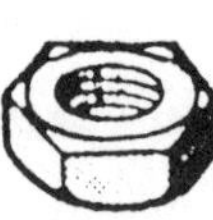
JAM

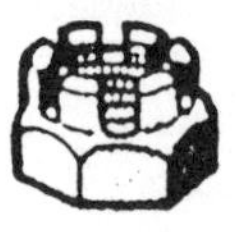
CASTELLATED

WING

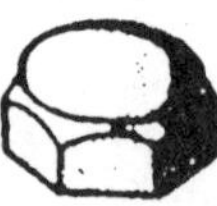
CAP

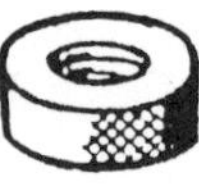
THUMB

STOP

The Three Types of Washers

Flat washers are used to back up bolt heads and nuts, and to provide larger bearing surfaces. They prevent damage to the surfaces of metal parts.

Split lock washers are used under nuts to prevent loosening by vibration. The ends of these spring-hardened washers dig into both the nut and the work to prevent slippage.

FLAT WASHER

SPLIT LOCK WASHER

SHAKE PROOF WASHER

Shakeproof lock washers have teeth or lugs that grip both the work and the nut. Several patented designs, shapes, and sizes are obtainable.

A Handy Shaver

The simple wood-shaver illustrated here is one of the handiest

tools to have around the house. Using it calls for no talent or experience. Manufactured by the Stanley Tool Co., and called Surform, it makes shaving down a door or drawer that has become too tight a simple job that can be done quickly. The blades last a long time before becoming dull, and they are replaceable.

Chiseling Technique

When chiseling wood, do not try to remove too much material at once. Shave off only small amounts at one time.

Tool Sharpening

When sharpening knives, scissors, and all types of tools and garden implements, keep the same bevel angles the tool had when new. Don't take off more metal than is necessary.

Sharpening Scissors

A quick way to sharpen scissors that are slightly dull but can stand a bit of honing is to make about six cuts into a piece of fine sandpaper. Extremely dull scissors will require conventional sharpening.

Disk Sharpeners

It requires more effort to cut with dull knives and tools. A variety of grinding tools and honing stones are available, but the old-fashioned disk sharpener is one of the least expensive and easiest to use. You can probably find one at your local hardware or variety store. Disk sharpeners can be mounted onto a wooden block or a counter. Pass the blade to be sharpened through the disks, exerting maximum pressure as you bring the knife toward you.

Shovel Sharpening

A shovel will give better service if its edge is kept sharp. File the bevel on the inside edge. The same treatment should be given spades and hoes.

Wood Files, Metal Files

When purchasing files, note that files for wood and files for metal are not the same. Wood files have fewer teeth which bite into the wood. A wood file will not work on metal and a metal file will not work efficiently on wood.

The Right Way to Use a Plane

A plane is used primarily for smoothing the edges of boards, and the best way to do this is to cut very fine shavings. Adjust the plane iron so that it barely protrudes from the bottom of the plane. Push the plane forward at a slight angle to the length of the

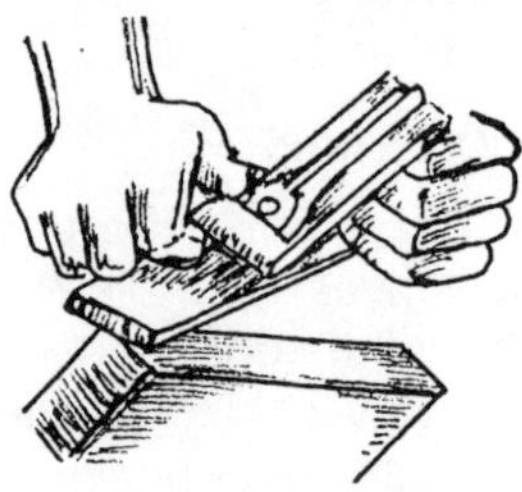

board for easy cutting. Several fine cuts are better than one thick one.

The Staple Gun

Staple guns are tremendous timesavers and are dependable for heavy and light work. They can accommodate quarter-inch to half-inch staples and will penetrate the hardest woods without much effort. The staple gun has dozens of practical uses, from holding glued parts in place until dry to making or repairing screens to installing ceiling tiles.

Small Parts Storage

Store nails, screws, nuts, bolts, and other small parts in plastic

jars that once contained baby food, applesauce, or mustard. Any kind of jar with a screw-on cap will do the job. (Glass jars with metal caps may be used, but there is the danger of breakage.) Simply pierce a hole in the center of the cap with a drill or a nail, then place the lid in position on the underside of a shelf and screw it into place. Use a washer under the screw to prevent the lid from turning when the jar is being unscrewed.

Keep Track of Small Parts

When taking apart equipment and appliances, it is easy to lose screws, bolts, washers, and other small parts. To prevent this, place all parts removed in a can or jar with a lid. Peanut cans are useful. Keeping track of small parts in this manner will assure that all parts removed will eventually be replaced.

Saving Washers and Nuts

Washers and nuts are easily misplaced. A good way to prevent them from becoming lost is to slip them over the open end of a large safety or diaper pin. Close the pin and suspend it from a nail or store it in a container.

Handling Steel Wool

To keep bits of steel from penetrating the skin when you are working with steel wool, cut a hollow rubber ball in half and place the pad in one of the halves. Bear down as hard as is neces-

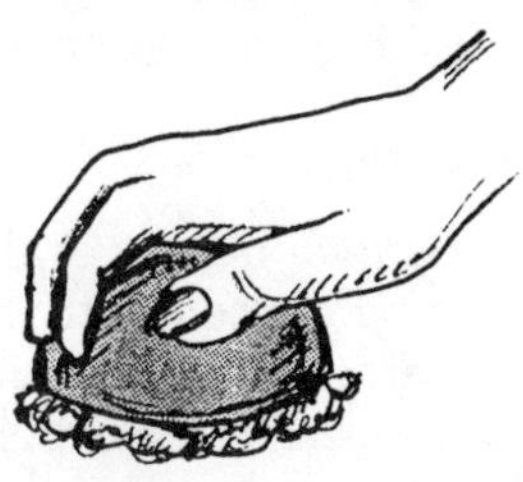

sary without worrying about picking up slivers.

Adding Life to Sandpaper

To add longevity to sandpaper, apply a stiff backing down the center of the sandpaper with a strip of masking tape. This will keep the sandpaper from tearing or creasing, even when you are using a sanding block on a relatively smooth surface. You'll get three times as much use from sandpaper this way.

Sandpaper Care

To add life and effectiveness to sandpaper, wet it slightly before wrapping it around a block of wood to do your sanding.

Steel "Sandpaper"

Pieces of this steel—tempered and of high quality—can do a better job than sandpaper—and they are easier to work with and cheaper in the long run. Usually called cabinet scrapers, the flat, thin (about 1/16 inch) implements usually measure two inches by six inches. Specialty hardware stores carry them in a few other sizes and shapes. You can scrape and smooth with them—and they work on wood, plasterboard, and most other surfaces.

Sanding Flat Boards

A bit of preparation will keep a flat board from slipping while being sanded. The idea is to place the board on a skid-free surface. Strips of foam rubber, such as a carpet cushion pad, will provide just such a surface. Foam rubber scraps are often available at no cost in stores that sell carpets. If not available to you, buy self-sticking weatherstripping in hardware stores. Either surface will prevent boards from slipping despite the vibrations caused by an electric sander.

Sanding Glass

To smooth the sharp edges of glass, fit a piece of sandpaper over the grooved end of a piece of wood flooring. Keep the sandpaper loose enough so you can fit the glass edge into the groove. Push back and forth with pressure applied. When the sandpaper is worn, shift the sandpaper on the block.

Cleaning Metal Files

In time, files usually clog up.

One good way of getting rid of embedded shavings and sawdust is to massage the file with an old toothbrush. After brushing, rinse the file with water, taking care to try to avoid rusting.

Saws That Bind

The cut, called the *kerf,* produced by a handsaw when a board is cut with the grain sometimes closes in on the blade and binds it. One way to avoid such binding is to push a nail or wedge of wood into the kerf at its open end. The insert will keep the kerf open until the sawing is finished.

To Make Sawing Easier

Rub a bar of soap either side of the blade of a handsaw and along the teeth. The blade will move through the wood with much greater ease. The soap will not stain the wood.

Saw Blade Treatment

Rust and resin often accumulate on saw blades, and this affects the effectiveness of the saw. This can be avoided by brushing sawdust from the blade after use, washing and drying, and then applying light oil to the blade when not in use. When ready to use the saw once again, wipe off the oil. Spray-can lubricants, such as WD40, are effective rust and resin removers.

Keeping Saws Sharp

You can avoid the time and expense of having to resharpen your handsaw or having to replace the blade if you get into the habit of sawing properly. It's therefore important to exert pressure only when you are pushing the saw down through the wood—away from the body. When drawing the saw back, lift it away from the wood slightly so no pressure is exerted against the object being sawed. Your blades will remain sharper longer, and sawing will require less energy.

Hacksaw Blades

Both coarse blades and fine blades can be used with hacksaws. Coarse blades cut faster and last longer. They should be used for most jobs. The thinner the surface being cut, the finer the blade that should be used. At least three teeth of the blade should engage the surface being cut. If, with the blade you have selected, only one or two of the teeth will be doing the cutting, choose a finer blade.

Cutting Glass

Wax will hold a ruler or a straight-edge in place when cutting glass. Normally, these have a tendency to shift. Make a heavy mark on the glass with a wax crayon and place your wood or metal ruler over the wax.

Cutting Plywood

When cutting plywood with a handsaw, place the good side face up so that any splintering will occur on the underside.

The same applies when using a table or radial saw, both of which cut in the downward direction.

When using a portable sabre or circular power saw, however, which cut on the upstroke, place the good side of the wood face down.

Protecting Circular Blades

Circular saw blades will stay sharp longer if protected when stored. An inch-wide cross-section of an old inner tube stretched around the blade of the saw will

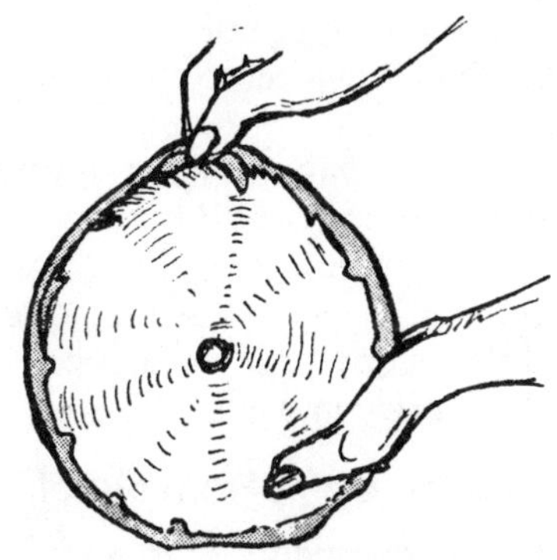

protect the teeth. Protect your fingers by wearing rubber gloves when putting the rubber around the blade.

Table Saw Safety

Keep your hands at least six inches from the blade when operating a tablesaw, and stand to one side of the cutting line, so that if the piece being cut binds and kicks back, it will not hit you. Above all, always use a push stick when pushing wood through to make narrow cuts.

Sawing Sticky Wood

Sawing wood containing excessive resin creates a sticky problem. To prevent sticking, squirt denatured alcohol along the line of the cut. Because the alcohol evaporates quickly, spray only about one foot down the saw line at a time. When the alcohol evaporates, the wood will not be stained.

Cutting Plasterboard

Plasterboard can be cut with a fine-toothed saw, but a better and easier method is to score and snap the material. Scoring should be done with a sharp utility knife drawn along a straight edge. Cut through the paper on the side of the plasterboard that will be facing the room. Be sure to press down sufficiently hard to cut through the plaster. Place a piece of wood under the plasterboard sheet with the edge of the wood along the cut line, and snap off the overhanging piece of plasterboard by pressing down on it. Cut through the paper backing on the reverse side to complete the job.

Preventing Wood Splitting

If nails (instead of glue) are used to join two pieces of wood, the wood will often split, especially if the nails are driven into the wood very close to the edge. The problem is easily solved either by drilling a small pilot hole before nailing or by cutting (or blunting) the point of the nail before hammering it in. Another method that often works well is to drive in the nail at an angle.

Drilling Through Plywood

To avoid splintering when drilling through plywood, drill through the good side. The splintering will occur on the backside. This can be avoided by clamping a piece of wood to the backside.

Homemade Bits

For work in soft wood, you can save on the cost of bits for electric drills by using nails for bits. Select a nail with the proper diameter for the job, and cut off the head of the nail with any metal cutter or hacksaw. Slide the nail into the drill as you would any bit. Tighten, and go to work! Nails used as drill bits will not penetrate metal.

Drilling Holes in Bottles

Drilling a hole through the side of a glass bottle that you are planning to convert into a lamp can be very difficult with an ordinary twist-bit and electric drill. The bit won't bite into the glass and will tend to wander over the surface of the glass. If this happens, use a spear-point carbide bit (not a masonry bit). Best results will be obtained if you use a variable speed electric drill that operates at very low speeds. Start your drilling at a low speed, and increase the rpm's as the hole begins to take shape. Lubricate the drill point with cool water from time to time as you are drilling, and do not press too hard.

Drilling Through Metal

A better drilling job will be accomplished, especially on metal, if you first drill through with a smaller bit and then redrill with the size bit required. Some craftsmen have found it effective to place a drop or two of turpentine, rather than oil, on the tip of the drill when piercing hard metal.

Slipping Nuts

To keep nuts from loosening, place a few drops of shellac on the bolt just before you give it the final, full turn. The shellac will hold the nut tight, but not so tight that you'll have difficulty loosening it later.

Another way to keep a nut from shifting is to add a second nut of the same size to the bolt. Tighten it against the first one, and the second nut will keep the first securely in place.

Removing Dents From Metal

To remove dents from a metal object, place the dented area on sand or another soft surface. Pound out the dents from the inside with a rubber mallet. If you do not have a mallet, convert a hammer into a mallet by putting a rubber tip over the face of the hammer. Use tips normally placed under chair and table legs. These are available at most hardware stores.

Stubborn Nuts

A badly rusted nut can sometimes be removed by repeated application of a penetrating oil, such as Liquid Wrench. Pour the oil, a few drops at a time, into the crack around the edges of the bolt. Allow the oil to sink in. After the second application, give the bolt several sharp blows with a hammer. Repeat this procedure several times until the nut loosens.

If this doesn't work, build a wall of putty around the frozen nut. Pour a little penetrating oil into the area inside the wall. Wait for several hours, remove the oil and putty, and turn the nut. If the nut is not freed after the first application, give it one more try with the penetrating oil.

Propane Torch for Stubborn Nuts

One way to remove a nut that has resisted your efforts with a wrench is to heat it with a propane torch. Best results will be obtained if the torch is adjusted to produce a small cone of flame. Direct the flame only at the nut. As the nut warms up, the hardened rust or paint will become loose enough to allow the nut to be turned with a wrench.

If All Else Fails . . .

Specially designed nutcrackers are available at better hardware stores. All that is required to crack the stubborn nut is to continue applying pressure to it until it splits. Other alternatives are to cut the nut off with a hacksaw, shear it off with a bolt cutter, or burn it off with an acetylene torch.

Taps and Dies

Bolts and nuts whose threads have become distorted can be restored to working order with special threading tools: *taps* (for nuts) and *dies* (for bolts). Though these sets are expensive, if you will be doing much machine-shop work, you might want to acquire a set.

Easy-out for Broken Screws and Bolts

If a bolt or screw breaks off in wood or metal, there is sometimes no alternative but to drill out the embedded stub. Once a hole is drilled in the screw or bolt, the remaining shell is removed with a screw extractor, also known as an "easy-out." Easy-outs come in sets of four or five in both rectangular and spiral configurations. Before drilling the hole, consult the recommendations printed on the easy-out packaging as to the diameter hole which must be drilled. A properly sized hole is imperative.

Cutting Metal Tubing

Before starting to cut through metal tubing, drive a short length of wood dowel into the tube. Then cut through both the tube and the dowel. The dowel will keep the teeth of the saw from catching against the edges of the tube with every stroke of the saw.

HIRING A CONTRACTOR

When to Hire a Contractor

Even if you are an ambitious homeowner, certain types of improvements will require professional help. When having major work done on a kitchen or bathroom, the expertise of more than one professional—a carpenter, plumber, electrician—will be required. In these cases, hiring a contractor is probably your best bet.

Interviewing Contractors

When interviewing a contractor for a job, learn as much about the company as possible. Make sure to determine if the person with whom you are speaking is an owner. Find out

- who will be running the job on a day-to-day basis;
- how long the company has been in business;
- how many people will be working on the job;
- where the company is presently working;
- the names and phone numbers of three recent jobs the company has done so that you can call for references;
- whether this company subcontracts its work or does all of the work on its own.

The Most Important Factor: Experience

Surely, you will want to find a contractor who will do the job as cheaply as possible. Even more important, however, is finding a contractor on whom you can rely to do a good job. The company you hire should have experience doing the kind of work you need done. If you plan to remodel a bathroom for example, you will not want to contract the job out to someone who has no experience laying tiles.

Understand the Contract

Before signing a contract with the person or company you have decided to hire, make sure that it specifies

- the exact nature of the work to be done. Materials to be used should be specified;
- how long the job will take;
- that the contractor is licensed and insured;
- how payments are to be made.

Be sure to read the fine print!

ADHESIVES

Gluing Guidance

To prevent glue from spilling onto nearby objects or onto the surface on which you are working, spread out a length of wax paper and do your gluing on it.

If the glued objects must be weighted down to keep them securely together while the glue is drying, there is a probability that the glue will seep out onto the piece you are using as a weight. Placing wax paper under the weight will save you a great deal of cleanup time.

Glue Application

When covering a large surface with a thin coat of glue, use a fine-toothed comb to spread the glue. The comb-spreader is especially useful when working on nonporous surfaces, such as veneer.

Gluing Clamps

To hold glued objects together while glue is drying, use spring-type clothespins and paper clips. If these are not available, use the clamps that can be found on some clothes hangers. For larger items, use spring or vise clamps available in hardware outlets. If the objects being glued are likely to be marred by the clamps, place a piece of cardboard or a thin piece of wood between the clamp and the object.

White Glue Stains

To remove white glue stains, apply very hot water. After the glue has softened, the garment can be washed in normal fashion by hand or in a washing machine.

Contact Cements

Although widely used for affixing plastic laminates to countertops, contact cements work well on metal, rubber, plastic, leather, fabrics, and wood. The two surfaces are bonded to one another by applying a coating to each surface and then bringing them together. The bonding is almost instantaneous, requiring no clamping. Nonflammable and fast-drying, contact cement is particularly effective on wood.

Cementing Nonporous Articles

Cements suitable for glass, glazed porcelain, plastics, and other nonporous articles are available under brand names such as Devcon Duco Cement. Slight pressure must be applied for a few minutes to create a successful bond.

Repairing Canvas With Rubber Cement

Canvas articles can be repaired with rubber cement. Hold the patch (which should also be canvas material) in place, and apply a weight to it after cementing. Leave the weight on the patch for several hours.

Plastic Resin Glue

For woodworking projects that require stronger adhesive than white glue, use plastic resin glue, which forms a bond stronger than wood itself. Plastic resin glue comes in powdered form.

White Glues

White glues work best on porous materials, including

wood, paper, and fabrics. They dry clear but are not resistant to moisture, so when more than average-strength bonding is required, a stronger adhesive should be used.

Epoxy Adhesives

Probably the strongest of all adhesives, and the most expensive, are epoxy glues. Epoxy glues come in two tubes: adhesive and activator. Small amounts from each tube are mixed together and applied to the area to be bonded. Since epoxy glues are cured by chemical interaction, the amount of time available for application is limited, since the mixture sets and dries in 10 to 20 minutes.

Epoxies will bond wood, glass, most plastics, metal, and ceramics, and are good for indoor and outdoor use. No pressure is required to hold pieces together.

New Epoxies

Some new epoxy products, such as those manufactured by the Devcon Corporation, combine the traditional two tubes into one syringelike dispenser. An equal amount of adhesive and activator is released by pushing down a double piston device that releases the ingredients. The two substances are then easily mixed and applied.

Instant One-drop Glues

One-drop instant adhesives, such as Krazy Glue or Super Glue, are best for materials such as glass, metal, ceramics, and some plastics. One drop will bond materials immediately. Only slight finger pressure is required to release the glue.

The adhesive must be used with great care because, if it gets on the skin, it is very difficult to remove. Using acetone immediately often helps, but this is hazardous if the glue is near the eyes, in which case immediate medical help is required.

Adhesive for Lightweight Objects

Instead of thumbtacks, which mar surfaces, use Holdit plastic adhesives to hold lightweight objects, such as posters, notes, and cards. Puttylike in nature, it never dries out, sticks to practically every surface, and can be used over and over again. If not available at your hardware or stationary store, write to the manufacturer, Faber-Castell. See the Appendix for the address.

Gluing Metal to Wood

When gluing metal to wood, first cover the metal surface with acetone. When the acetone has dried, join the metal to the wood with a regular household cement.

Gluing Glass

For gluing one glass surface to another, shellac is an excellent adhesive. First, set the shellac in an old dish and put a match to it. This will burn up the alcohol. What is left will be an excellent adhesive that can be used to join glass to glass, leather to metal, plus many other combinations of materials.

Gluing Ceramic Pieces

Epoxy resin glue is the proper adhesive to use for fixing ceramic pieces. Be certain that the surfaces being glued are especially clean.

Gluing Plastic and Plexiglass

When applied to plastic surfaces, acetone will dissolve the plastic enough to allow the pieces to bond. Set the plastic or plexiglass on a secure foundation and tape in place the parts to be joined. To apply the acetone, use a glass or metal applicator, such as a hypodermic needle. (A plastic needle would dissolve.) Apply the acetone to the edges where the two pieces meet. Leave the tape in place until the melted plastic has firmly set.

Repairing Holes in Plastic

To mend holes in plastic items, such as buckets and toys, start by sanding the area around the hole. This will roughen the area so the bond will be stronger. Place another piece of plastic, preferably of the same type, over the hole (on the inside if possible), and use a soldering iron set on low heat. First, dip the tip of the soldering iron in oil, then fuse the patch to the plastic being repaired.

The plastic inside lining of the caps of most aspirin bottles, and the plastic covers of coffee and peanut cans, are good for patching small holes.

Softening and Loosening Glue

Most glues that have hardened can usually be softened by pouring a few drops of vinegar into the container. If you want to loosen joints that have been glued together, apply a liberal amount of vinegar to the joint.

Glue Container Tops

Glues, shellacs, or other adhesives usually adhere to the top of the container in which they are stored, and it is often difficult to open them. Spread petroleum jelly (Vaseline) over the parts of the lid that touch the container before closing. The glue will not stick to those areas, and you will have no difficulty opening the container.

19
Caring For Your Car

Introduction

The computer age has become firmly entrenched in automotives, and caring for one's car is no longer the chore it once was. The foremost improvements are in the starting and fuel metering systems. With electronic ignition, the mandatory yearly tune-up is now largely a thing of the past.

The budget-minded car owner can do much to reduce the cost of car maintenance. Once the drain plug and filter have been located, oil and oil filter changes can be accomplished quickly. Lubrication, too, is a straightforward operation if the car provides sufficient undercarriage clearance. Changing spark plugs requires only a spark plug socket wrench and an inexpensive gapping tool. Flushing the radiator and adding new antifreeze is no more difficult than removing the drain plug, and changing an air filter may not require any tools at all. Whenever performing any car service operations, always wear work clothing, make sure that the car is properly braked, and be aware that a hot radiator operates under pressure and can be dangerous.

Even if you choose not to service your car, you should make a weekly inspection. Even without a pressure gauge, it is easy to tell whether a tire needs air. Inspecting each tire will reveal embedded nails or glass. A careful look under the hood will verify that the radiator, battery, power steering, and break fluid levels are correct; that there is sufficient oil in the engine crankcase;

and that all of the belts are unfrayed and sufficiently tight. Going through this checklist weekly will prevent harrowing highway breakdowns.

Lastly, every driver should know how to use the jack and replace punctured tires. Because several years sometimes pass without using the jack, it is sound advice to remove the jack every six months and review how it is used.

GENERAL AUTOMOTIVE HINTS

Buying vs. Leasing a Car

There are advantages and disadvantages to buying and leasing a vehicle. The decision to buy or lease should be based on your financial situation, whether you intend to use the car for business, and other factors. Consult an accountant or a person familiar with the pros and cons of the two methods before making a final decision.

Car Trade-in

When a car has traveled about 60,000 miles, many experts suggest that it is time to trade it in. Although there are certainly exceptions, at that point maintenance and repair costs generally start to escalate.

USED CARS

Before buying a used car, have it examined by a mechanic. But before doing that, here are a few tests you can perform yourself:

1. Test the shocks by pushing down on each bumper in turn. Note whether the car levels off quickly without bouncing.
2. Check the oil. Remove the dipstick. If the oil clings to it, this may indicate that the seller has added a very heavy oil to cover up a defective engine.
3. Most engines sound good once they finally get started, so pay special attention to the sound of the motor when you *first* start it. If it sounds peculiar, beware!
4. At a cruising speed of around 25 miles per hour, push the accelerator to the floor. A sound engine will quickly and steadily pick up speed.
5. Be aware of how the shift feels when you take off on your test drive and how it feels after you've been on the road for a while. Some dealers attempt to silence a noisy transmission with oatmeal or bananas!

6. Test-drive the car in uncongested traffic. At 35 miles per hour, take your hands off the steering wheel. The car should steer itself straight for about 50 yards. Also, be sure there is sufficient play in the steering wheel. You should be able to turn the steering wheel about one and one-half inches before the front wheels start to move.
7. Test-drive the car over some bumps. If the suspension is in good shape, the car should take the bumps smoothly and quietly.
8. Check the automatic drive for proper acceleration on an average uphill grade. There should be no slippage. Then, back the car up a short hill. It should make the climb smoothly.
9. When applying the brakes suddenly, the car should not pull to one side. If it does, consult a mechanic.

Put It in Writing

When purchasing a used car, be sure to get all promises and guarantees in writing. They should be indicated on the bill of sale and should be signed by the owner or dealer.

When purchasing a used car on the installment plan, be sure to get an itemized accounting of the cost, including down payment, monthly payments, interest charges, and additional charges. Check carefully before signing the agreement.

Safe Car Colors

Experts tell us that light-colored cars (yellow, green, white, cream) are most visible and are therefore safest on the road. Dark colors (red and black) are the least safe.

Shopping for Car Insurance

Before buying car insurance, the National Insurance Consumer Organization (NICO) suggests that one get a quote from GEICO, which sells insurance by mail from Washington, DC (Telephone: 1-800-841-3000).

Save $ on Old, Battered Cars

If your car is old, battered, or for any reason has little market value, you would be well advised to raise to the maximum the deductible on your collision and comprehensive insurance. Instead of a $250 deductible, make it $500. The higher the deductible, the lower the rate you pay. Or, better yet, if your car is more than ten years old, consider not carrying collision and comprehensive at all.

Insurance Coverage for Glass and Towing

You may be one of many motorists who is not aware that most car insurance policies provide complete coverage, with no deductibles, for glass breakage and for costs of towing a vehicle. Check your policy to be certain.

Car Insurance for Present and Past Military

Present or former military officers, including their spouses, widows, and widowers, may find good insurance rates from USAA in San Antonio, Texas (telephone: 1-800-531-8080).

Car ID

A suggestion often made is that a new car owner slip his or her business card or a piece of paper with name and address on the side of one of the car door windows. If the car is ever stolen, this will be a good means of proving that the car is yours, because even if the car is dismantled for parts, chances are the door and its window will not be separated.

Car Wheel Lock

When buying a car, make sure to ascertain whether the wheels have a locking lug. If so, a special round "key" about three inches long and one inch in diameter is needed to remove them. Be sure you know where that key is (it's usually placed in the glove compartment) because without it you'll be unable to change your tires.

Avoid Car Pockmarks

If you want to reduce the chances of the sides of your car getting pockmarked, try to park next to cars with four doors. The doors on these cars are not as wide as those on two-door models and, hence, are less likely to make contact with the body of your car.

Parking Space

When parking, select a space in between or next to new cars. Owners of new cars are usually more careful when opening and closing doors and are less likely to damage your car.

THE CAR EXTERIOR

Car Washing Water

When washing a car, use cool or lukewarm water. Hot water may damage the car finish.

Dry After Washing

Don't expect a car to become perfectly clean if it is washed with detergent and then allowed to dry itself. Unless the car is dried with clean towels, water stains will appear. Do not use dirty towels: the grit in them may scratch the finish.

Squashed Insects

To remove insects squashed against the hood of the car, use a dampened linen or nylon net. Without scratching the surface, the fibers will act as a mild abrasive.

Rust-proofing New Cars

It is standard procedure for a car salesman to try to convince the buyer to have the underpart of the car rustproofed. This is an unnecessary expense because all new cars are rustproofed when built.

Rust Protection

By the time winter is over, the underside of most cars harbor an accumulation of salt and other corrosive chemicals used by highway departments in the snow and ice removal process. Hose off the underside of your car thoroughly, particularly the underside of doors, fenders, and the exhaust pipe.

Undercoating Caveat

The cost of undercoating a car is high. So, before having your car so treated, check out the reliability of the firm that will do the work. Many outfits promise more than they deliver, and most consumers are not able to determine for themselves whether an undercoating job has been done properly.

Car Glass

Windshields and car windows can be cleaned from traffic spatterings by rubbing them with a damp sponge on which baking soda has been sprinkled. Rinse with clean water and wipe off with paper toweling.

Squeegees

The most effective way of cleaning a windshield is with a squeegee. It washes the windshield clean and removes the excess water. To be sure no streaks are left behind, wipe off with a damp chamois.

Windshield Wiper Blades

If windshield wiper blades are not cleaning the glass well, or if a wiper blade chatters when running, wax or some other material may be on the blade or windshield. Clean with a nonabrasive cleanser. The windshield is clean if beads do not form when rinsing with water.

Reaching the Wiper Blades

In order to reach the wiper blades, place the wiper switch in the "low" position and the ignition switch in the "accessory" position. When the wiper blades are approximately vertical on the windshield, turn off the ignition switch.

Windshield Wiper Conditioning

Improve the effectiveness of your windshield wiper blades and lengthen their life by cleaning the edges with a detergent from time to time. If the wipers are slightly nicked, rub fine sandpaper over the edges. To avoid damage to wiper blades, do not use gasoline, kerosene, paint thinner, or other solvents on or near them.

Homemade Windshield Fluid

Windshield wiper fluid offers two advantages: it will not freeze in cold weather and it will not form deposits common to water. If you run out of windshield wiper fluid, to one cup of water add one quart of rubbing alcohol and two tablespoons of liquid dishwashing detergent. Pour into the container under the car hood.

Window Stickers

Inspection stickers on a car windshield are often difficult to remove because of the slope of the windshield. Use a putty knife to scrape off as much as possible, then remove the remainder with a cloth or sponge moistened with acetone or nail polish remover (which contains acetone as a basic ingredient).

Whitewall Tires

To restore the whiteness of whitewall tires, mesh kitchen soap pads are effective. Occasionally, rubbing with a scouring powder may be needed to complete the job.

Car Polishing

Keep your car looking good by polishing it whenever necessary. You can tell when it needs polishing by dropping water on the hood. If the water forms into beads, the old polish is still intact.

Autobody Repair

Plexus is a new adhesive that car owners will find effective in bonding broken plastic and metal parts on cars. A strong bond is achieved in 15 minutes and a full-strength bond in less than two hours.

Protecting the Car Surface

Wax improves a car's appearance, and it also protects the surface against rusting and fading. Wax the car right after you've washed and dried it.

Shellacking Chrome

The chrome on your car will stay bright indefinitely if you protect it with shellac. Apply one or two thin coats of fresh white shellac every six months.

CAR MAINTENANCE AND OPERATION

Tire Pressure

Keep tires inflated to the pressure recommended in the owner's manual. In some late-model cars, recommended tire pressure can be found on a plate attached to the doorframe on the driver's side.

Driving with less than the recommended pressure can reduce the life of the tires by as much as 25 percent. Too little pressure makes for a very spongy ride; too much pressure makes for a very hard ride.

Note that recommended tire

pressure varies with the seasons of the year. In general, less air is required in summer (when air expands) than in winter.

Tire Checks

Small cuts and breaks in tires tend to grow deeper, and they invite the entry of dirt and water, which in time destroy the cord structure. Check tires frequently for embedded nails and glass.

Tire Longevity

Rotate your tires every 5,000 miles to be sure of even wear. Include the spare in the rotation. When treads wear unevenly, a shimmy will develop, making for a very uncomfortable ride. Also, tires will last much longer if you make sure the brakes are well adjusted and if you avoid screeching halts and sudden starts.

Wheel Alignment and Balance

When tires are out of balance, the result is that the wheels shimmy and the tires wear unevenly. If you notice uneven wear, have your wheels aligned and balanced by an experienced mechanic. Beware of a mechanic who installs too many weights when balancing tires.

Don't Curb Your Car

Every driver tries to avoid potholes, but not all drivers are careful enough about staying away from the curb. When a tire is scraped against a curb, the tire fabric is crushed against the rim, snapping the cords in the tire and cutting or scraping the sidewall.

Proper Engine Lubrication

Keep your car in good condition by following the oil lubrication advice in your owner's manual. It will pay off in added power, better gas mileage, and longer life for the engine. Use lightweight oil in cold weather and heavy oil in warmer months. Using the wrong oil results in wasted gas consumption. Do not forget to change the oil filter with each engine oil change.

Fill 'er Up

When you add gas to your tank, fill it up. A full tank leaves no room for condensation. Condensation adds water to the fuel, which is harmful to the engine.

Watch Oil Level

When there is not enough oil circulating in your car, harm can be done to vital engine parts. Monitor the engine oil level by checking the dipstick regularly. As engines age, oil consumption increases. Consider disposing of a car with insatiable thirst for oil.

Check the Clutch

Be aware of how far you have to push the clutch in when shifting. A clutch that goes in all the way doesn't have much wear left. If the clutch is in good shape, the pedal will have about an inch of play.

A clutch that slips uses more gas than needed, robs the engine of power, and reduces its lifespan. Have it relined as soon as possible.

The "Grabber" for Oil Filters

A specially designed oil filter removal tool, made with oil-resistant handles in two sizes, has been recently introduced by the Pine Vally Co. If not available in your auto parts store, write to the company. See the Appendix for the address.

Carburetor Adjustment

There is no need to burn too rich a mixture of fuel. A carburetor that is not adjusted properly can provide too rich a mix. Monitor your gas mileage and, if it declines, consider a carburetor adjustment. Worn spark plugs and worn engine valves and pistons are other causes of reduced gas mileage.

Battery Terminals

Check the car's battery terminals from time to time. If covered with a white, powdery substance, clean off with a rag or a brush with fiber bristles. Do not use a brush with metal bristles.

Extending Battery Life

Before discarding a battery that seems to be used up, disconnect and rub all grime off the points of contact. In many cases, you will find that there is much life left in the battery.

Check Wiring Regularly

Do not rely on service station personnel to tell you when wiring in your car is worn or frayed. Regularly look under the hood yourself and check out the wiring. If you see wiring that appears damaged or defective, make an appointment with a mechanic. In general, wiring should be as far away as possible from hot engine parts. If you notice wiring that seems too close, move it away.

Spark Plugs

Weak spark plugs can prevent complete combustion of fuel. To avoid the accompanying higher consumption of fuel, have spark plugs, along with distributor points and battery ignition coil, checked regularly.

Temperature Gauge

An engine that's too hot can cause damage to the pistons and cylinder walls as well as other parts. To be sure the cooling system is working properly, check the temperature gauge regularly. The best temperature at which to operate an engine is between 170 and 190 degrees Fahrenheit.

Spray Lubricants

The ideal way to eliminate squeaks in car doors and hinges is to apply a spray lubricant, such as WD40, which has the ability to penetrate hard-to-reach areas and displace moisture. These nongreasy lubricants, available in all hardware stores, will protect metal parts and surfaces against rust and loosen badly corroded and sticky joints.

Before Starting the Car

Different engines have different starting procedures. Frequently, the accelerator pedal is depressed several times before the ignition key is turned. The number of depressions will vary with the outside air temperature and the length of time since the car has been used. It is not always proper procedure to keep the pedal depressed when starting the engine. Check your owner's manual for precise information.

Wait Before Rolling

After the engine has started, a car should be idled for a period of time to allow the engine to warm up. If this waiting period is not observed, the car may stall, particularly in cold or damp weather. Check the owner's manual for the recommended waiting period.

Checking Gas Mileage

To determine how many miles a car gets per gallon of gas, fill the tank completely and jot down the mileage on the odometer. The next time you need gas, fill up the tank completely once again and note the mileage on the odometer. Subtract the lower number from the higher one and you will know how many miles have been traveled.

Now, divide the number of miles you drove by the number of gallons you put in. For example, if the tank was filled with 14 gallons and you drove 350 miles since the last fill-up, divide 350 by 14 to find out that the car was getting 25 miles per gallon (mpg).

Mileage and Octane

Some people think that high-octane gasoline gives a car more miles of travel per gallon. Octane does not affect gas mileage. The best way to get better mileage is to reduce the rate of speed at which the car travels, which is not always easy with today's fast roads and highways.

Car Fuses

You can save yourself considerable money and anxiety if you can locate the small box under the dashboard that houses all the fuses for the car. These fuses very in amperage, and they control the windshield wiper, signal lights, radio, air conditioner and heater, cigarette lighter, and other accessories.

In the car manual you will find a diagram of the fuse box showing exactly which fuse controls which function.

When you find that one of the above-mentioned items is not working, do not run to your mechanic before checking the fuse yourself. He may charge you $10.00 or more to correct something you could easily do for under a dollar.

If, for example, it is the windshield wiper that is not working, locate the position of the wiper fuse in the fuse box by checking its location in the manual. Remove the fuse by simply pulling it out. Take the fuse to any store that carries automobile accessories and purchase an exact duplicate, one with the same number of amps. Push into place. If the wiper works, that was your problem. If the wiper still doesn't work, the problem is elsewhere, and your mechanic will have to help you.

Note that for fuse-testing purposes you can "borrow" an adjacent fuse with the same amp rating, if available.

Air Filters

Much gasoline is wasted if the air filter is not cleaned or changed as recommended in the auto owner's manual. To burn less fuel, keep the air filter clean.

When to Replace Belts

Automobile alternator and fan belts often develop cracks in their V-shaped walls, some extending as far as the cord material which surrounds the outer circumference of the belt. If the belt appears about to break, replace it.

Beware of Belt Fraud

One of the favorite ruses of disreputable service stations, especially those located just off highway exits, is to slit fan and alternator belts when the owner is in the restroom, point out the problem when the patron returns, and milk a quick and profitable repair. It is best, when frequenting such vulnerable service stations, to be in the presence of the attendant as he inspects the car. Be aware, too, that attendants at service stations located near highways are sometimes not qualified mechanics; their diagnoses often carry little value.

Engine Racing

Avoid racing a cold engine. Racing the engine burns gas and results in a lot of engine wear.

Speeding

High-speed driving not only consumes a great deal of gas but also increases tire wear. Particularly, when you speed while negotiating curves, you are decreasing the life span of the tires tenfold.

Riding the Brake

By resting your foot lightly on the brake when you do not intend to slow down or stop, you can overheat the brakes and wear out the brake lining and pads much faster than would normally happen. You are also wasting fuel by forcing the engine to work against the brakes.

Pump Gas Pedal and Brake Evenly

In normal operation, the brake and gas pedals should be depressed smoothly. Sudden, heavy depressions of either pedal puts strain on the car and causes an uneven, jerky ride.

GAS-SAVING TIPS

1. Turn off your engine if you plan to stop for more than a minute. Restarting uses less gasoline than a minute's idling.
2. Avoid pressing the accelerator all the way down when climbing hills and long grades. It wastes gasoline.
3. Jumpy starts and fast getaways will burn over 50 percent more gasoline than normal acceleration.
4. Pumping the accelerator when waiting at a traffic light consumes a great deal of gas. So, refrain from doing so.
5. Check tire pressure every month. Low tire pressure increases rolling resistance, causes increased tire wear, and reduces gasoline mileage.

DEALING WITH EXTREMES OF WEATHER

Cold-weather Care

Keeping a car in a partially heated garage in cold weather ensures that the car won't freeze up. A garage temperature of 40 degrees Fahrenheit is ideal. But whether or not you garage your car, never let the radiator be filled with water only. Antifreeze should be mixed with the radiator water and kept in the car throughout the year. Ratios of antifreeze to water depend on the climate. A 50-50 mixture is a good guideline.

Check the radiator when it is cool to see that fluid levels in both the radiator and the plastic overflow tank are as they should be.

Frozen Car Locks

One of the easiest ways to unfreeze a car lock is to insert a hot key. Heat the key with a cigarette lighter or a match. Protect your hands from the heat by wearing gloves, and heat only the tip of the key.

Cold Weather Start-up

If your car has a carburetor and the car fails to start in cold weather, try the following. While the car is still in the garage, blow hot air on the carburetor with a workshop vacuum, a hair dryer, or similar item.

Icy Windshields

To avoid having to scrape hard ice from the windshield of your car on a freezing winter morning, cover the glass with a sheet of vinyl plastic the preceding evening. Place magnets over the vinyl sheet and position them against the metal windshield molding. In the morning, simply pull away the plastic and the windshield will be free of ice.

Warm Water for Icy Windshields

Pouring a bucket of warm water on ice-covered windshields will remove the ice successfully and without effort in all but the coldest weather.

Windshield Treatment

In cold weather, warm the windshield by putting on the defroster before using the window washer spray. This will prevent ice from forming on the glass.

Foggy Windshields

If your windshield tends to get fogged over on the inside in cold, damp weather, clear it up by spraying with an ammonia-based cleaner (such as Windex) and wiping it clean with newspaper or paper towels. But first start the car and let it warm up so the defogger can take over.

Opening the car windows a crack in damp weather will often relieve fogging.

Antifreeze as Windshield Washer?

Do not mistakenly use radiator antifreeze as windshield washer. It could cause paint damage and cloud the windshield.

Car Ventilation

To improve car ventilation and bring in a fresh flow of air, clear snow and ice from the hood and from the air inlet in front of the windshield. This helps the heater and defroster work better and reduces the chance of fogging the inside of the windshield.

Removing Trapped Hot Air

On hot, muggy days, before putting on the car air conditioner, open the car windows for a minute or two to allow trapped hot air to escape. By doing so, you will cool the car interior much faster.

Air Conditioners in Cars

In many car models it is advisable to start the air conditioning system at full power and after a few minutes to turn it down to normal. At full power the vent is closed and the car cools off more quickly. When reducing the power to normal, the vent opens and air circulates in the car. Consult the owner's manual for more information.

Air Conditioner Life

Add to the life of your car's air conditioner by running it once a month for at least ten minutes, summer or winter. This procedure will preserve the condenser.

Rocking Your Car

If you find your car stuck in mud or snow, rock the car forward and backward in a steady rhythm to help gain enough momentum to extricate it. Shift between forward and reverse gears while pressing softly on the accelerator. Varying the direction of the front wheels can sometimes provide the additional bit of traction required. Prolonged rocking, however, may cause the engine to overheat and result in transaxle and tire damage.

Radio Antennas

Radio antennas often get pitted by weather and become difficult to move. You can prevent this by coating them with wax, especially in winter.

Driving Through Flooded Areas

Do not drive through water that is higher than the bottom of the wheel rims. If you do, the brakes will stop working.

CAR SAFETY AND EMERGENCIES

Car Recalls

If you want to find out if the model car you own has been recalled due to a defect in manufacture, call the National Highway Traffic Safety Administration hotline at 1-800-424-9393. There is no charge for the service.

Headlights and Windshield Wipers

Several states have passed legislation requiring that whenever car windshield wipers are used, the headlights must be turned on as well. Check with your Motor Vehicles Bureau to find out if this law is in effect in your state. Fines can amount to $100.

Driving While Under Medication

Do not drive after taking any drug that may induce drowsiness. These include prescription drugs such as valium and over-the-counter drugs in the antihistamine family, including cold suppressants.

When Most Accidents Occur

Most accidents occur at night and on weekends. So, driver, beware!

Drugs, Alcohol, and Driving

It is unwise to consume even small amounts of alcohol when you are on drugs of any kind—especially before driving. Drowsiness caused by many common medications is increased considerably when even a little bit of alcohol is consumed. Be aware that some cough medicines contain enough alcohol to produce the same effect as wines and liquors.

Spare Keys

It is wise to have spare keys squirreled away so you are not locked out of your car. Many people keep a duplicate car key in their wallet or the coin compartment of a pocketbook. A duplicate house key can be hidden in the garage or in an obscure crack in the house wall.

Stuck Car Locks

If you can't get your key into the door lock or into the ignition, squeeze powdered graphite into the keyhole and it should free the lock. If this doesn't work, or if you do not have powdered graphite handy, rub the lead of a soft pencil against the sides of the key. Give the key a good coating and then push it into the lock, moving it in and out a few times before turning. A drop of oil on the key can also be effective in releasing stuck locks.

Ignition Key Difficulty

If you have trouble turning the ignition key to start the car, try moving the steering wheel to the right or left until the key turns freely.

Car Fails to Start

If your car fails to start, the problem may be a defective battery or a malfunctioning alternator. However, before replacing either, make sure to check the alternator belt. Often the only thing required is that the belt be tightened. After this is done, the battery will need to be jumped or charged.

Brake Light Warning

If after releasing the parking brake, the brake light remains on, this indicates a malfunction in the brake system, which requires immediate attention.

Testing the Shocks

If you feel that your car ride is not as smooth as it should be, test the condition of the shocks by sitting on the car fender and moving up and down. When the car is bouncing, jump off. If it bounces up only once, the shocks are OK. If it keeps on bouncing, the shocks are shot. You need new ones.

Drying Wet Brakes

When a car has been driven through water deep enough to wet the brake components, and sometimes after a car has been washed, it might not decelerate at the usual rate, or it might pull to the right or left. If you cannot wait and allow time for the brakes to dry out naturally, drive very slowly and apply pressure to the brakes lightly. This procedure will dry out the brakes in several minutes.

Engine Overheating

If you have an old-model car (1985 or earlier approximately) and the engine is overheating, turn off the air conditioner (if it is on), move off the road, and shift to neutral. Let the engine idle for two or three minutes. If the temperature does not start to drop, turn off the motor and leave the car. Call for assistance.

If you have a late-model car (1986 or later) and the car is overheating in heavy traffic, in the summer months turn on the air conditioner and in winter turn on the defroster. A special fan kicks in automatically, which will prevent the car from overheating.

Shift Gears

Continuously pressing on the brakes will cause them to overheat. When descending a long or steep hill, shift to a lower gear.

Escaping Steam

If an engine has overheated and you see or hear steam or coolant escaping, wait before opening the hood. Never remove the radiator cap or the coolant recovery tank cap while the engine and radiator are still hot.

Cruise Control

Do not use automatic cruise control on slippery roads.

Avoid Skidding

To avoid skidding and losing control on slippery roads, do not downshift into first at speeds above 20 mph when driving an automatic transmission and above 5 mph when driving a manual transmission.

Car Jacks

Since cars have to be jacked up quite a bit to change tires, you can take some of the strain off the jack by putting it on a platform made from two-by-fours or four-by-fours. This will raise the jack sufficiently to avoid the arching that often occurs when the jack is raised. You will also find that the car will stand more firmly if a platform is placed under the jack.

Don't get under the car while it is in a raised position. Also, to prevent the car from rolling accidentally, place short two-by-fours or bricks under the wheels that are not being raised.

Jack Helper

It is a good idea to keep a large piece of ⅝-inch or ¾-inch plywood in your car trunk for an emergency tire-changing. Often, the ground is soft where the jack is placed, and the firmness of the plywood will make the difficult task of jacking up the vehicle quite a bit easier.

Tire Traction

If you are stuck in mud or snow and can't get a push, you might try to get more traction by putting boards or ashes under the tires or by letting some air out of the back tires (or front tires if the car has front-wheel drive). Accelerate slowly in low gear so the wheels won't spin as fast. Reinflate the tires at the nearest service station.

If you use chains on your tires to get traction, keep them loose rather than tight. This provides better traction and does the least amount of damage to the tires.

Distress Signal

If your car breaks down on a highway, the best way to summon help (unless you are near a telephone) is to raise the car hood. This is a universally understood call for help. The other method of calling attention to one's plight is to put on the car blinkers.

Police Alert

It is wise to keep a large sign handy to alert police in case you are stuck on the road. Print the words CALL POLICE on a piece of cardboard or cloth and keep it in the trunk.

Exhaust Fumes

Do not idle an engine in closed areas (in a garage, for example) and do not sit in a parked or stopped car for any length of time with the engine idling. You may be overcome by potentially lethal carbon monoxide gases.

Reclining Seatbacks

If the back of the driver's seat and front passenger seat is kept in a fairly upright position, the chances of personal injury are reduced in the event of a sudden stop or a collision.

If the seatback is positioned at more than a five-degree angle from the most upright position, protection afforded by the seat and shoulder belts is considerably reduced.

Car Restraints

The cushioned head restraint on the back of each of the front seats should be positioned so that the top of the cushion is approximately on the level of the ears. It should not be positioned to cradle the neck.

20
Gardening

Introduction

Gardening is said to be America's most popular hobby and, indeed, it can be practiced by people of virtually any age, at any time of the year, in open rural spaces and in cramped city apartments. Those who live in the suburbs or the country can tend large vegetable gardens and fruit orchards which will provide food throughout the year; those with smaller spaces can tend delicate flower gardens and pamper postage-stamp-size lawns; those without open-air space can cultivate houseplants and terrariums. No one who loves to tend plants need be idle at any time during the year.

Garden Help

If you have difficulty growing grass, flowers, or vegetables, a soil analysis by your county agriculture extension agent or state agriculture department might provide an explanation. Check the telephone book for phone numbers and addresses. County and state agriculture officials will explain how to take a proper soil sample.

Allergy-prone Gardeners

Pollen counts are highest between 8:30 a.m. and 5:30 p.m., so if you are allergy-prone, do your gardening at other hours. Wear a mask to filter out the pollen. Some doctors advise their patients to take an antihistamine as a precaution.

Nail Dirt

It's easier to get dirt under your nails while gardening than it is to get it out. Avoid the problem by scratching your nails against a bar of soap before beginning garden work.

Wet-weather Gardening

When gardening in wet weather, slide plastic bags over your shoes or sneakers and it will be easier to slide on a pair of boots. It will also provide additional protection against wet feet.

In general, it is a poor idea to work wet soil, since it will tend to clump and compact. Further, moisture activates fungus spores on wet leaves. Touching wet plant leaves might encourage the spread of disease.

Garden Kneeler

For more comfortable kneeling while doing garden chores, make a knee pad by stuffing old nylon stockings in a hot water bottle.

Commercially manufactured knee pads are sold at garden centers and through garden catalogues.

A Child's Garden

Even if it's only a row or two, set aside a portion of the vegetable or flower garden for your young children to plant some seeds. Let them do some of the spading and raking in preparation for planting, and give them the responsibility for weeding and watering their rows.

Losing Garden Tools

Garden tools left on the lawn are often hard to find because their coloring is so close to that of the landscape. To save the time and energy the search takes, dip the handles of your garden tools into yellow or orange enamel outdoor paint. The coating will last for years, and the tools will always be easy to locate if lost on the lawn or in the brush.

Protecting Garden Tools

During a long winter of disuse, moisture is apt to attack unprotected garden tools, encrusting them with rust. To avoid wasting the time you would have to spend removing the winter rust, spray oil over your rakes, shovels, and pruning shears before putting them away in the fall. (A thin coating of mechanic's grease will achieve the same result.) After spraying with oil, protect them further by wrapping each with rags or newspapers.

Repairing a Garden Hose

A small hose or crack in a rubber garden hose can be repaired with a rubber patch and some adhesive tape. Sand the surface around the hole lightly with fine sandpaper. Also sand the surface of the rubber patch, which can be cut from an old tube. Apply contact cement to both sanded surfaces and wait until the cement is dry to the touch. Press the patch over the hole very firmly. Wrap the patched area with vinyl electrical or rubber tape.

Hedge Trimmers

When using an electric-powered hedge trimmer, you may run into the common problem of finding the extension cord accidentally cut by the trimmer blades. An excellent way of preventing this is to slit a three- to five-foot section of old garden hose down the center, spread it apart, and let it wrap itself around the electric wire cord. Wind some electrical tape around both ends of the garden hose and continue to wind it until secure. The thick garden hose will prevent the trimmer's teeth from cutting the electrical wire.

Making a Garden Walk

Use flat rocks to create your own garden walk. Stepping stones need not have a cement base. Slates at least two inches thick can also be used. Allow the grass to grow in around them so that they will stay in place.

Sagging Garden Gates

To correct a sagging garden gate, use a turnbuckle. Buy a buckle and rod set that will fit the gate. Or, buy only the buckle and use two turns of heavy galvanized wire for the rod. The buckle will raise up the side with the hinges to the level of the lower side (the swinging side).

Preserving Fence Posts

If water collects on the top of a wooden fence post, the post will

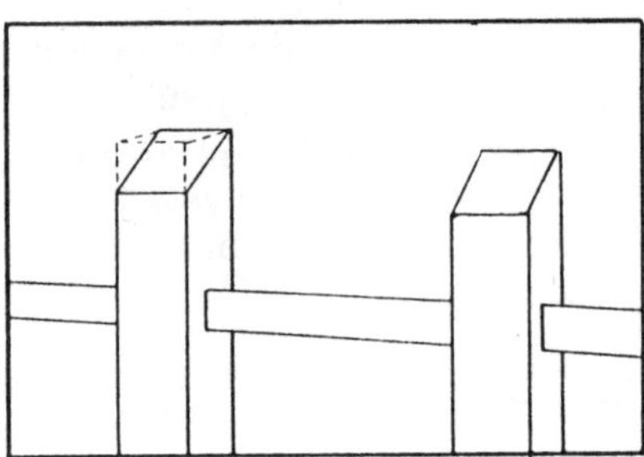

rot. To prevent this, slant the top of the post, as shown here.

Rapid-growing Trees

Do not buy trees advertised as "rapid-growing," because they usually have brittle branches and are short-lived. Poplars, willows, and silver maples fall into this category.

Transplanting Trees

The best time to transplant a tree in northern climates is late fall or early spring, when the ground will be workable but the tree dormant. In fall transplant after the first hard frost, and in spring before the buds begin to swell. Most roots will grow at temperatures above 45 degrees Fahrenheit, so if you are able to transplant right after the first hard fall frost while the ground is still relatively warm, or several weeks before the buds emerge in spring, by which time the ground will have warmed up sufficiently, the tree will have time to establish its root system before winter sets in or before spring growth begins.

Evergreens for Foundation Plantings

A house is more effectively tied into its surroundings if squat, low-growing plants are placed around its foundation. Evergreens, such as azaleas, work well for this purpose. Tall-growing evergreens that block windows and require constant pruning are not recommended. In choosing foundation shrubbery, consider available light. Azaleas, hemlocks, and rhododendrons perform adequately in reduced light. Yews, boxwood, and junipers do not.

Shade Trees Near the House

It is inadvisable to plant shade trees within fifteen feet of a house. Tree roots spread quickly, and they could damage the foundation of the house.

Balled Trees

When planting a balled tree, it is permissible to leave on the burlap, which will eventually rot. However, remove the wires holding the burlap to the ball of earth. The wire will inhibit the growth of the tree and, in time, might kill it.

Protecting Tree Limbs and Shrubbery

After a snowstorm, clear off as much snow as possible from shrubbery and tree limbs. When snow turns to ice, the weight can break branches. Using an upward sweep, brush off the snow with a broom.

How to Prune a Branch

When a large, heavy branch is pruned from a tree, it often strips the bark off the main stem as it falls. Avoid this by making a series of three cuts in the branch. First, make a cut one-quarter of the way through the bottom of the branch, eight to 24 inches from the main stem (1). Next, cut three-quarters through the width of the branch, from the top side, about two to four inches further out on the branch than the first cut. The branch will crack and break at (2). When the main part of the branch is severed, a small stub will be left attached to the tree. The small stem can then be removed by making a third cut flush with the main stem without stripping bark from the main stem (3). The flush cut should be made as close to the "collar" as possible (the collar is the raised bark area that demarcates the branch from the main trunk). Cutting inside the collar inhibits healing.

Felling Trees

Before cutting down a tree, consider the wind direction, the natural lean of the tree, and whether the trunk is sound, hol-

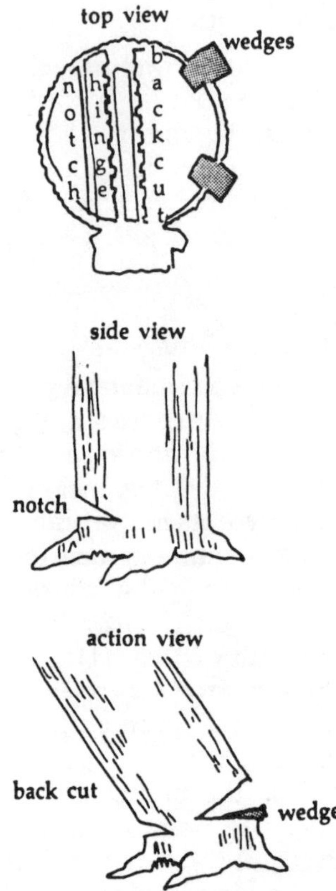

low, or partially rotted. Watch for dead limbs overhead. Then, cut a notch one-third the diameter of the trunk in the direction of the line of fall. Make the back cut at least two inches higher than the notch, leaving a hinge of uncut wood to guide the tree over. If there is a chance that the tree might not fall in the desired direction, use wedges to open the back cut and tilt the tree in the desired direction of fall. Never let a wedge make contact with a vibrating chainsaw because the wedge will kick back.

Trees Are Not Always Forever

In landscaping open land, the question of how much space to allow between trees and shrubs arises. Spacing young trees and shrubs so that they have an immediate presence will prove inadequate several years later, whereas trees and bushes planted with the proper spacing for mature specimens might appear as orphans for a decade or more.

One solution is to plant young specimens at half the spacing that mature specimens would require with the intention of removing every second tree or bush when they start to crowd. Simply cut the plant off at the ground line. Such a planting strategy is more expensive than planting at spacings that will accommodate mature trees, but it provides a settled look much earlier.

Lawn Weeding

The best time to weed a lawn is early spring, before the weeds have flowered and begun to disperse new seeds. Early spring is also the best time to apply most chemical weedkillers (herbicides).

Chemical Weedkillers

Be wary of using chemical weedkillers on lawns on which children and pets play. Many chemicals are toxic. Allow weedkillers to be absorbed into the soil or by plant tissue before allowing children or animals to play in the treated area.

Removing Dandelion Seed Heads

Gardeners are often unable to dig out dandelions before the heads set seed. The seeds soon blow around and multiply the

dandelion problem many times over. To solve this problem, attach a vacuum cleaner to a long extension cord and sweep up the seed heads.

Grass in Cracks

Eliminate grass that grows in walkways or between wall bricks by pouring on salt or a strong saltwater solution consisting of at least two tablespoons of salt to each quart of boiling water. The same result can be achieved chemically by using the substance glyposate (sold commercially as Round-up and under other trade names). Glyposate will kill grasses and other weeds in their entirety without being residually active in the soil. Glyposate is thus a good material to use in order to clear an area of weeds in grass before planting trees, shrubbery, or a vegetable garden. However, since glyposate will kill plants that it contacts, it must be used with extreme caution.

Cut Grass Regularly

Grass should be cut when it has grown one inch higher than its intended height. Often, long grass suffers shock when being cut.

The correct height for grass varies with the variety and the season. Cutting height is generally between one and one-half to three inches, with shorter heights in the cooler part of the year. Maintaining taller heights in the summer shades out weeds that seek to establish themselves.

Mowing Wet Grass

Mowing wet grass produces an uneven, sloppy result. In addition, because grass sticks to the mower blade and housing, it causes the motor to work that much harder and can cause damage to the machine.

Transferring Seedlings Outdoors

When the soil is warm enough, young plants started indoors in peat pots should be transferred outdoors. For each peat pot, dig a hole large enough so that each pot will rest one-half inch below the level of the ground. Fill each hole with water and allow it to drain. Put each peat pot in a hole and fill in around the pot with dirt. Press firmly around the pot and base of the plant, then add a liquid fertilizer.

Testing Seeds

Seeds lose their vitality with age, and most of the more commonly used vegetable seeds are good for only one to three years. Before sowing seeds stored from a previous year, make sure it is viable. Place a few seeds between two damp sheets of paper towel. Keep them in a warm spot for five to ten days. If 75 percent of the seeds send out sprouts, the seeds will germinate when planted.

Depth to Plant Vegetable Seeds

The depth at which vegetable seeds are planted is important for their germination and survival. Follow the directions on the seed package. As a rule of thumb, seed should be planted at a depth three times the seed's diameter. Fine seed should be scattered on the surface of the soil and pressed down lightly.

Vegetable Gardens and Tree Roots

All too often, well-tended vegetable gardens fail to meet expectations. Growth is scrawny and yields are meager. One cause may be encroaching roots from adjacent shade trees which sap the garden of nutrients and moisture. Tree roots can easily extend fifty feet from the trunk. If you have no alternative tree-free location, it is sometimes possible to reduce competition from neighboring trees by digging down to a depth of one to two feet with a spade and severing any encroaching roots.

Plastic Mulch to Establish Ground Cover

Weeds can become a real problem before ground cover plants are established. Plastic mulch helps overcome this problem. Place black plastic over well-prepared soil. Cut an X slit in the plastic over each planting hole. Make each hole three inches in diameter and set a plant through it. A mulch of pine bark or wood chips can be used to obscure the plastic. The plastic can be left on permanently to reduce weed growth between the ground cover plants.

Correct Way to Set Bulbs

When planting bulbs, the sides of the holes should be straight and the bulbs planted so that their

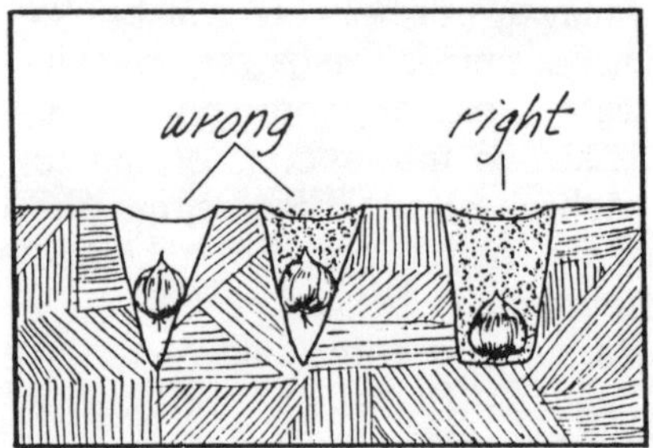

rooted bases face down. There should be air space around the bulbs.

Caging Tomatoes

If tomatoes are allowed to develop on the ground, they often rot. Therefore, it is necessary to support most tomato plants off the ground. You might want to try caging rather than staking tomato plants. The cage can be

made from a section of wire fencing 48 to 60 inches tall and 18 inches in diameter. Although it will rust, concrete floor reinforcing wire is an economical choice. Caging requires less labor than staking and tying tomato plants, and often results in increased yields. It is wise to secure the cage by tying it to stakes driven into the ground. At windy sites this is imperative.

Rotating Crops

Crop rotation is important in a vegetable garden, regardless of size. Planting the same vegetables in the same spot year after year depletes the soil of its nutrients and encourages certain types of insects. It is advisable to rotate leguminous plants (peas, beans, etc.) with nonlegumes (lettuce, onions, etc.).

Bean Yield

You will get a better bean yield if you pick the pods while they are still young (about one-quarter inch in width). This will encourage the flowers to be more productive.

Vegetables in Flower Beds

If you don't have a vegetable garden, consider growing vegetables in your flower garden. Vegetables in a flower bed can serve the double purpose of providing food and making an attractive display. Suggestions for vegetable edging plants are: parsley, leaf lettuce, bibb lettuce, endive, and herbs of various kinds.

Remove First-Year Strawberry Blossoms

The first season that strawberries are set out should be primarily for the purpose of their becoming established, not for fruit production. To ensure that most of the plants' energy goes into growth rather than fruit, blossoms should be removed the first year. Remove the flower stalks of June-bearing strawberries as soon as they appear. Remove the blossoms of everbearing types as they appear until the middle of July. Then, allow flowers to set fruit for harvest during the remainder of the first season (August-September). Blossoms should not be removed after the first year.

Plants That Attract Bees

Bees are the principal pollinators of garden plants, and many vegetables will not produce fruit unless properly pollinated. Therefore, it pays to attract bees to your garden area. Berganot, lemon balm, and thyme are especially good bee-attracting plants.

Unwanted Animals

Dogs and other unwanted animals can be kept out of flower and shrub beds by sprinkling mothballs over the area.

Keeping Out Rabbits

Rabbits have a strong aversion to talcum powder. Sprinkle a liberal amount around your plants and they will keep their distance.

Fencing the Garden

When fencing a garden to keep out animals, remember that some animals are diggers and can go

under normal fencing. Bury garden fencing at least six inches to keep the diggers out.

Herbs as Insecticides

Basil planted near tomatoes will discourage worms and flies. And mint, sage, dill, and thyme usually will protect cabbage, cauliflower, and broccoli from attack by cabbage moths.

A Suggested Herb Garden Design

A separate herb garden can be an attractive part of your land-

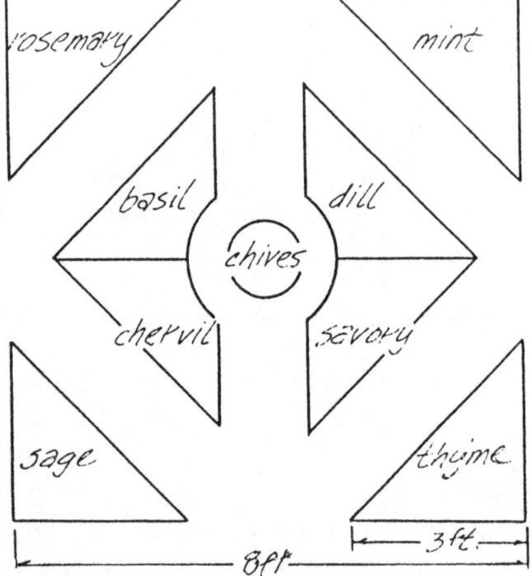

scape. The diagram is a suggested design.

Rosemary Warning

Extremely cold temperatures kill rosemary plants. If you live in a cold climate (below freezing in winter), it would be wise to first pot the rosemary and then place the pot in the ground in the spring. In the fall, at the first sign of cold weather, simply remove the pot from the soil and place it indoors in a sunny location.

Drainage for Houseplant Containers

Good drainage material should be placed in the bottom of pots and other containers used for houseplants. This keeps the potting soil from becoming waterlogged and damaging plant roots. Place two inches of broken clay pot material or coarse gravel in the bottom of containers used for houseplants.

Increase Humidity for Houseplants

Most houseplants need higher humidity than houses provide. To solve this problem, group houseplants together and place a few glasses filled with water among the pots. The water that evaporates will be trapped by the dense canopy of foliage and increase the humidity content of the air surrounding the plants. Or, better still, use a humidifier.

Giving Houseplants a Summer Vacation

Most houseplants will prosper outdoors during the summer; but if plants are not sunk into the soil, they will turn over from the wind and will quickly dry out. Therefore, dig a hole deep enough to sink the pot containing the plant under a sparsely leaved tree, such as a honey locust. The leaves of the tree will allow in sunlight while preventing sunscald. Place three inches of stone in the bottom of the hole for drainage and fill around the pots, up to the rim, with peat moss. Once placed outdoors, houseplants should not be neglected. Because they are contained in pots, they will need additional watering. Turn the pots periodically to break any roots that may penetrate the soil through the drainage holes. Return plants to the house in early fall before frost threatens.

Watering Houseplants

So as not to shock your houseplants, water them with tepid water or water that is taken from the tap and kept in a jar for about an hour, so that it is at approximate room temperature.

Giving Houseplants a Turn

Plants have a tendency to grow *toward* light. If plants are left in one position, they will become misshapen by the accelerated growth of parts nearer the light. To prevent this, periodically turn your houseplants, each time exposing a different side to the light source.

Fresh-cut Flower Care

Flowers should be cut at an angle with a knife before being placed in water. Extend the life of cut flowers by keeping the vase water clear and fresh. Do this by adding one-quarter teaspoon of liquid bleach to each quart of water poured into the vase.

Another recommended method for adding life and vitality to flowers is to mix into a quart of water two tablespoons of white vinegar and two tablespoons of cane sugar. The sugar serves as food, and the vinegar prevents the growth of harmful bacteria.

Keeping Flowers Fresh

Cut flowers will stay fresh longer if all leaves are removed from the stems that are underwater. Life of the flowers can further be extended by refrigerating them (vase and all) at night.

Hairspray on Flowers

Cut flowers will not shed their leaves as quickly if they are coated with hairspray. Spray in an upward sweep at least one foot from the leaves.

Hastening Springtime

If you have fruit trees on your property, you have an opportunity to celebrate an early spring. Place prunings or cut branches in a vase of water in a room set at 65 to 70 degrees Fahrenheit. In one to three weeks, simulated spring temperatures will "force" the buds to flower. Always choose branches that have abundant flower buds. (Usually, the round, plump buds are fruit buds and the pointed ones leaf buds. Apple and pear branches work particularly well, as do forsythia and flowering quince.

Splitting Stems

Before placing flowers in a vase, split those with thick stems,

thus making it easier for moisture to be absorbed.

Changing Flower Colors

To change the color of cut flowers, mix food coloring in warm water and place flower stems in the solution. The coloring of the flowers will change overnight.

21
Managing Money

Introduction

There was a time not long ago when managing money was easier. Banks offered savings and noninterest-bearing checking accounts; brokerage houses essentially sold stocks and bonds. But, we now live in an age of financial "products," and weeding through them requires constant vigilance by anyone expecting to realize maximum yields from investment dollars.

Banks still provide five to ten varieties of certificates of deposit (some with fixed interest, some with variable interest), interest-bearing checking accounts, and money market accounts offering variable interest rates, with and without checking. Many of these accounts provide for fees and penalties if withdrawal restrictions and balance minimums are not adhered to. Virtually every bank has a different list of products, and each depositor has no option but to read carefully the catalogue of restrictions that each bank is required by law to provide, lest the depositor find a list of unexpected bank charges on the monthly statement.

Brokerage houses now offer a parallel savings option with their money market accounts which sometimes offer somewhat higher yields than banks. Money market accounts are insured up to $100,000 by the Securities Investor Protection Corporation (SIPC) and are a convenient place to hold money while waiting for more favorable long-term investment opportunities to develop. For those who deal in stocks and bonds, maintaining a brokerage money market account facilitates transactions.

As with financial institutions, the area of marketing also has undergone a revolution in recent years. The distinction between discounters and full-price retailers has been blurred, and a wise consumer today shops solely by price, ignoring store classification. And he shops the year 'round (a person in the habit of making the bulk of his purchases right after Christmas is likely to discover that all of the choice merchandise has been sold in pre-Christmas sales).

Like never before, stretching one's dollar is a full-time job.

What to Keep in a Bank Vault

It is wise to keep birth and marriage certificates and other important family records in a vault. But it is unwise to keep in a vault your original will, cemetery deeds, or other things that might be needed on short notice. Banks generally seal a safety deposit box when they learn that the owner has died.

The Safety of Safe Deposit Boxes

Only money kept in bank accounts is insured for theft. Money or valuables kept in safe deposit boxes are not insured.

Protecting Valuable Papers

If you can't get to your bank vault to store precious documents, protect them from fire by placing them in waterproof containers in the refrigerator or freezer until you are able to transfer them to the vault.

FDIC Protection

The Federal Deposit Insurance Corporation (FDIC) protects individual accounts for up to $100,000 and a limited number of joint accounts in the same bank for an additional $100,000 each. Your banker can advise you on how to open more than one account in the same bank and yet be fully insured. Generally, the FDIC is able to sell all the deposits of a failed institution to a healthy one, and service to customers continues uninterrupted.

CDs in Savings Banks

Money invested in savings bank CDs (Certificates of Deposit) is a safe investment. CDs are insured up to $100,000 by the federal government. If you have more than $100,000 invested in CDs in your name in any one bank, the excess is *not* covered by insurance. Play it safe and use the excess to open new CDs in other banks.

CD Advice

Don't keep all your money in one CD. Take out at least two, one with an early maturity date. In an emergency, you can withdraw money from the quick-maturing CD and thus sacrifice less interest and suffer a smaller penalty for early withdrawal.

Beware of ATMs

The automatic teller machines in banks are a boon to customers who are in need of cash after bank hours, but it is unwise to make *cash deposits,* even if a transaction receipt is given. If a bank claims that it did not receive cash with the deposit, your transaction receipt, according to federal regulations, will not qualify as legal proof that cash had indeed been deposited.

Credit Card Loss

Keep handy at all times a record of your credit card numbers and the toll-free numbers you must call immediately if the cards are lost or stolen.

Stale Checks

Under the Uniform Commercial Bank Code, banks are not obligated to cash checks that were issued more than six months earlier. Nonetheless, they sometimes do. To play safe, and to keep your account straight, stop payment on all old checks you have issued.

800 Number

Making use of an 800 number can save you many dollars. Most large companies have toll-free numbers. To find out if an out-of-town company you wish to contact has an 800 number, dial 1-800-555-1212. The operator will give you the company's 800 number if it has one.

Occasionally, companies limit 800 number use by not listing their numbers in the general directory. A dealer might be willing to share these numbers with you.

Money-saving Coupons

Always check the price of a coupon item against the price of the house brand, because often national brands are more expensive, even with a coupon. If a newspaper has coupons for items you use frequently, get several copies of the paper—that is, if the newspaper is not too costly. Note the expiration dates on coupons. Some manufacturers' coupons carry no expiration dates.

Calculating Price Differences

Keep a pocket-size calculator with you when shopping so that you can compare prices in an instant. If one brand of detergent is being sold at $1.25 for a 12-ounce box and another brand is being sold at $2.99 for a 16-ounce box, you will be able to calculate that the first brand will cost 11¢ per ounce while the second will be more expensive at 19¢ per ounce. Some stores provide the public with per-unit price information.

Buy Big and Save

Generally speaking, you save money when you buy detergents, lotions, etc., in large, economy-size boxes and bottles. However, it is often awkward to use the product in such large containers. To take advantage of the savings, save small bottles and containers and transfer the contents of the large containers to smaller ones.

While larger is generally cheaper, this is not always true. Store promotions on smaller sizes sometimes reverse this pattern, so always compare before buying.

Eye-level Merchandising

Products featured on eye-level shelves in retail stores have been estimated to sell very much faster than those products featured on top or bottom shelves. Therefore, merchants often display the more expensive items on eye-level shelves. For bargains, cast an eye on the upper or lower displays of merchandise.

Credit Card Membership Fees

If you are among the one-third of all credit cardholders who pay off their balance monthly, the card company's annual membership fee should be of concern to you. Fees can range from none at all to as much as $60.00. You can get valuable fee information at a minimal cost from Credit Card Locator, Credit Card Rating Service, P.O. Box 5219, Ocean Park Station, Santa Monica, CA 90405. This organization will provide you with the names of over one hundred institutions that charge no annual fee at all and about two hundred that charge less than $15.00.

If you send $1.50 to The Bankcard Holders of America, 560 Herndon Parkway, Suite 120, Herndon, VA 22070, they will send you a list of banks that charge no fee at all.

Credit Card Bargaining

You can sometimes use your credit card as a bargaining chip. A small merchant may be willing to drop the price if you offer to pay him in cash rather than by credit card. After all, a merchant sometimes pays a credit card company a fee as high as seven percent to process a transaction.

Supplying Additional I.D.

When making purchases with your credit card, the merchant should not request that you supply additional personal information, such as address and phone number. Only provide this information if it is essential for shipment or delivery of merchandise or if, for any reason, the merchant is unable to obtain proper authorization from your bank. Other than for these reasons you are not obligated to supply personal information.

Beware of Credit Card Cash Advances

Do not regard cash advances taken through Visa, MasterCard, or another credit card as simply another transaction. First, there may be a fee of up to five percent of the total cash advance. Second, the interest charges against the advance begin on the day of the transaction, not some weeks later, as in the case of most credit card purchases.

Canceling Credit Cards

When canceling a credit card, make sure you cut the card in half and return both halves to the bank with a cover letter.

Sales Slips

Always keep sales slips or credit card slips for the purchases you make. If ordering by mail, keep a copy of the order and make sure to hold on to canceled checks or credit-card billing slips. When returning merchandise, make sure to get a receipt from the shipping organization that states when, where, and how the item is being shipped. When filing a complaint, never send original documents. Send photocopies only.

On Saving Instruction Booklets

In the long run, you will save money and effort by getting into the habit of saving all booklets and manuals that come with the manufactured items you purchase—from cars to toasters. Keep all such booklets together in a drawer or file. It is a good idea to reread instruction manuals after you have become familiar with the basic operation of the item.

For Insurance Claims

When filing an insurance claim after a burglary or fire, you will have to prove that you owned the items that you are claiming were stolen or damaged. Therefore, hold on to all receipts of purchases and take pictures of all the articles in each room of your house. Keep receipts and photographs in a fireproof vault at home or in a bank.

Low-cost Life Insurance

Before buying life insurance, contact a company equipped to advise you on the best buy. Companies like Insurance Information, Inc., in Hyannis, MA (telephone: 1-800-472-5800) provide such a service for $50.00 (1990). Based upon your age and health status, they will research the field and send you the names of five suitable insurance companies with the best rates for your situation. They also provide the phone numbers of these companies, who will direct you to their local representatives.

Estate Planning

Financial planners advise that one should review his or her will every five years at the least to take into account changes in the law and in one's financial situation. The birth or death of one of the beneficiaries, change in marital status, and change of residence from one state to another are factors to be considered when re-evaluating one's will.

Funeral Expenses

In 1984 the Federal Trade Commission (FTC) issued a series of rules requiring funeral parlors to provide consumers with itemized price lists and telephone quotations upon request. Compare prices before committing yourself to one funeral parlor.

Free Tax Information

The IRS can supply you with information on almost every subject. Ask them for Publication No. 17, Your Federal Income Tax, issued annually, which contains 200 pages of information that can be useful when filling out your return. Ask a local IRS office for a copy or call 1-800 TAX-FORM and request that a copy be mailed to you.

Free Assistance for Taxpayers

The Volunteer Income Tax Assistance (VITA) program consists of IRS-trained volunteers who assist low-income, elderly, handicapped, and non-English-speaking taxpayers in the preparation of their tax returns. These volunteers offer their (free) services in libraries and other community institutions during the filing season. Check with your local IRS office for the VITA site nearest you.

Tax Information by Phone

You can get answers to specific questions about tax preparation by calling (in most states) 1-800-829-1040. Check the instructions that accompany your 1040 form for the number to call in your state. Be aware that the answers given to your phone questions by the IRS "experts" are not always error-free, and the IRS assumes no responsibility for the accuracy of the information provided by their employees.

Old Tax Returns

If you want to obtain a copy of one of your old IRS tax returns, write to the IRS office where you send your annual return. Request Form 4506. In 1990 the charge for information relating to any one particular tax year was $4.25.

IRS Suspects

Those who have worked for the IRS tell us that individuals fitting into one of the following groups are more likely than others to be examined by the IRS:

- doctors and dentists
- airline pilots and flight attendants
- waiters and cabdrivers
- teachers and college professors.

Individuals in these groups often are suspected of taking unwarranted deductions for fictitious expenses, and others of pocketing undeclared cash income. Travel and entertainment deductions that seem unreasonable usually trigger an audit.

The IRS Audit

Do not be overly upset if the IRS audits your tax return. More than 1,000,000 other Americans are audited each year, including the president and vice president of the United States.

Gaining an Advantage With Auditors

Former IRS revenue agents report that the longer a case is on file with them, the better are the examiners chances of a favorable resolution of his or her case. Agents are often under pressure to complete the cases assigned to them in a prescribed period of time. So, if you are called for an audit and can repeatedly stall the interview, you probably will be ahead of the game. When the auditor finally gets to you, he will be more anxious than usual to dispose of the case.

Change of Address

If you move, notify the IRS of your change of address, especially if you are expecting a tax refund. In one recent year, the Postal Service returned to the IRS $40,000,000 in tax overpayments that were undeliverable because taxpayers did not inform the IRS of their new addresses. If you have a specific question in this regard, contact your local IRS office.

Declaring Miscellaneous Income

If you have been paid over $600 in any one year for services rendered on a freelance basis, the IRS has been advised of it by the payer on Form 1099-MISC. This category includes royalties, prizes, and awards received, all of which must be declared as income.

Social Security Income

If you are married, receive social security, and have an income exceeding $32,000 ($25,000 if single), you will have to pay tax on half of the social security income.

Real Estate Taxation

When your property is assessed for tax purposes, be aware that anything on the property that is movable—that is, not permanently affixed—should not be included in the valuation. A tool shed is an example of a structure that is not subject to real estate taxation.

Tax-free Treasury Bonds

Interest earned on all U.S. Treasury bonds is exempt from state and local taxes, but federal tax will have to be paid on such earnings.

Tax-free Municipal Bonds

Interest earned from tax-free municipal bonds is entirely free of federal, state, and local taxes. Some states, however, do tax the interest if bonds were issued in a state other than the one in which the owner resides. Check before purchasing.

Deductible Interest

As of 1990, none of the interest paid on consumer debt, such as student or car loans, credit cards, etc., will qualify as income tax deductions after 1990. Interest on home equity loans up to $100,000 continues to be deductible.

Tag and Garage Sales

Income earned from selling personal belongings at tag, garage, or yard sales is not subject to income tax since the prices for which articles are sold at these sales generally fall far below the original cost, and therefore no profit is made.

Tax-free Gifts

You can give up to $10,000 per year to anyone, and the recipient will not have to pay income tax on the gift. A husband and wife can reduce their taxable estate by jointly giving up to $20,000 per year to family members or others.

22
Tips for Travelers

Introduction

For most travelers, it is the unexpected—an intimate chat on an airplane with a perfect stranger, negotiating one's way through the subway in a European city whose language you don't understand, coming across a shopping steal in an Oriental bazaar—that makes excursions exhilarating. But, to heighten the joy of the unexpected, it is wise to pay careful attention to the basics.

Especially if traveling during peak seasons, make sure that your travel tickets and accommodations are arranged well in advance to avoid disappointment. And take the time to research your destination fully. If you are intent on visiting the Tivoli Gardens in Copenhagen, seeing a bullfight in Spain, or attending a performance at the Moscow Art Theatre, make sure that the facility will be open when you arrive and that tickets will be available. Often, if you have your heart set on seeing something in particular, it is possible to make advance reservations through the concierge at the hotel at which you will be staying. Your travel agent can send a fax for you, or you can telephone the hotel directly.

To facilitate an orderly vacation departure, work with checklists. Note all the purchases and preparations required for the trip and check them off as they are completed. If you are a frequent traveler, you will find that by retaining your basic list and modifying it from trip to trip you will avoid last-minute frazzles as well as the disappointment of arriving in Tahiti without your bathing suit.

Neighborly Assistance

Homes with a lived-in look are rarely troubled by burglars. If you are going to be away for a while, leave a key with a trustworthy neighbor. Ask the neighbor to remove mail from your mailbox daily and remove circulars and debris from the walk. Also ask the neighbor to vary the positions of your drapes and blinds daily.

Itinerary

Before departing on a journey, be sure to give friends or family a copy of your itinerary. The itinerary should include the hotels at which you will be staying, airline flight numbers, and telephone numbers where you can be reached in case of emergency.

Travel Checklists

Make a list of all the things you want to take with you on your trip as well as a list of things to do before leaving. The latter include notifying the post office, leaving instructions with a neighbor, and so on. Check the list just before departing to be sure you've remembered everything. Frequent travelers may wish to keep a copy of the list and amend it from trip to trip to simplify future trips.

Shopping for the Cheapest Fare

Before purchasing an airline ticket, ask the ticket agent to quote you the lowest possible fare on that route. It is a good idea to check with more than one carrier because agents will occasionally only quote prices for which tickets are available. Thus, if no tickets at the lowest price are available for the date you request, you will not be aware that a lower fare exists. It is wise not to pay for tickets until the date required in case cheaper tickets materialize in the interval.

Travel Information

Though there is no shortage of travel maps and guidebooks which can be purchased for both domestic and international destinations, many states and foreign countries maintain tourist offices in major U.S. cities. Consult phone books and 800 directories. Much of what these offices offer—usually without cost—is more current than what is available commercially.

Special Airline Meals

If you are planning to travel on a flight on which a full meal will be served, be aware that there are food options available to you. Besides the standard menu, when booking your flight you can request strict vegetarian, lacto-ovo vegetarian, Eastern vegetarian, fruit plate, kosher, fish, and other types of special meals. When you arrive at the airport, be sure to check that the special meal has been ordered for you.

Unnecessary Travel Insurance

Before buying extra travel insurance, check your existing

policies. It might be that you are already covered for all possible travel mishaps and that additional coverage would be superfluous. Some credit card companies provide various forms of travel insurance when the trip is charged through them.

Advance Seat Assignment

For many flights, airlines are able to assign seats and issue boarding passes at the time reservations are made. Inquire when purchasing your tickets. By making advance arrangements, you will shorten your check-in time on the day of departure.

Boarding Assistance

If you are in any way disabled and will need a wheelchair or other special assistance, give advance notice to the airline with which you will be traveling or the airport from which you will be departing. They usually will be able to accommodate your needs.

Duty-free Shops

The best items to buy in duty-free shops are liquor, cigarettes, perfume, and wine. These are generally taxed high when purchased locally. Other items offered for sale at airports are often overpriced.

Duty-free Gifts

According to the U.S. Customs Service (Washingon, DC), duty-free souvenirs can be sent from abroad to as many persons as you wish. The value can be up to $50.00 of gifts per day per person. Packages should be marked "Unsolicited Gift" and contents and value should be indicated on the appropriate forms. Alcohol, tobacco, and perfume *cannot* be sent in this manner.

Travelers Checks vs. Credit Cards

When going on an overseas trip, plan to use credit cards rather than traveler's checks. You can save as much as several percent on exchange costs.

Money Exchanges

When traveling abroad, you will generally do better converting dollars into local currency in banks rather than in hotels or business establishments. Airports are one of the least reliable places to obtain favorable exchange rates.

Money Chart

If you are one of those who are daunted by foreign money, prepare a money conversion chart—from U.S. to foreign and from foreign to U.S.—before your departure. List in convenient denominations: 1¢, 5¢, 10¢, 25¢, 50¢, $1.00, $2.00, $3.00, $4.00, $5.00, $6.00, $7.00, $8.00, $9.00, $10.00, $20.00, $30.00, $40.00, $50.00, $60.00, $70.00, $80.00, $90.00, $100.00, $200.00, $300.00, $400.00, and $500.00.

Advance Money Exchange

Before leaving the United States for an overseas destination, change a small amount of money into the appropriate foreign currency. By doing so, you will spare yourself having to stand on the long lines that sometimes build up at exchange windows in airports. Make sure to change enough money for cab fares, phone calls, tips, and the like.

Before changing money, be sure to put aside some American currency—including coins for telephones—for use upon your return home.

Black Markets

In countries where the local currency cannot be freely exchanged for foreign currency, there often exists a vigorous black market where foreign currency can often be sold for from 10 to 20 percent to several times the official exchange rate. Sometimes, these black markets exist with the wink of the government.

While there is no general rule as to whether a traveler should or should not deal in the black market, two hard rules should be followed if you decide to use them: (1) *Always* count the other party's money before handing over yours. (2) *Never* allow yourself to be left with more money than you can reconvert when leaving the country. Most countries will reconvert local currency upon exit *if* you have a receipt to prove that it was converted legally.

Before dealing in the black market, inquire as to the best rate by getting a quote from several dealers.

Hotel Rooms

Before your bags are carried up to the hotel room that has been assigned to you, ask to see the room. It may not be to your liking, and this is the time—before unpacking—to make the change. Although sometimes offering inferior views, bear in mind that rooms off the street will generally be quieter.

Hold on to Your Hotel Key

There is less chance of your hotel room being ransacked if you keep the room key with you all the time instead of returning it to the desk. Employees will not know as readily when you are in and when you are out.

Money and valuables should be kept in hotel safes, and suitcases should be locked before you leave the room.

Passport Backup

When traveling overseas, keep a photocopy of your passport in a place other than where you keep the passport itself. In the event that the passport is stolen or misplaced, having a photocopy will help speed up the replacement process.

Keep Extra ID Photos

Keep an extra set of passport/visa-type photos with you when traveling. You may wish to obtain additional visas or forms of identification in the country you are visiting, and having photos on hand will speed up the process. Inexpensive snapshots are often acceptable for such purposes.

Learn Basic Phrases

It's worth taking the extra time to learn a few basic phrases in the language of the country you plan to visit. If the language uses an alphabet unfamiliar to you, make the effort to learn that alphabet so that you will be able to sound out street names, store names, and the names of tourist sites. Learning to count in the foreign language can also be extremely helpful.

Car Rental Insurance

Nowadays, many credit card companies give cardholders free insurance when renting an automobile and paying for it with that company's card. Inquire as to the policy of your credit card company. If it covers you, be sure to waive the car rental company's coverage (which can amount to as much as $15.00 per day) when signing the rental agreement.

Federal Tax on Overseas Flights

When flying from one city to another to catch an overseas flight, you should not be charged the federal air tax for that flight. Show the agent your ticket to prove that this is the first leg of an overseas journey.

Duffel Bags

Seasoned travelers often pack their belongings in a 24-inch-long duffel bag that can be carried on board the plane and stored under the seat. This eliminates the need to wait to reclaim luggage and also reduces the possibility of loss. Depending upon the carrier, it is sometimes possible to bring two carry-ons into the cabin.

Luggage Advice

Be aware that the luggage you carry with you onto the plane is not insured against theft or loss. Luggage stored in those small front closets should be marked with a colored piece of tape along its sides or with a colored string around its handle. Someone will be less likely to mistake luggage for his or her own if the luggage bears unusual markings.

Traveling Light or Heavy

If you plan to visit many destinations on your trip, it is wise to travel as light as possible, even if weight limitations are not a consideration. Carrying lighter bags will prove less of a physical strain—especially when traveling by train—and unpacking and repacking less of a chore. If, however, you are heading to just one destination, there might not be much advantage in restricting yourself.

Luggage Straps

It's a good idea to invest in a pair of sturdy luggage straps. The

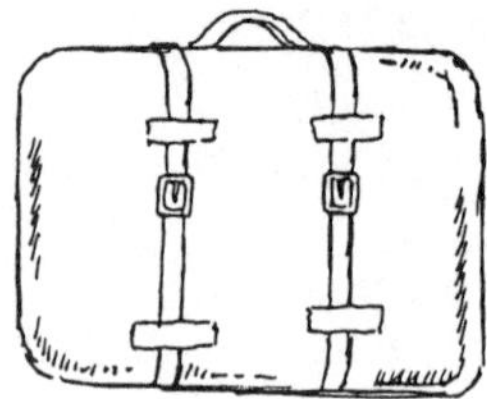

straps give extra strength to the luggage as it is thrown about by airline personnel. In the event that a lock or zipper should break, the straps will prevent the luggage from opening completely. For added security, tape the straps to the case with heavy-duty plastic tape.

Luggage Carrier

Some travelers find wheeled luggage carriers, which look like shopping carts without the carrying area, helpful in avoiding back strain. The drawback is that these carriers are a nuisance to transport when not in use.

Supplementary Luggage

International tourists virtually always return home with more luggage than they departed with. To prepare for this contingency, it is useful to pack an extra canvas bag inside your suitcase, which you can call upon should the need arise. Should you not have such a bag, it is often possible to purchase inexpensive bags made of nontear materials such as polypropylene. Bags of this type, which come in a variety of sizes, are not sturdy enough for constant use, but serve well in an emergency. Avoid placing breakables in such bags. Some airlines, upon request, will supply cartons in which supplementary luggage can be shipped.

Luggage With Wheels

If you have difficulty carrying heavy luggage, consider buying suitcases with wheels. When making such a purchase, check to see that the wheels are sturdy

and that the luggage can be pulled with ease—that is, without having to bend over and risk straining your back. Luggage wheels work well on smooth floors; they do not perform well on rough pavements.

Travel Comfort

Airline seats are generally bad for the back. Lessen back pain by placing an object under your feet, thus raising the knees and reducing the stress on the lower extremities. A rolled pillow placed in the small of the back will also help.

Nonsmoking Sections

Do not assume that because you have requested a seat in the nonsmoking section, you will not be affected by the smoke coming from the smoking section. In airplanes, the two sections are divided merely by a few feet. If you have an aversion to cigarette smoke, inquire as to where the smoking section ends and ask to be seated as far from it as possible.

Airplane Ear Pressure

Ear pain affects many people, particularly when a plane is preparing to land. Caused by a sudden change in cabin pressure, the problem can be alleviated by chewing gum, holding one's mouth wide open, or yawning or swallowing frequently.

Dental Work and Flying

Dentists advise that one would do well not to take an air trip on the same day that dental work has been done. Atmospheric pressure can cause pain in the teeth treated.

Travel Sickness

People suffering from motion sickness should be conscious of where they sit when traveling. On a plane, choose a seat near the wings; in a car, sit in the front; on a bus, avoid sitting over the wheels.

Motion Sickness Capsules

Recent research seems to indicate that taking two capsules of powdered ginger (available in health food stores) about ten minutes before a flight is effective in reducing motion sickness.

Overseas Health Emergency

Travel agents recommend that when taking an overseas trip you keep with your passport the following information relating to health: types of allergies, blood type, medications you are currently taking, name and telephone of your home doctor. In case of emergency, this information could save your life.

Water in Foreign Countries

When traveling in countries where water is likely to cause illness, it is best to boil the water for five minutes before drinking. If this is not possible, carry water purification tablets with you. Many pharmacies carry them. Bottled water is not always safe, so when in doubt, avoid it. Better hotels in countries where water is not potable sometimes provide specially treated tap water for their guests.

Just in Case

When visiting underdeveloped countries, take along items that may not be easily obtained, such as feminine hygiene products and bathroom tissue. It is a good idea to always carry bathroom tissue in your day bag.

Emergency Eyeglass Repairs

If you are fully dependent on your eyeglasses for vision, it is imperative to take a spare pair of glasses on your trip. In addition, if you are not keen on having to shift to a second pair of glasses, it is often possible to make repairs on frames by yourself. Purchase extra optical screws and an optical screwdriver. You might also wish to take along spare temples and nose pads.

Lodging a Complaint

If you wish to lodge a complaint against an airline, bus, or train company, get in touch with the U.S. Department of Transportation, Office of Community and Consumer Affairs, 400 Seventh Street SW, Room 10405, Washington, DC 20590. You might also call them at (202) 366-2220.

Free Advice for U.S. Train Travelers

If you travel by train, Amtrak will send you a kit with maps and information about low-cost hotels. Call 1-800-USA-RAIL. You can also write to Travel Planner, Department N, Amtrak Distribution Center, P.O. Box 7717, Itasca, IL 60143.

Travel Agent Complaints

If you are peeved at the way a travel agent has handled your booking, complain to the American Society of Travel Agents: (703) 739-2782. Or write to ASTA, Consumer Affairs Department, 1101 King Street, Alexandria, VA 22314.

Plan-ahead for Repeat Visitors

If you intend to revisit a country in the near future, it is a good idea to take a small amount of that country's currency and put it in a safe place upon your return home. This will be a time-saver on your next visit.

23
Homeless Hints & Tips

Introduction

Many of the insights we gain and shortcuts we learn in the course of a lifetime are randomly acquired, and they can't be easily categorized. If we jot them down at all it is on scraps of paper or in the margins of instruction manuals rather than in tabbed looseleaf binders. We conclude this book with a group of hints and tips which don't fit clearly into any of the established categories. In so doing, we encourage you to collect your own hints and tips, to delve into the principles behind them, and to write them down so that they can be modified with additional experience and passed along to others.

Insect Attractions

Insects are attracted by both black and brightly colored clothing. They are also attracted by perfumes, hairsprays, and body lotions. So, be aware not to use these items when working outdoors or walking about in heavy grass.

Bleach in Swimming Pools

Bleach is excellent for cleaning and refreshing swimming pools and water tanks in recreational vehicles. For details write to Clorox Company (see address in Appendix), or call their toll-free number 1-800-292-2200.

Beach Umbrellas

You can lengthen the life of a beach umbrella or an awning if you open it up after a rain to allow the air to dry it out. Material not exposed to air and daylight will mildew and rot. The same applies to lawn chairs with fabric seats.

Renewing Umbrellas and Awnings

Faded canvas umbrellas and awnings can be given a new lease on life with a fresh coat of paint. Use canvas paint and a wide brush, applying the paint with quick, even strokes to avoid streaking.

Repairing Outdoor Plastics and Vinyls

Torn vinyl and plastic products used outdoors, such as pools and beach balls, can usually be mended with new, durable Tough Tape, produced by the 3M Company. The tape is available in hardware, stationery, and department stores.

Lightning Protection Out of Doors

If you are out of doors during a lightning storm, try to get indoors as quickly as possible. Leave open areas and do not wait under trees, particularly isolated ones. It is safe to stay in an automobile, but turn off the engine and avoid touching metal parts. Do not park or stand near power lines or under a trestle.

Outdoor Furniture

Red cedar and redwood are naturally resistant to decay. Red cedar is commonly used for house shingles and clapboards. If you are going to make outdoor wooden furniture or bird feeders, use redwood. A pigmented stain is all the finish you need for furniture. Bird houses or feeders can be left unfinished and will turn a silvery gray without decaying.

Pitted Aluminum Furniture

Remove the black pockmarks from aluminum by rubbing firmly with fine steel wool. Apply a thin coat of paste wax and polish well. Allow 20 minutes for drying before buffing. Waxing once or twice a year thereafter will prevent subsequent pitting. Between waxings, wash the aluminum monthly with mild detergent to keep it fresh-looking.

Pipe Legs

To make a table that can be quickly dismantled and transported (for picnics, for example) use ordinary pipe threaded at one end for the legs. Attach a standard pipe flange under the tabletop, and screw the pipe into the flange. To protect finished floors, slide rubber crutch tips over the bottom end of each pipe. The pipe, the flange, and the tips can be found at hardware stores.

Fishing Sinkers

If you like to fish, don't discard the old nuts, bolts, and large washers that you come across from time to time. Save them for use as sinkers when you go fishing.

Tennis Balls Bounce

To restore their bounce, wrap bounceless tennis balls in aluminum foil and place them in a 200-degree Fahrenheit oven for about twenty minutes.

Golf Club Care

A simple way of keeping new golf clubs looking good is to rub them with clear shoe polish wax. This will preserve their shine and prevent early rust and corrosion.

Candle Power

Candles set aside for blackouts and other emergencies should be at least three-quarters of an inch thick and six or seven inches high. Acquire a glass chimney to shield the candle. Uncovered candles tend to flicker in the slightest draft and are a fire hazard, while a candle inside a glass chimney provides a warm steady light, burns slowly, and can be carried around without flickering or being extinguished.

Candle Drippings

To avoid excess candle dripping, sponge the candles lightly with rubbing alcohol. To this end, you might also want to leave your candles in the freezer for an hour or two before using.

Decorative Candles

Decorative candles that have lost their luster can be enlivened by rubbing with a soft cloth dampened with denatured alcohol.

Smoking Candles

Candles will smoke less if the wicks are trimmed with scissors before use. Long wicks tend to smoke. Cut the wicks straight across so that the flame and candle burn evenly. Remove pieces of wick, matchsticks, and other foreign particles from the top of the candle, near the wick; they can be a source of smoke.

Wilting Candles

Candles have a tendency to wilt in hot weather. You can prevent this by dipping them in shellac that has been thinned with turpentine. Hang candles by the wicks, and allow them to dry. The shellac will stiffen the candle but not interfere with its burning. Three-pound cut shellac is best.

Dog Cleaning

Keep your dog clean and odor-free by rubbing baking soda into his or her hair and then brushing it out.

Warped Records

To prevent records from warping, it is important that the shrink-wrap be removed from the covers as soon as possible. When shrink-wrap heats up, it contracts and often warps the records.

To straighten out a warped record, place the record (in its dust protector) between two pieces of glass large enough to cover the full diameter. Allow the record to sit in the sun for two or three hours, and the record will reassume its original shape.

Splicing Cassette Tapes

One tiny spot of nail polish remover or acetone will join the ends of a cassette tape.

Preserving Batteries

If you have unused batteries, you can preserve their energy by storing them in the refrigerator carefully wrapped in an airtight plastic bag. (Suck out the air and seal with a wire twist.) When ready to use, allow the batteries to warm up to room temperature, then wipe off any moisture from the contact point.

Battery Corrosion

Ordinary carbon-zinc batteries will cause corrosion in a flashlight if they remain in the case for any length of time after they are "burned out." Remove the batteries from the case if the flashlight is not used frequently; replace the batteries only when you are planning to use the flashlight.

Lubricating Carriage Wheels

Baby carriage wheels that squeak can be lubricated with oil or Vaseline.

Telephone Savings

If you want to cut down on your long-distance charges, time your own calls. Keep an hourglass egg timer next to the phone, and it will let you know when those first three minutes are up.

Long-distance Telephone Calls

The cost of a long-distance telephone call depends on how long you talk. You can talk less and still get your information across if you jot down ahead of time the topics you want to cover. But an even greater saving will be yours if you check with your long-distance carrier and become aware of the hours when the rates are cheapest. Usually, night rates and holiday rates are least expensive.

Removing Prices From Packages

When giving a gift, you will surely want to remove the price. If the price sticker cannot be removed intact, you will at least be able to remove the price by pressing Scotch tape over the sticker and then pulling off the tape. The printed words (and part of the label) will come off.

Typewriter Keys

For a light cleaning of the keys on typewriters rub them lightly with a cloth dampened with alcohol. For clogged type, press into keys the puttylike, soft plastic materials available in stationery stores.

The Value of a P.S.

Psychologists tell us that if you want the letter you write—particularly a letter with a sales pitch—to emphasize your point, add a P.S. The P.S. is usually read even if little attention is paid to the rest of the letter.

Envelope Sealant

Dab a little nail polish on the flap of a nonsticking envelope. It will dry fast and not leave a smudge. The seal will be so secure that even steam will not be able to open it.

Label Protection

If you want to be sure the label you have written to mail a package will not become smeared, rub a candle over the writing. The wax will form a weatherproof coating. A coating of Scotch tape will also keep the label legible.

Hi-Liter Pens

When reading a book, magazine, or newspapers, use a Hi-Liter pen to mark off passages you will want to refer to again. These pens, which are like magic markers with see-through ink, are available in stationery stores. Use only yellow ink if you plan to make photocopies, unless you want the marks to show up on the copies.

Cleaning Gold Jewelry

The best way to clean gold jewelry is to soak the items in sudsy lukewarm water to which a drop of ammonia has been added. Allow the items to be immersed for two or three minutes, then dip an old toothbrush into rubbing alcohol and brush the jewelry clean.

Stringing Beads

Stringing beads without the use of a needle is not difficult if you use the right kind of string. Nylon fishing line is ideal for the purpose—it is strong, flexible, and stiff enough not to require a needle. Dental floss is good, too. Dip one end into nail polish. After it dries, the end will be firm enough to use as a needle.

Quick Patina

To obtain the greenish effect on copper (and bronze) which normally occurs only after years of exposure to air, you can rub buttermilk on the object. Parts of it will turn green.

Needling a Thread

The best way to thread a needle is to cut the thread at an angle, moisten it, and then hold the thread steady while pushing the eye of the needle into the thread.

Reviving Sports Jerseys

An old sports jersey that has been outgrown is still of some use. Sew up the neck and sleeves and stuff it with old rags, then sew up the open ends. It will serve as a good knock-around pillow for a youngster's room.

Storing Christmas Bulbs

Egg cartons, especially the styrofoam kind, are ideal for storing Christmas bulbs and ornaments. For larger ornaments, cut the tops off two boxes, then place the bottoms together. Secure them with rubber bands or string. The lids can be used for storing odd-shaped decorations or candles. Tubes from rolls of paper towels or toilet tissue are likewise useful in storing candles and small electric bulbs. Stuff the bottom with paper first, and label each tube.

Storing Flammable Liquids

When you store a flammable product, make sure it's kept in a metal container. Fuels and solvents stored in glass containers may expand during a heat wave and explode. If a spark or flame is present when this occurs, fire will result. Whatever the metal container you use, make sure the lid is on tightly.

Adding Life to Film

Photographic film has a limited shelf life. The expiration date is marked on all film. You can greatly prolong the life of film by wrapping it in an airtight plastic bag. (Suck out the air and seal with a wire twist.) Then, store the protected package in the refrigerator until needed.

More Hints to Remember

(Jot down new hints here as you come across them.)

Appendix

Black & Decker
10 North Park Drive
Hunt Valley, MD 21030

Consumer Information Center
Dept 684 E
Pueblo, Co 81009

Devcon Consumer Divsion
780 A.E.C. Drive
Wood Dale, Il 60191

Dremel Company
4915 21st Street
Racine, WI 53406

DuPont Company
1007 Market Street
Wilmington, DE 19898

Durasol Drug Company
1 Oakland Street
Amesbury, MA 01913

Faber-Castell Corp.
551 Spring Place Road
Lewisburg, TN 37091

Johnson & Johnson
Grandview Road
Skillman, NJ 08558

Johnson Products
2072 N. Commerce Street
Milwaukee, WI 53212

Krazy Glue Company
53 W. 23 Street
New York, NY 10010

Magic American
23700 Mercantile Avenue
Cleveland, OH 44122

Medi-Source, Inc.
50 Gordon Drive
Syosset, NY 11791

Red Devil Paints and Chemicals
30 North West Street
Mt. Vernon, NY 10550

Reliable Paste Company
3560 Shields Avenue
Chicago, IL 60609

Rust-Oleum Corp.
2301 Oakton
Evanston, IL 60204

Sprayway, Inc.
484 Vista Avenue
Addison, IL 60101

3M Eastern Public Relations
530 Fifth Avenue
New York, NY 10036

3M Consumer Stationery Division
3M Center
Bldg 223-45
St. Paul, MN 55144

Stanely Tools
600 Myrtle Street
New Britain, CT 06058

Turtle Wax Company
5655 W. 73 Street
Chicago, IL 60638

U.S. Borax & Chemical Company
3075 Wilshire Blvd.
Los Angeles, CA 90010

WD-40 Company
1061 Cudahy Place
San Diego, CA 92110

Index

About the Author

JAMES SANDERS, a devout "do-it-yourselfer," has written various articles on consumerism that have appeared in newspapers and magazines throughout the country. Mr. Sanders, who is retired, spends his time researching the hints he collects.

Mr. Sanders currently lives with Charlotte, his wife of forty years, in Burlington, Vermont. They have four children and six grandchildren.